JESUS THE CHRIST

THE
STORY OF JESUS CHRIST

An Interpretation

BY

ELIZABETH STUART PHELPS

AUTHOR OF " A SINGULAR LIFE," " THE GATES AJAR," " THE SUPPLY
AT SAINT AGATHA'S," ETC.

BOSTON AND NEW YORK
HOUGHTON, MIFFLIN AND COMPANY
The Riverside Press, Cambridge
1897

5/95

G. J.

"A man whose soul is absorbed in a great life's work is apt to disclose his own mental history only in glimpses. Christ was no exception to this."

AUSTIN PHELPS.

To the friends and critics whose sympathy and scholarship have made it possible for me to overcome the difficulties under which this work has been done, I owe a gratitude beyond words.

E. S. P. W.

NOTE

THIS book is not theology or criticism, nor is it biography. It is neither history, controversy, nor a sermon. It makes none of the claims, it assumes none of the pretensions, of any one of these. It is not a study of Jewish life or Oriental customs. It is not a handbook of Palestinian travel, nor a map of Galilean and Judean geography. It is not a creed; it speaks for no sect, it pleads for no doctrine.

It is a narrative, and will be received as such by those who understand the laws of narrative expression. Beautiful romances have been written upon the subject which these pages venture to approach; but this is not fiction. The great historical facts that revealed the Founder of Christianity to us have been carefully considered. No important departure from the outlines of his only authorized biography has beguiled the pen which has here sought to portray the Great Story with loving docility. The few, unfamiliar strokes by which these outlines have been sometimes filled have been reverently and studiously adjusted to the composition of the picture, — it is hoped without offense to probabilities. It is believed that these probabilities are so reasonable that they may serve to

deepen, not to dissipate, our respect for such knowledge as we possess concerning the life of Jesus
Christ.

A student of this subject, who comes to it from
outside dogmatic prepossessions, is amazed — one
almost says appalled — at the conditions of thought
through which he must approach it. The Christic
literature is one vast controversy. Critic contends
with critic, and theologian with theologian. Bio-
graphers and commentators differ with an intensity
which, though it startles, not always pleasantly, is a
tribute to the powerful interest of the topic, and a
stimulus to its study.

The memorial of the Gospels was written by plain
men who knew little of literature, nothing of science,
but much of the central Figure of their times. As a
fragmentary biographical record of ancient origin,
this memorial is necessarily subject to more or less
personal interpretation. Among what we may call
its secondary features, there are few in the treatment of which scholars are agreed.

The writer of this narrative is not unaware of the
differences among New Testament critics when she
chooses between them such aspects of many events
or conditions as seem to her best for the purposes
of this book.

The life of Christ was lived to inspire, not to
confuse. Little things are restless; the great repose. Scholars are tenacious of detail, for they hold
the values of accuracy in their keeping. But Christian scholars are generous in feeling, for they hold
the treasures of their faith in trust. They may con-

tend about the unimportant. On the essential they
will agree.

What does it signify whether the star of Bethlehem was a meteor or a miracle? What does it
matter whether Jesus was born in one year or the
next, in this month or that? It is of no consequence whether he was baptized in Jordan River or
Jordan region. It is quite immaterial whether the
misfortunes of Mary Magdalene were mental or
moral, or, indeed, which of the Marys she was. The
precise chronology of the unknown feast is a little
question. Whether Jesus revisited Nazareth once
or twice is a point not worth two pages of controversy.

The important things — all that any of us need,
all that most of us care for — are few, clear, and
unquestionable. Jesus Christ lived and died, and
lived again after death. He lived a life explicable
upon no other view of it than his. He founded a
faith comprehensible upon no other interpretation of
it than his own. He himself is Christianity. He
is the greatest force in civilization: the highest
motive power in philosophy, in art, in poetry, in
science, in faith. He is the creator of human
brotherhood. To apprehend him is to open the
only way that has yet been found out of the trap
of human misery. His personality is the best explanation yet given of the mystery of human life. It
offers the only assurance we have of a life to come.

The butterflies of immortal hope are delicate
organisms, easily impaled by skeptical naturalists,
and eagerly catalogued with other lost ideals.

Modern interrogation has raised many queries with which no student of this theme can be unfamiliar, but on which it is not the mind of this book to dwell.

It is the fashion of our times to trouble one's self about the supernatural; as if (for aught we know to the contrary) the supernatural might not be the most natural of all things! It is the intellectual mode, and Christian scholarship has not altogether escaped it, apologetically to investigate what are called miracles.

There is not, there never was, there never may be, a miracle as strange as the life of Jesus the Christ. He was the Miracle. Explain him. There will be no difficulty with any lesser wonder.

Biographies of Christ are many. They are all learned, and most of them are long. They are crowded with the erudition which scholars have demanded of each other, and possess, in spite of it, much of the interest which the ordinary human being seeks and needs, but which he needs without being obliged to seek too hard for it. To this mass of instructed work I am a thankful debtor. It is with confidence in the kind tolerance and welcome of students obviously far wiser than myself, that I venture to add this unpretending book to a stately company.

But men are many and scholars are few. It is with more confidence in the warm, human world outside of books, that this one hopes to find its friends.

There has come to me, during the time given to

the growth of this work, an experience always full
of wonder and of charm.   Often, on waking in the
morning, after days of the most absorbing and
affectionate study of the Great Life, the first conscious thought has been: " Who was with me
yesterday? What noble being entered this door?
In what delightful, in what high society, have I
been!" I felt as if I had made a new, a supreme
acquaintance.

I pass over this feeling to those who can understand it, or who may share it; and wish it, from my
heart, for those who do not.

CONTENTS

LIST OF ILLUSTRATIONS

THE STORY OF JESUS CHRIST

PRESAGE

I

CALL it the year of Rome 749, or the year 5 before our era. The land was Palestine.

Fifteen hilltops watched the village. This high country, eighty miles away from the capital, shut in the inhabitants of little towns with much the same general effects that we find to-day, in mountain regions where the people cannot easily get away from their silent homes and close horizons; they depend more for such knowledge of life as they have upon the world's coming to them, than upon their going to it.

There was a valley, cutting these hills from east to west. It threw up a small plateau, on which a settlement condensed rather than straggling, hung with a certain half-melancholy, half-cheerful picturesqueness; an effect peculiar to a limestone country, where the low tints of gray and the cold tones of white weigh the landscape; but where " green things growing " find generous hospitality in the cultivated soil.

There was a fountain; the only one in the village. The women went with their urns on their shoulders to get water for the family supply; they stood, graceful, slow of motion, lazy and lovely, taking each her turn. It was approaching the cool of the day. The women chattered like birds; they raised their eyes to the mountains indifferently. The sky was taking on a great preparation of color; but the women preferred to hear what was to be said.

A girl put down her urn, and looked at the sky. She did not talk. She moved away a little from the other women, and leaned against a high, white rock. Her chin was lifted, her eyes upraised; her mouth had a sweet expression; her thoughts were high. She had the manner of one who preferred to be alone without knowing why.

The other women rustled, gossiping, away. The girl followed slowly, with obvious reluctance; she walked alone. The urn stood steadily upon her head; her carriage was straight and noble. She was of middle height, or possibly a little above it. She had a fair complexion, blonde hair, and bright, hazel eyes. Her eyebrows were arched and dark; her lips ruddy, and full of kindness when she spoke. Her face was long rather than round; her hands and fingers were finely shaped. "She had no weakness of manner, but was far from forwardness. She had no pride, but was simple, and free from deceit. She showed respect and honor to all. She was very gentle, in all things serious and earnest; she spoke little, and only to the purpose."[1]

[1] Tradition.

The women of her race are easily beautiful at any time; and the region in which she lived was remarked for the attractiveness of its feminine inhabitants. Their very dress was more ornamental and effective than in some other portions of the province. To this day the same is true. In the hill and valley country to which the village clung, there was a special richness of growth; foliage, fruit, flower, and woman developed gracefully and with luxuriance.

Now the maiden was a poor girl, born of working people, reared by them, and living among them. Yet she came of the lineage of a powerful and popular king. This country maid, this laborer's child, was born, not to the purple, but of it. She might be called a royal peasant. Her veins ran with the richest blood of the nation; her hands knew its commonest toil. A patrician ancestry and a plebeian training make, for certain ends, the most desirable inheritance that can befall one. She had it.

To call her devout, is to say that she was something more than a good churchwoman. In a girlish way she was a sweet student of the Law and the Prophets, but she was more than that. She was one of the rare natures in which faith is like breath. We see its gentle pulsations, and respect them unconsciously as we would a law of physiology. Many phrases have been invented to describe the soul that seeks the divine because it is the perfectly natural and inevitable thing for it to do; but none of them are satisfactory to us; perhaps because most of us are too far from that type of being ourselves to understand it. We can honestly revere dedication when we believe in it, however, and hers it is impossible to question.

She was one of those exquisite spirits that are able to rely on truth which they cannot comprehend, without any waste of the nature in doubt or evasion. She believed so utterly in the God of her people that He was more real to her than any other fact of life.

The month was April; and this is to say the bloom of the year in Palestine. The early spring and quick, luxuriant growth of the warm climate gave to that month something of the characteristics of our own June. It was the time of sun and splendor. It was the time of leaf and blossom. It was the time when hope and fulfillment met in the face of the fields, and when the countenance of the sky and the breath of the atmosphere hold that something separate from this earth which appertains to all perfect beauty. The dullest of us are conscious of it, when the fire burns in the young grass-blade and the color in the opening flower, the dazzle in the air, and the depth in the heavens.

The Galilean girl felt the holiness of beauty, for she was capable of feeling everything pure and exquisite; and she kept herself alone, to dwell upon the gentle thoughts developed in her by the divinity of the day elected for the marvel which glorifies the name of one little mountain town forever.

The hour of evening prayer among her people fell at the setting of the sun and the coming of the stars. But hers was no ordinary, mechanical nature, such as prays because it is ecclesiastical and civil law to do so at an ordered time. Prayer with her was the luxury of the soul.

She trod the village street abstractedly. Her feet, from modest habit, led her home. Without speaking, she emptied her urn into the water-jar that stood near the door, and quietly freshened the herbs that floated on the top of the water. She wished to be alone. The commoner minds about her were still dissipated in their distractions; hers had already entered into that revery which is neither wholly thought nor wholly prayer, but partakes of the reality of both.

In the space between the sunset and the twilight the girl stole up, unnoticed, to the roof of the house, — the flat roof, in all hot countries the place of family meeting, of relief from the scorching weather, of indulgence in private grief or of prayer ; in fact, among the poor, it was the only possible place of retirement at home. Her poverty was not of the squalid, but only of the strenuous kind ; and the usual conveniences or the usual comforts of a respectable home were hers. But these, in the East, were always few enough.

The hour of the evening sacrifice arrived. The cool breeze from the west died down. Peace fell with the calm.

The sun had set over the valley. The view from the house-top was not a broad one ; it was restricted by the hills. A little farther up the great slopes, a wide panorama (often called one of the fairest in the world) opens splendidly. But the scenery apparent from the young girl's home, was not of the kind

that carries the mind far into vague dreams of
beauty; rather of the sort which defines familiar
outlines, — the architecture of the closing hills,
the cleft of the narrowing valley, the sights of the
village street; the kind of outlook which makes
humility and duty seem more natural than restlessness, acceptance, than interrogation.

But the luxuriant vegetation of Nazareth was
fair to see, even if one saw little more. The green
that is half gold melted over the hillsides, and ran
riot in the valley. Flowers were at a high tone.
The red lamps of the pomegranates were burning
freely. Fruit gardens touched in rich, metallic
colors to the landscape; gold of apricot, with pale,
silver leaves, purple of grape, and yellow-green
of fig, passed each in its time. Hollyhocks, rose
and red and yellow, unfurled their banners. All
in their season, too, lilies of differing hues and
petals would be abloom; the fairest of them, tall,
white, slender, maidenly, like girls in sweet procession, or like angels in a vision.

In the village, roof-gardens sometimes added flowers to the gentle joys of home. One of these sky-
gardens belonged to the poor home of which we
think, — a little, cubic dwelling looking like a block
— and tall, white flowers stood above the vines, leaning against the evening sky.

The girl crept among them. Her eyes were on
the heavens. There was an aureola in her heart.
Her prayer had passed the phase of words. She
had ceased to address God, she had come so near
Him.

The flood-tide of the sunset ebbed away from the houses of the villagers, her neighbors. These houses were white, of limestone; vines and the shadows of vines crept freely over the houses, softening their dazzle. Flocks of doves swayed over and settled upon the roofs; when these were of delicate shades, softly darker than the roof, the effect was charming; as the twilight fell, the doves scattered to their cotes or slept in those which they had found within the house itself.

One of these lovely birds, — in all ages and in most countries the symbol of purity, — dipping across the dusk, and hanging over the roof, called the maiden's attention to the appearance which had awaited the slow turn of her head, and the concentration of her gentle eyes from their devout abstraction, upon itself.

There is always something which makes one hold the breath when a bird of the air brushes one, or even swings near enough to have been caught if one had wished. It is not to be wondered at that imagination has connected the spirits of the unseen, or the departed, with the visits of birds. In Palestine the dove was especially loved and cared for; it was sacred to the uses of the Temple, and religious association was always busy with it. A gentle mind like that of this girl would turn tenderly to the movements of the soft wings which arrested her notice.

Then, did she see the Angel? Did he break a stalk of one of the white flowers, as he stirred, and so hold it in his hand, smiling to reassure her by the ease and cordiality of the act?

Whence came he? Had he swept from the heights of distant Lebanon, whose white head, turning gray in the twilight, was darkening as if the mountain drew a mantle over it? Had he floated on the departing cloud that rode like a chariot of fire past the sun whose own face was hidden from the marvel? Or had he formed from the ether, where he stood, against the faint sky, quietly and naturally, as inspiration forms in the soul, and faith in the heart that is fit for it? Whatever of the strange was in the manner of his coming, the angel came.

II

There have been in all ages three kinds of persons: those who never see mystical appearances, those who think they do, and those who do; and the three types may be confounded. It is also to be suggested that visitors from an invisible life, if such there are, and whoever such there are, may be responsive to the absence or the presence of welcome, like any other superior or sensitive being. Angels, like people, might come where they are wanted, trusted, or expected.

In fact, there are laws of spiritual hospitality, breach of which may, for aught we know to the contrary, deprive a human creature of the mystical privileges. The soul of this Hebrew girl was hostess to all that was pure and perfect, delicate, ethereal, devout. As the flower receives the sun at dawn, as the earth the rain at drought, she instinctively received the divine.

The angel stood quietly. He seemed to wish not to alarm the girl. She thought him a spirit of high rank. He spoke with the tenderness natural to strength and to superiority alone. Was he used to stand in the presence of God? Yet he said, " Fear not, Mary."

How astonishing the conversation which followed! The scene moved on steadily to its solemn climax. Question and answer succeeded with increasing courage on the part of the Galilean girl, and with growing definiteness on that of her celestial guest. Clearly but gently she was given to understand that she had not been made the subject of an inconsequent apparition, such as were frequent enough in Oriental experience or imagination; but that she was the medium of the most tremendous revelation which this planet has ever known.

Chosen out of all the world, the Hebrew maiden whose qualifications for her solemn mission were the simple, womanly ones of a pure heart and a devout life received the angel's message as she who could be chosen by it would be sure to do. The fiat of Deity was in the magnificent attitude of the angel; he stood tall, erect, majestic. Awed, the woman fell upon her knees before the messenger of God, and veiled her face from sight of him. " Be it unto me," she said, " according to thy word."

Now, when he perceived that Mary understood the import of his embassy, the angel left her. Gabriel, a great spirit, mighty in rank, went his way to that mysterious condition of life from which invisible beings may wander — why not? — not for petty purposes, but when sufficient cause exists to summon a superior to an inferior creature from a higher to a lower system of things.

The woman was left, in a world like ours, to her unique experience.

She had received from the vision a prediction whose nature so utterly transcends all mortal laws and all mortal experience that he would profane the very courts of mystery who should descend to offer for it any human explanation.

There is no quibbling possible with the marvel. It must be rejected or accepted on its own great grounds. No compromise between fact and fancy has dignity in the isolation of the case.

Shall we be less high-minded than the instinct of the race and the faith of the ages?

Take the wonder as it is told.

The incarnation of Deity is an idea older than the time when the Galilean girl in Nazareth received a spirit's message. This mystical possibility has been a favorite with certain crude and ancient religions. Instances might be given of it, but not here; they jar upon the lofty and beautiful character of the Christian story, which so far surpasses them in purity, in pathos, and in philosophy, that one has not the rudeness of heart to introduce them in its matchless, opening chapter.

Was all the fable but a perplexed, prophetic yearning for the fact? At last, in this simple, hallowed way, has history met it?

Gabriel seems to have been something of a philosopher (as well as altogether an angel) when he reminded the astonished woman, at the close of his announcement of the incredible facts, that with God nothing is impossible. These were astute words under the circumstances, and worthy of a superior intelligence. The argument admitted of no reply.

Mary listened to it gently. Her soul was a lily. All motherhood has been dignified forever by the spotless mystery. All humanity is nobler for the delicacy of the womanly nature from which the Son of the Highest should be born into a low world.

III

The story of the Gospels was written by men. Men have studied and expounded it for two thousand years. Men have been its commentators, its translators, its preachers. All the feminine element in it has come to us passed through the medium of masculine minds. Of the exquisite movements in the thought and feeling of Mary at this crisis of her history, what man could speak? Only the hearts of women can approach her, when, quite without angelic endorsement or even human protection, she is left to meet the consequences of the will of God upon her life.

The angel had disappeared in his own ether. The music of a celestial voice was replaced by the chat of the villagers, the plain, usual people to whom marvels did not happen; who would understand nothing. She who had heard the accents of heaven shrank from the tones of earth. Fragments of family conversation — the note, though most familiar, often least sympathetic to the listener — had a foreign sound.

Had Mary a mother living? or loving? It is touching to know that the first act of the wondering girl, after the angel had explained the nature of her future to her, was to seek the sympathy of another woman, and that woman not of her own household.

There was a village, Juda by name, in the south of Palestine in the hill country of Judæa; it was a hard journey of about five days from Nazareth. There Mary had a friend. She took the journey.

An elderly woman, reticent, dignified, devout, herself the subject of a strange experience, received the girl. Mary crept into her arms; she found it hard to speak, even to Elizabeth. Then she found it harder to be silent. Her sensitive nature vibrated between exaltation and anxiety. There is a song famous and sacred in musical history — an inimitable outburst of religious and poetic feeling. In the home of Elizabeth Mary uttered the Magnificat. The two women confided in each other. Mary thought of the hard journey back to Nazareth; of the caravan of curious neighbors or kinsfolk which she must join; her heart sank. Oh, to stay on and on, protected and respected, quiet, and safe! Dreading to return to her own home, she lingered in the house of her relative. Shielded, trusted, understood, how should she face the cruel storm that awaited her? She clung to this brief, slight anchorage.

The suffering element in the life of the son began

early in the soul of the mother. A desolate maternity forecast the melancholy of the child.

And now, the inexorable action of the greatest drama in the world began to move. The claims of her father's [1] roof summoned the absent girl. Her kinswoman might shelter her no longer. With dignity, with sweetness, and in silence, Mary gathered her courage, and came back with her secret to her home and her neighbors.

The angel of the mystery had borne a significant name, — Gabriel, the Might of God, or a Mighty One is God. But Gabriel had vanished. No angel was visibly courier to Mary, when, in the weakness of woman, she took the weary journey back again to face her unknown fate.

IV

In his shop in Nazareth, Joseph the carpenter worked drearily. Hammer and saw fell from his dispirited hand; his basket of wooden nails lay unused. His dejected eyes wandered through the opening which served as door and window to his simple place of business. His heart was far from his work, and heavy as doom.

This grave, honest man,[2] a middle-aged person, with experience of life behind him, loved the girl to whom he was betrothed. His restrained and unselfish tenderness had chosen her with that decision

---

[1] Joachim, born in Nazareth; her mother, Anna, native of Bethlehem. Tradition.

[2] A widower. Tradition.

which belongs to mature affection, whose depth is to
a youthful fancy as the Mediterranean Sea beyond
the mountains was to the spring at Nazareth. The
whole nature of the man was involved. His mind
moved heavily about the central fact. The cruelest
of disasters seemed to have struck his promised
wife — this sweet, this saintly girl. The marvel
that had befallen her was scoffingly received.

This elect and tender being was bearing in patient
loneliness an unspeakably pathetic lot.

Thus again, the awful law of sacrifice which was
to become the ruling passion in the life of the son,
began in the courageous and noble maternity fore-
shadowing his character.

Joseph, the betrothed of Mary, meditating on her
virtues and her beauty and her danger until he was
sick at heart, fell asleep at last, from weariness, in
his shop among his tools. It is easy to see the carpenter, almost as he was. Ages move and customs
vanish, but certain facts remain, — the shape of a
shaving cut by a sharp edge from wood is the same,
and so is the fashion of a manly heart.

The betrothed of Mary woke from his sleep,
resolved. The Jews were a people accustomed to
place great significance upon dreams, especially
upon those of a sacred character, and Joseph had
dreamed the dream which was to decide, from a
practical point of view, the fate of the world.

Had he carried his terrible perplexity in prayer
to the very gates of sleep? And had God met it
there, because it was ready to be met? The carpenter rose, refreshed and relieved. He had in this

manner, occult to us and to our time, but perfectly natural to him and to his, received the command most welcome to his loyal heart. He had been directed to trust and to wed his promised wife.

Betrothal was an important rite among his people, not less so than actual marriage. Betrothal was beautifully called "the making sacred." It was a formal, festive occasion, lasting several days. A great social affair was made of the whole scene.

Joseph and Mary, being poor, had been quietly betrothed. No invitations to a costly feast were sent out; they passed their vows in the simplest and severest manner. Nevertheless, the vows were passed. The sanctity of the relation was unimpeachable. Mary awaited, in the seclusion of her troubled home, the will of God and of men upon her future. Her eyes widened and darkened with patient sadness. How piteous her position no man has ever told us; few have guessed, and none could understand.

At this crisis in the story one straightforward, chivalrous act set everything right. Joseph the carpenter, being of royal blood, strode like a man through the gossip of the village, and took his promised bride to be his wife. In the Oriental phrase and custom, this "redeemed" her. In the shelter of her husband's home misapprehension could not touch her, and gossip might forget her. Has history, or has reverence, ever done justice to Joseph? It seems hardly. In our admiration for the ever-womanly which Mary's ideal has left in a world that needed it, we have a little overlooked the ever-

manly, the simple, noble, loyal deed, the gentleman
mechanic who knew how to love a woman and to
protect her, thinking more of her and less of himself,
as a man should do.   And of this ideal, too, the
world has need.

V

The political situation among the race to which
Joseph and Mary belonged was, at this time, extremely interesting.   The Hebrews were above all
things a hero-loving nation ; and their heroes were
dead.   They were a people of a marked literary
quality, and their literature was a thing of the past.
Their poets, like all other men of importance among
them, were of a religious temperament and bore the
name of prophets.   The Jews revered their prophets.   Now, at the time of which we write, there
were no prophets.   Most nations undergo crises in
which the higher qualities among their leaders sink
underground for a time like subterranean rivers.
Such a crisis was now drawing down the Hebrews.
The hero - worshipers were without heroes.   The
idealists were perishing for ideals.   The thinkers
were suffering for stimulation.   The common citizen was dully and thoroughly disheartened.

The Jews were notable in this respect, that they
had experimented at a theocracy and had failed in
it.   Their dejection was proportional to their defeated aspiration.   It was, after all, a fine idea, that
of selecting the Almighty for a chartered Ruler, and
accepting nothing less than his personal control.
This superb national conception was apparently a

doomed one, for the Hebrews were a conquered nation, and had been for nearly forty years.

In certain respects, more humiliating than enslavement to Babylonia, Greece, or Egypt, was enslavement to Rome. By the irony of fortune these proud people were now subjects in their own land, were but the disdained provincials of a vast empire. This is to say, that Cæsar Augustus occupied the Roman throne, and Herod, his vassal king, the palace at Jerusalem.

From a time near the beginning of the national history the religious poets of the Jews had foretold a strange event. Even Moses, the law-giver, had intimated it. The great poet Isaiah had sung of it like a sibyl. The strenuous Daniel had insisted on it like a homesick captive. The national records preserved it as dreary mines preserve the secret of a strange and cheerful jewel.

The theocracy, in a word (that was the idea) had not been neglected by its invisible King. Jehovah had never forgotten the people who had elected to be his subjects. A substitute appointed by Him would appear before the ruin of the nation was complete; would unite the scattered tribes, would mend the broken machinery of government; would grasp the shattered power, restore the lost glory, and make the future splendid.

The appearance of this deputy of God was expected by this wretched and poetic people with a confidence which is the more striking when we come to the dénouement of the story. Whoever, whatever, he should be, — wherever, however he should manifest himself — the Wonder was to come. To this unknown, unseen, unborn, was given the name of the Messiah, or the Anointed ; a recognition of a fact which the mass of the people were exceedingly dull at understanding : that he was to have a sacred as well as a political character. The rich imagination of the nation had always been smouldering about this being. But a touch was needed to set it afire. He was the Hero of heroes. To his mysterious image all their disappointed hero-worship clung.

In the year of which we speak, " all the world " (such was the imperial audacity of the phrase) was complaining under especial grievance. A census preparatory to extra taxation was ordered ; and the consequence was a tumult. The people were extremely angry ; but escape from the great hand of Rome was impossible. Cæsar Augustus was ruler of the world. Herod, his creature, controlled more territory than any dead Jewish King had ever done. The once splendid and sacred throne of David now existed, a pitiable farce, only to extend the forces of execrated and alien heathenism. Raging and impotent, the subjects prepared to obey.

To Nazareth, as to other villages in Palestine, the Roman fiat came.

Long and severe were the journeys required of the country people who must answer to this enrollment edict. Every citizen was obliged to register himself at the town whence his family had sprung. This involved a national commotion. The Jews were not only in the stir of revolt, but in the irritation of travel, — poor of pocket, uncomfortable in body, and sore at heart.

VI

Two plain people of Nazareth started at dawn one winter day to take one of these annoying journeys. Joseph and Mary, husband and wife, traveled as poor people must; on foot, or with one beast of burden between them.

There was a little town, about six miles south of Jerusalem, between seventy and eighty from Nazareth. Bethlehem was the birthplace of David the King; and Joseph the builder, descendant of David, must register there.

Mary, his wife, went with him. Why? She, too, was a daughter of kings. Did she own some bit of property in Bethlehem? — real estate, perhaps, unmarketable, but taxable, such as only made her "land poor;" giving her no income, but yielding some to Rome? Did she, too, register? But this was not necessary. Women were not obliged to present themselves personally; a written report of their property sufficed for them. Why, then, did Mary — who had the gravest of reasons at that time for wishing rest and shelter — take that cruel journey over one of the roughest of Palestinian pathways?

Precisely because she had reasons for doing the thing that her heart craved. And her heart craved that she should at that time of all others be near her husband, who understood her. Joseph must go to Bethlehem, and go just then. Mary would not allow him to leave her behind alone. The circumstances were too unusual. Her need of him was absolute. Indeed, it might not have been safe for her to stay at home unprotected.

There was another reason; but how far this influenced her only the heart of Mary ever wholly knew. Did she share this visionary idea with the quiet man who loved and guarded her, as they came down from the hill-country into the caravan route? Or did she keep it shyly to herself?

Her child would have been born in Nazareth, but for this accident of the census. But *was* it only an accident that the census must come into the question just then? — that the family must register, and in Bethlehem? Was it one of those divine incidents in which the great Will rides over little human wills, and brings everything out as no one could possibly have expected, as no one could have planned? For Mary was a reader of the poets of her people; and learned in all their Scriptures. A thousand years ago those ancient dreamers had associated strange things with the town of Bethlehem. Did she remember them? If she did, could she discuss them? There, it had been written, the Governor of her people should be sought. There the Wonderful should enter the world. Could she dwell on this, and hold her courage? Could she forget it, and be Mary?

Strictly speaking, there were no roads between Nazareth and Bethlehem. Rome built roads, but not at this time for her enslaved Hebrews. The caravan routes that traversed Palestine were hard traveling. Rough past rudeness were the foot-ways

BETHLEHEM

and the hoof-ways that led from Nazareth down
through the valley, over mountain side, and rolling
rock, and jagged limestone, and through sliding
dust; a severe journey of five days or more, as you
might make it, according to one's means of locomo-
tion or the strength of the travelers.

The wife's store of strength was small, and the
journey dragged. She was such a young creature!
— a mere girl — and delicate of organization, as we
know.

Think of it as December, too, and that means the
chilly season in Palestine, with roads across the
plains in bad condition. The rains were over; sun-
shine smote the hills, and the silver leaves of the
olives glanced like little steel swords in the wet
light. Even frost was possible at that time of the
year. Snow was not unheard of.

The two travelers arrived in Bethlehem at night,
foot-worn and chilled and faint. The wife, perishing of fatigue, had passed the stage of physical suffering when one takes any care or thought for what
is to happen next. Because of her weakness, they
had lagged behind the other travelers, and the town
was already brimming over with strangers like themselves. Every house was crowded. Her anxious
husband took her from threshold to threshold in
vain. The climb to the village up a steep hill had
added a last hardship. A faint light, swinging on
a rope across a doorway, signified the village inn.
They toiled up; the woman half dead of this last
effort. But the khan could not admit them.

Alarmed by the condition of his wife, Joseph

persisted manfully in his determination to find her shelter. Mary asked no question, expressed no concern. Her head fell upon her breast. The poor, homesick, young creature was dumb with suffering. Oh, the mistake of coming on this miserable journey! She thought of her home at Nazareth, of her bed, perhaps of her mother's face; or of that other, Elizabeth, who had understood and cherished her.

Dully, at length, she heard her husband say that there was a stable behind the inn, and that for the common humanity of the deed, the people of the khan would let her in. He carried her to the stable: she crept among the straw, like the animals around her; and there — hastened probably by her cruel journey — the anguish of motherhood overtook the exhausted wife.

VII

. . . .

Mary, presently, looked about the stable. Women are merciful to each other in this one respect at least, and we are not forbidden to think that some matrons of the inn had ministered to the unfortunate young traveler. The child was not dressed, but wrapped tightly in a long band, — the baby - clothes of the East. The women had left the young mother, now, with her husband and the cattle. She faintly regarded the stable.

The khan to which Joseph and Mary had applied was not a comfortable place; and the stable in which the baby was born was a rude affair. Mary

saw that it was a cave in the heart of a rock; a
species of grotto. A little flat lamp of clay whose
wick floated in oil, or a rude kind of lantern
made by straining waxed cloth over a frame of
rings, was allowed her. It struggled feebly with
the damp darkness. By the weak light she saw the
cattle, prevented from sleeping by the presence of
their unusual neighbors, and perplexedly rumina-
ting. Straw was about, and hay and provender.
Mud was beneath. The walls of the grotto dripped.
She and Joseph were alone — no, not alone : there
lay the child, breathing beside her.

It must have been far on in the night, probably towards morning, that she stirred uneasily, and,
out of fitful slumber, broken by conscious suffering, turned again, broad awake, and looked about
her.

No, it was no dream. She was not at home in
happy Nazareth. Strange to the eye, strange to the
ear, strange to the heart, were her rude surroundings. She was used to decent poverty, not to outcast, squalid scenes like this. Joseph sat silently
regarding her. Had Joseph not slept? A tired
man, himself in need of rest — how loyal was he
to his precious charge! But Joseph had arisen,
and stood straight and strong between her eyes and
the entrance to the grotto. Voices were audible.
Joseph was speaking. Question and answer followed. Visitors were in the stable.

Day was breaking. The gray light crept in with
a kind of reverence, as if the morning were on its
knees. In the cold color Mary saw the visitors.

Their calling was stamped on their dark, weather-tinted faces, and on their rough, warm clothing. They wore mantles' of woolen stuff, and heavy, sheepskin cloaks. They carried powerful sticks, strong enough to kill a wild beast. They were shepherds. Some fierce dogs accompanied them. Mary did not speak. She lay on the straw, and listened perplexedly. The court of the khan was quite open to the public. The poor young mother had not been even allowed the privacy sacred to her emergency. That had been hard enough; but visitors! And now! She winced when the intruders, all speaking fast in their excitement, pushed their way towards her. Their eyes were fastened eagerly upon one object. She heard exclamations and answers, and the low, controlled replies of Joseph. She saw the great, tanned fingers of the men pointing at the baby. She heard one say to another : —

"That was the sign ! "

And another answer : —

"In a manger ! There he is ! "

Then the shepherds spoke all together, their sentences falling over each other. But Mary — for her ear was delicate and quick — made out as much as this : in their pastures, a mile or more out of Bethlehem, these strong, not untender men, iron of fist to wolves and robbers, silken of touch to sheep and lambs, — men wakeful of eye and ear by profession, apt to see or hear what others slept through, suddenly, in the deep of the night, had seen the sky blossom with celestial forms and faces, and heard the ether ring with celestial tongues and songs.

ARRIVAL OF THE SHEPHERDS

Half in terror, half in delight, they had hurried up to the town to tell and to test their wonderful experience. Had the baby been in a respectable bed, had he been born like a comfortable child, they could not have found him. Only one newborn infant in Bethlehem lay in the manger of a public stable.

Now these were not ordinary, coarse herdsmen, but men selected for a superior position — that of guarding the flocks dedicated to the uses of the Temple; therefore they and their ewes, and the lambs destined for sacrifice, were encamped within easy distance of Jerusalem all the year round. Winter, like the summer, found these men at their posts of duty. They were important servants of the Temple, not without respect among the people, certain to command a hearing. They went straight out from the stable, and told their experience to anybody and everybody in the crowded town. The village, overflowing with guests from all parts of Palestine, listened to this strange tale; and travelers, returning to their homes, carried the rumor of it widely.

The shepherds went back to their sheep. They had seen their only angels. The next night, the next year, brought no more. They talked all their lives about this one great experience. Did they search the skies midnight upon midnight for that flower of life ? Did they tell their children's children how the splendid Oriental zenith burst that only time into celestial bloom ? How the soft, winter wind broke into articulate speech ? How he

looked — the mighty one, who was General of the
Heavenly Host? And how they found that spirits
spoke the truth. For there was the child; and the
manger.

But the young mother did not speak when she
heard about the angels, and the sign. She was
glad when the shepherds were gone out of the stable.
She looked at the baby mutely. Her heart was like
a white flower, closing over a drop of dew. She
kept these things, and pondered them.

Joseph, too, was quiet. He was one of the plain
men who make no fuss about duty; but he had been
in a hard position. He thought about the shepherds,
the angels, their startling message, and the dream
of his in Nazareth. It was impossible to think how
it would have been, if he had not trusted it, and
her. The eyes of the girl wife questioned her husband gently. The mysterious child slept beside
them. The hand of Joseph silently clasped that of
Mary.

.   .   .   .

VIII

Kepler, the astronomer, in the year 1604 had a
pupil superior to the common run of students, — a
thoughtful man, with his eyes open, and not afraid
to say what he saw with them. In December of
the preceding year, a conjunction of two of the
superior planets (Saturn and Jupiter) had interested all scholars of the sky. In a few months, Mars
had marched into the society of these celestial com-

rades, making one of the important stellar events of the time. Following this conjunction, in the autumn of 1604, there flashed into the sky a new and short-lived star. This the pupil of Kepler pointed out to his master, and this the master studied. It was a very brilliant star, more like a diamond than a comet, and sparkling with changing colors.

This star burned for a year, waned and wasted out of sight. But its life was long enough for the great astronomer to conceive a great idea.

Kepler was familiar with astrology, as all masters of an accurate science ought to be with its kindred imaginative studies ; and he knew quite well how the dreamers of the East in the times of which we are thinking were governed by the speculations of that art. Kepler, from the astronomer's point of view, fell to studying certain events which are interwound with the opening scenes in the history of Christianity. The result was one of the dramatic theories of science, liable to be held only by men of imagination.

According to the calculations of the great astronomer, in the Roman year 747, or at a time closely preceding the birth of the strange child in the Bethlehem stable, a similar conjunction of Saturn and Jupiter had appeared in the Oriental heavens, and Mars had joined the two in the spring of 748, making a brilliant exhibition. Kepler boldly hazarded the belief that the course of this conjunction was followed, like that of 1604, by a temporary star. His position has not been altogether approved by modern astronomers, but it is far too interesting to omit from any record of a curious historical fact on which astronomy has a peculiar judicial claim.

Persia at that time, as more or less at all times, was a camp of dreamers and astrologers. The study of the skies was a passionate pastime. The sagest of men gave their lives to it. All men were interested in it. Accurate knowledge of the skies they had not, but its place was filled by what they thought they knew, or wished to believe. They were constantly on the watch by night.

The Eastern sages knew little enough about astronomy as Kepler knew it; but they saw the great conjunction, and it produced a strong effect upon them. They took note that the conjunction occurred in the Constellation of Pisces, which was supposed by Chaldean astrologers to be immediately connected with the future of Judea. Thus the thoughts of the sages were naturally turned in that direction. Whether they had been studying the subject for a year, or more or less, is not important, and cannot be averred. The point of interest is, that a few of the star-gazers of the East were so profoundly impressed by this planetary movement that they left their homes and occupations, and formed a little traveling company to investigate its meaning. But this extraordinary journey was not entirely a scientific expedition. It had a political or historical character. Mystical or devout motives influenced these men. A rather remarkable reason for this existed.

IX

Astrologers from the earliest times had always associated heavenly disturbances with the birth of great men. The expectation of the advent of an extraordinary being among the Jewish people was not, at that time, entirely confined to the Jews. Rome, Persia, the far East, the civilized world to a certain extent shared it. Perhaps the Hebrew captives, scattered past collection among alien peoples, had tried to console themselves by whispering the proudest hope of their proud nation in their captors' ears. Perhaps the social conditions of the times — too miserable for the heart to dwell on, and too corrupt for the modern pen to describe — had given force to the rumor. Decent men who thought, and studied, and aspired had reached the stage of desperation which precedes despair. They were ready for any social or political experiment; they were attentive to any sign of the times.

Each man took out his private fears or hopes for the condition of his age, in his own way. The sensualist sank, the tyrant tortured, the slave despaired, the politician schemed, the rebel fought, the captive conspired, the dreamer slept, the devout prayed, the mystic mused.

The students of the sky followed the march of the stars.

The Eastern travelers, coming by an unknown route, reached Jerusalem. Here, these idealists asked strange questions, and they received significant replies. Arrived at the capital of the Jewish nation, and at the very altar of the Jewish faith, they found themselves still perplexed. These " peculiar people," these educated slaves, did, indeed, confidently expect to be freed by a heaven-born deliverer, to be ruled by a divinely appointed King. But nothing had been seen or heard of him. The Magi, with the persistence of men who have sacrificed too much for an idea to abandon it easily, betook themselves to the palace. Here they had an interview with one of the most abhorrent and abhorred of monarchs.

Rome, like the rest of the world, was acquainted with the rumors about the yet unidentified Jewish King. The haughty Roman eagle hung upon the Jewish Temple, but the powerful Messianic expectation had reached the Roman intellect. Herod was a coward as well as a tyrant, and he feared nothing more than the renationalization of the enslaved people.

He appealed to the priests and teachers of his remarkable and dreaded captives. Their governing body, the Sanhedrin, was called together. The question was officially put to them : Where was this King of theirs to be expected, or to be sought ? With ecclesiastical precision the anxious monarch was referred to the records or Scriptures of the Jewish people, which indicated Bethlehem as the birthplace of their national hero.

The capital was now on fire with the matter. The visit of the Eastern strangers had become the event of the day. With a stroke of imperial and diabolical diplomacy, Herod feigned a warm interest in the errand of his guests, and suavely directed them to Bethlehem; the condition of the royal politeness being that they should report the result of their investigations to himself.

The group of mystics, a little awed by the splendor and affability of the palace and the monarch, but less than commoner men, started at once for Bethlehem.

Men who have cast down all the affairs of life to travel for seven months, or a year, or more, over deserts and mountains, and through fords and forests, and in peril of beasts and of robbers, in pursuance of an idea, are not the men to be too much impressed with political power or splendor; still, they accepted Herod at his word, — being foreigners and not fully aware how little that was worth. A brilliant appearance in the skies, evidently temporary, and which had for some time puzzled them, now seemed to them to point towards Bethlehem; to confirm their own astrological beliefs and the Jewish traditions and directions.

Were the hardships of that long itinerary drawing to an end? Does the star know and love the student of the sky, that it will not mislead him? The Magi trod the streets of Bethlehem with arrested breath.

The mysterious child was now some weeks of age; the family were no longer boarders in the stable of the khan. They may have been house-guests or lodgers at the inn; but this they could not afford for any length of time. If the mother of Mary had been born in Bethlehem, had she not relatives there? — people whose home had been too full, or whose welcome had been too chilly at the time of the registration, to admit the travelers?

Then, remember, had come the sacred shepherds of the Temple, talking everywhere, telling a wonderful tale. Then, the strange birth of the strange child became the topic of the town. Then, the outcast family became respectable, interesting. Then, the love of the dramatic, which is strong in the Jewish nature, took hold of this vivid situation. Did some of Mary's relations, moved by the sudden publicity given to family affairs, perhaps stirred by some higher feeling of regret, or shame for neglected hospitality, persuade her to accept a tardy welcome under their roof?

At all events, the Eastern travelers found the family readily. All Bethlehem was talking of them, and their affairs. The temporary star looked down on the village gossip coldly. Its light and its life were beginning to waste.

Were the travelers Persians? Arabians? Princes or astrologers, or both? How many were there? What tongue did they speak? Greek, perhaps, — then the Court language of the East. Or did interpreters connect them with the Aramaic as spoken in Bethlehem?

We only know that they found the object of their wearisome and romantic journey. The star and the child had met at last.

Mary, his mother, was with him. She was used, by this time, to a certain amount of public curiosity in her child. Many visitors had come to see her; but none like these.

THE HOLY FAMILY

The grave group in their foreign garments, these serious men, travel-worn, and travel-wise, regarded the girl mother for an instant critically. Then their glance fell and rested upon the baby. Their eyes questioned and answered each other as they consulted together in their own tongue, probably never heard before by the Galilean girl. The study of a scroll, the march of a star, the dreaming of dreams, the daring to come out and be different from other men, the energy of ideas that could not be proved until one had trusted them — all this, all these, were justified at last.

Here was the Star Child.

Moved by a mute and common impulse, the Magi fell upon their foreheads. Startled, the young mother turned her sweet face and mildly looked at them.

Thus and then, we have the first worshipers (many centuries have given us many millions) bowed before the Madonna and the Child. But the Eastern sages did not kneel to the woman. It was the nature of the men and of the times to forget the woman. They had not traveled all that distance, all that time, to see a Jewish mother.

The Magi bent their mitred heads, and knelt before the child. Deeper than the impulsive curiosity or even the deference of the Temple Shepherds was the profound, intelligent reverence of these learned foreigners.

Mary, looking on, perplexed and gentle, saw suddenly that the visitors, still upon their rug before the baby, were opening and offering to the child strange things — products of the far East.

Joseph, coming in, and being wiser than Mary about such matters, perceived at once the meaning of what he saw.

For the gifts in the hands, on the laps, of the Magi were the typical offerings of subjects to a King, and in no other wise to be interpreted. There could be no doubt about it. Here was the child — to whom Joseph and Mary were becoming quite accustomed, already wondering if the baby were so very different from others after all; a little, helpless, human, nestling being, to be warmed and cherished on a mother's heart.

And there were the sages worshiping a monarch. The glitter of gold shone out of dusky bags; it did not attract the baby's eyes. Spicy, Oriental odors filled the air. Frankincense sent up its pungent perfume, strong as the heart of love. And there, — ah, there was myrrh, bitter as life, and as old to the fancy of the East as the ceremonials of death.

Only the wise recognize power in the weak. The Eastern scholars knelt humbly and happily before the babe of Bethlehem. It would have been difficult for the learned to follow their thoughts. Mary could not. But she clasped the child, and wondered.

The visitors went away quietly.

Their faces wore a rapt and reverent look. They were found to be men not inclined to talk, and local curiosity made but little out of them.

They quickly vanished from the village, and lost themselves in the first convenient caravan to Arabia. For one of those mystical reasons which often have

the most practical effects on human affairs, they
struck Jerusalem from their homeward route, and
omitted the courtesies of the palace on their return.
A royal murderer, scowling from his windows,
watched in vain for his Eastern guests. He had
miscalculated their shrewd simplicity.

X

Dreadful rumors of more dreadful facts ran whispering at this time about Judea. In the palace at
Jerusalem, Rome was represented by a monster.
Cruelty was his pastime, and murder his passion.
One of his worst manias was a senseless jealousy
of any possible or imaginary claimant, present or
future, to the throne which he disgraced. He slew
whomever came in his way, or whomever crossed
his fancy, with no more compunction than any gentleman of that age felt in the whipping of a slave.
Priests, nobles, the Sanhedrin, political suspects, the
people, his own family, those he feared, those he
loved, and those he hated, fell indiscriminately before his deadly will. He smote, he strangled, he
starved, he burned, he tortured. His morals were
past speaking of. He had the vices of his times
"carried up" by the Satanic ingenuity of his own
abnormal abominations. In consequence of them,
he was dying slowly in a manner of which modern
delicacy does not speak. But life was in him yet;
and all there was left of it was expended in the in-
fliction of torment. His name rang like an alarm-
bell through a wretched land.

In the homes of the oppressed people, ghastly stories circulated.

It was said that something had befallen the High-priest, a young, noble, and attractive man, brother-in-law to Herod. " Drowned ! " in pretended jest — " drowned before the king's own eyes, and by his order." The tale of worse than this stole from caravan to home : " His own sons, three of them, murdered." And still a worst ! " His wife, Mari-amne, beautiful, a Princess, passionately adored ; the only being whom the butcher ever loved, — Mariamne strangled ! " With paling lips men told each other about the great golden eagle which hung above the Temple gate, and how the people, insulted to frenzy, tore the haughty Roman emblem down one desperate night. Hideous things were said : for the rioters were students, and their leaders learned and eloquent ; and forty of them roasted alive for their escapade.

Now, in Bethlehem, Joseph and Mary shuddered as they caressed the child ; for there had come to them startling news in a strange way. The fearful gossip had not reached the village. None of the neighbors had heard it. No other mother fainted before it. No father barred his doors in mortal terror of the hired assassins of the king.

But Mary had married a dreamer ; and one night Joseph, standing tall and solemn, awaked her sud-denly. His voice fell below his breath. He looked over his shoulder.

" Arise," he said. " Take the child ! Fly ! "

Without question or argument, for that was her

THE MADONNA

sweet nature, Mary obeyed the vision and the authority of her lord. The child, of whom Joseph was now the legal protector, was clasped to her heart. The three stole out into the night — the fugitives of a mystical order. For this builder was a visionary beyond his calling or his kind. Like his lovely wife, he was more than usually accessible to delicate agencies. The condition may not have lasted his life out, but it served its uses in its time with significant effect. It led this thoughtful family as the break of a wave on a cliff may lead a poet, or a touch of the sun on a leaf may move an artist, or the hymn of the winds may stir a devotee.

Scarcely had the three vanished from the village when Bethlehem became the scene of one of the most piteous of tragedies, but of the least proportions in the life of the monarch who ordained it.

What was the butchery of a few babies in the catalogue of the crimes of Herod? — he who, knowing himself to be about to die, could command the slaughter of all the priests and nobles whom he could entrap in the Hippodrome, in order that his death should be received with public mourning instead of the frenzy of delight which was otherwise inevitable.

There were but a score of little corpses in Bethlehem. Who could have supposed amid the shrieks of that bleeding night, that the insignificant massacre should become one of the most memorable and familiar in human history?

Egypt, at all times the natural shelter of Palestinian refugees, could be reached by steady traveling in a few days' journey from Bethlehem. The boundary line, a little river with a long name, secured the protection of the fugitives. The infant Egyptian traveler, clasped to his mother's heart, across the Rhinokolura River, slept safely while the first martyrs to his name, coevals of his own brief age, went to their fate. Did the child dream? Who knows?

The expense of this unexpected journey was something which the family of a poor mechanic were ill prepared to meet. Now, behold the supply of gold which the Eastern star-gazers had poured at the baby's feet, hoarded by the young mother with the awe of a poor girl who had never handled so much wealth in all her humble life before! Protection against the poverty and discomfort of this sudden uprooting was at least secured. At the outset of his struggling life a breath too much of exposure, of suffering, would have killed the child. He seems to have been sheltered at this time of his utter helplessness, like a tiny, trembling flame, by the inclosing motion of an unseen Hand. The pure, white light went straight upward to its appointed end, unquenched by wind or weather, like the flames of the camp-fire in the desert, familiar to us in that most impressive of the pictures that have portrayed the Egyptian journey, wherein Joseph, flat with fatigue, keeps watch upon the sands by the fire, while Mary sleeps with the sacred child on her breast in the arms of the great Sphinx: — the mysteries of womanhood and of infancy, of divinity

THE REPOSE IN EGYPT

and of humanity, of the past and the future, of solitude and of family, of sacrifice and of love, clasped
together in silence and in night.

Joseph, for a dreamer, was a practical and able
man, and fully capable of managing the affairs of
the extraordinary family of which, in so singular a
manner, he found himself the head and protector.
The slow-traveling news of the day reached the
carpenter in due, though dilatory, season. Herod,
calling wildly on the spectre of his beloved and
murdered Mariamne, had gone to his miserable tomb.
The little Bethlehem babies were sleeping in their
graves, forgotten by all but their parents. Joseph
brought his family back to their own land, where
the first information that he picked up told him that
the new monarch was no improvement on the old
one. Therefore he abandoned altogether the idea of
revisiting Judea, and turned his face by way of the
coast towards Galilee.

Neither he nor Mary had a whole heart for living
in Nazareth, where their associations were not entirely pleasant ; but with the limited choice which is
left to the freest of us in the decisions of life, — a
choice which was narrow enough for two plain work-
ing-people who knew little of the world, and had less
wherewith to conquer it, they struck root in the old
familiar, self-satisfied, and suspicious village, where
they had lived and loved ; where they had been betrothed and wedded, had suffered, and wondered,
and prayed, and accepted their strange and sacred
lot.

Thus Nazareth, an unpopular mountain town,

became the home of the family; and the Child —
known from that day to this, for the space of two
thousand years, by a Jewish epithet of contumely,
as the Nazarene — bears in history the great name
of Jesus the Christ.

CHAPTER I

THE BOY

THE boy of Nazareth lived with his parents in a little, plain house, such as one must see everywhere to-day in Palestine. It was white, with a flat earthen roof, protected by a low parapet prescribed by law; it had one door, and it might be, no windows; there were vines blending the rectangular outlines of the dwelling; there were birds and flowers dipping and springing on the roof and about the place.

Inside the building, one room accommodated the family. A bench ran around the side of the room; in the daytime the boy neatly rolled upon it the rug, or bright quilt or mat, upon which he slept at night. Meals were spread upon a round and movable table, which was pushed in and out of its place as needed. A decorated chest stood against the wall; in it were stored the valuables of the family, their best clothes, and copies of the sacred writings of their people. Tall water-jars flanked the door, and a few herbs floated in them to keep the water cool. There was in this simple household, practically, no more furniture. Housework was reduced to its elements. Everything was scrupulously neat. The Jews were always washing, for the incessant use of water was prescribed by Levitical law. The lad bathed before he ate, before he prayed, before he slept, after touching anything which was ecclesiastically unclean. Moses had a genius for cleanliness, and in this respect was the most peremptory of law-makers.

Palestine was not a quiet place except in the heat of the day. In the morning the village began early to echo with chatter, pious or otherwise. The Jews, like all religious polemicists, were great talkers. The first conversation which the little Jesus had heard concerned the affairs of church and state, these being always one. One of the earliest words which the ear of the child had caught was Yaveh, — Jehovah. He had listened, ever since he could remember, to the neighbors and the customers droning perpetual talk about burnt-offerings and sin-offerings ; Moses, the prophets, David, the exile, Babylon, Rabbinism, unleavened bread ; the priests, the Synagogue, and the Law ; the Sabbath lamp, feast-days, fast-days ; phylacteries, paschal lambs, Passovers, — an endless and pompous iteration. He was scarcely more than a baby before he knew what the parchment meant attached to the door-post, and he watched the visitors who, on coming in or going out, reverently touched the Name of the Most High, and then kissed the fingers that had approached the holy inscription.

When he was five, the little boy was put to the study of the Law; for all well-brought-up Jewish boys were mimic theological students. We have our occasional tiny prig who learns the Greek alphabet at three, and is a Hebrew scholar at seven, but to a Jewish man-child a certain amount of pious precocity was a matter of course. He began to be learned at five. At thirteen he was a man, and able to enter upon full ecclesiastical privileges. Marriage was expected at eighteen, and was not unknown even earlier.

Schools were abundant everywhere on Jewish soil, and between the ages of five and thirteen Jesus had been compelled by law to study with his mates. The little fellows applied themselves to the cheerful topic of Leviticus, then to other portions of the Pentateuch and to the Prophets. The lad had learned the schedule of holy times, — all about the feasts of Purim, of the New Year, of the Tabernacle, and the Fast of Atonement. Then came the Commandments and the Law, an interminable and devious procession of "Thou shalts" and "Shalt nots." But it was at least sure that he had committed to memory much of the fine literature of his people.

Now it is impossible to overestimate the importance of this fact in the environment of the child, — that he was a Galilean. The Jews had the vices of their virtues, like other races, and their ecclesiastical aristocracy was one of the most obstinate.

Judea was the seat of the capital, of the Temple, of scholarship, of bigotry; of social, political, and religious position and importance; of asceticism, of experts in the Law; of Rabbinism, or the rigid and conservative school of theology, of every learned, hard, haughty assumption and assertion. Galilee was rustic, liberal, worldly, more or less heretical, crowded with traveling and even hospitable to settling Gentiles, — unconscious and happy, full of lovely scenery and lovely women and children, not troubled about too many things in theological dispute, agricultural and cheerful, fond of planting fruits and flowers. There was a proverb which told how it was easier to raise ten olive orchards in Galilee than one child in Judea. It was the fashion in the metropolis and suburbs to speak slightingly of Galilee ; " Galilean — fool ! " was a common fling. The Galilean village of Nazareth was the special object of general contempt; it was difficult to say precisely why. Probably the village was too liberal in theology to be tolerated by the more ecclesiastical Judea. Possibly it was too hospitable to the heathen guests whose diverse routes met in or around the town.

The Nazarenes were quick-tempered, being ardent, generous, and impulsive. They were sometimes taunted as uncultivated, a common and untrustworthy adjective in all ages tossed from the city at the country. It was the fact that the Nazarenes, indeed that most Galileans, admitted foreign words into their vocabulary, and spoke with a distinct brogue of their own. A learned lady once contemptuously addressed a distinguished Galilean scholar because he had used two unnecessary words in asking her the way to a distant town. The Nazarenes were considered as uncouth, out of the mode, out of society. Jerusalem regarded Nazareth much as New York regards the winter population of a Catskill hamlet, or as Boston views the affairs of a remote parish on the northern Vermont line.

But metropolitan scorn is sometimes only the syn-

onym for metropolitan ignorance. Like some other
country villages, Nazareth was really less provincial
in certain respects than the urban mind could understand. This was largely owing to the single circumstance that she had access to the caravan routes. One
ran through Nazareth to Samaria, Jerusalem, and the
south. Damascus travelers, by one of two routes,
came behind or below Nazareth at no great distance;
and, in fact, the village was a crossing-place of many
nationalities. Greeks, Romans, Arabs, Syrians, and
Phœnicians poured through the region ; brought the
culture, such as it was, of the heathen world, and
perhaps its morals also.

At all events, they brought the current of the
stream of life. They brought movement, change,
knowledge, breadth of thought, sparkle of feeling.
Nazareth was not a stupid place. This little mountain village, shut in like a flower in a walled garden, was alert and vivacious. It had a variety of
languages. Her people had intellect; they had imagination, and they had some knowledge of the world.

The Jews were devoted to their religious festivals,
— those pleasing occasions in which it is easy for
people of any faith to unite the sense of being as
devout as possible with that of having a very good
time. Of these festivals the Passover was the most
brilliant, exciting, or solemn of the year, according
to the temperament of the worshipers.

Egypt and Israel both remembered yet the story
of that black night when the first-born child in
every unsanctified household in the land was smitten
by death, and when the trembling slaves marked

their door-sills with sacrificial blood, that the destroyer might pass them by, as we are told he did.

This thrilling, national event was the centre of commemoration. Around it many penitential vows and prayers and mysteries clung. Passover was the annual sacrament of the people. No devout Jew would fail to visit Jerusalem at Passover time if he could help it.

The boy Jesus was now twelve years old, that is, coming into his thirteenth year; after this time he would ecclesiastically be of age; would be permitted to sit with his male relatives and friends at the Passover supper, and allowed to take his part in the public services of the synagogue.

His mother and Joseph were about going up to Jerusalem for the national feast. The child had been promised that he should go with them. It was his first visit to the capital.

No, not his first. Mary his mother remembered that other when, going over from Bethlehem, she carried the baby before the ecclesiastical authorities in the Temple as the Jewish law required, and an old priest and a prophetess created some excitement by openly worshiping the wonderful child. What startling thoughts had stirred the heart of the young mother at this first public recognition that hers was not like other women's children, — who shall say? She had never expressed them, but silently offered the two doves, the smallest sacrifice made by the poorest of women; she, a dove herself, as mild, as patient, as the helpless winged things with whose lives the red altars of that age and that faith smoked steadily.

As silently the child lay against her heart. They passed in and out of the Temple like two mute spirits hovering apart from the ecclesiastical ceremonies to which they were gently subject.

Now, the country lad, growing tall and sturdy, a strong walker, like other Eastern boys, came down the rough highway through the mountain passes that led from Nazareth to the plain of Jezreel. There is something delightful about the intense, quiet excitement of a thoughtful boy for the first time admitted to any knowledge of the world. Nothing else even in the charm of youth is quite like it.

It needs no history to tell us that this was a lovely boy. The omitted chapters in his young years speak for themselves. No man develops as he did from a rude or from a thoughtless boyhood. It must be a delicate root that throws out so fair a flower. The lad was a well-ordered child, giving no anxiety to parents; obedient to family rule, amenable, docile, sweet. But he was a manly boy, and he was a little student. He obeyed his mother, but he studied the Law. Now the Law taught him that a man has more privileges than a woman, such as even mothers do not share. When he went up to the capital on that first journey he remembered this.

April was Passover month, and Palestine was at her blossom. The boy's first sight of the world was a dream of delight. He descended the rugged path, past the rich Nazareth gardens, down the mountain sides, through the great plain, in an ecstasy of color, perfume, sound, and scene. Pomegranate and orange, olive, fig, and grape and grain cast tints

and scents upon the soft, hot air; the gay and abundant birds of Palestine darted like messengers of an
unknown life about the pilgrims; the pious chatter
of the travelers had a joyous tone; a subdued and
happy excitement pervaded the company; the familiar outlines of home scenery disappeared; the
caravan route became crowded with people; at night
the tent was struck in a strange place; every man's
face turned towards the city when he prayed, — the
sacred city which the young Jesus had never seen,
of which he had dreamed as an imaginative child
dreams of the most wonderful thing known to the
experience of the world in which he has been reared.
The boy looked up at the blazing Oriental stars with
thoughts that he shared with no one — thoughts
which he could but half understand himself.

On the fourth day the pilgrimage drew towards
its end. The massive city walls came in sight; the
topmost outlines of the Temple rose solemnly, —
gleaming gold and flashing white marble. The
crowd thickened. Shouts rent the air: Jerusalem!
Jerusalem! As the throng climbed the sacred hills,
they sang the famous Songs of Ascent written by
David their king. A trained flute-player led the
exultant music.

The lad bowed his young head. This was his first
entry into Jerusalem. The voices of his mother and
father seemed to him a good way off. The talk of his
relatives and friends sounded indistinct. He did not
shout. He could not explain how he felt. He might
not sing. He could not speak.

All through the days and nights of the great fes-

HIS FIRST VIEW OF JERUSALEM

tival his subdued excitement increased, unnoticed, or, if noticed, not understood by his family. He observed everything acutely; he received a sunburst of impressions; he took on, like a sensitive plate, the finest lines and shades and lights of the stirring and solemn scenes to which he was for the first time admitted; his mind and heart were full to throbbing.

The panorama of this great and sacred pageant aroused in him a deep and naïve enthusiasm. In all ages and all faiths, the coldest scoffer finds it hard not to respect a sincere and devout boy.

Passover lasted a week, but attendance was obligatory only for the first two days. During that time every household had baked and eaten its unleavened bread, had killed and offered its sacrificial lamb. Two hundred and fifty-six thousand of these poor creatures were slaughtered in the holy week, — a piteous sacrament! The court of the Temple reeked in blood. The hands of the priests dripped. The great altar ran. But upon this dark view of their consecrated anniversary, no Hebrew mind of that day dwelt. Animal life had no value in a time when human life had little enough. What was a lamb? Innocence born to suffer for guilt, the symbol of purity, of pain, and of forgiveness. The boy of Nazareth, sensitive above his neighbors, thought about the lambs. It was like him to pity them; to remember the signs of their suffering, to wonder at it, to count its cost.

During these two days the Passover supper had been eaten; whether or not the precise age of Jesus had admitted him to a share in this impressive cere-

mony, in either case its effect upon him was intense.
His solemn emotion waxed with every hour. The
grandeur of Jerusalem, then a little city, but immense to the imagination of every Jew; the splendors of the truly magnificent Temple; the swelling
of the vast numbers of pilgrims through the streets
and up the terraces; the magnetism of his first experience with crowds; the religious nature of every
sight, sound, thought, feeling which appealed to
him, — these accumulated like a mighty wave in
which he was swept. He strolled from his mother's
side, his father's protection. Lost in wonder and in
admiration, stirred with a deepening unrest, and
overcome with a kind of awe for which he had no
name, he wandered about the city and through the
Temple. Nazareth, the carpenter's shop, the country synagogue, the dull, daily lesson, the dry, daily
task, home, mother, father, were forgotten. Nothing
familiar kept him company. The boy walked about
in a grave, bright dream.

On the third day of the great feast it was quite
lawful to return home, and many families availed
themselves of this permission.

Two millions of people sometimes came up to
these festivals; the city brimmed over; the press,
the discomfort, were considerable. It was not lawful to let lodgings within the city gates, and even
Oriental hospitality was heavily taxed among the
residents. The immense throng began to break here
and there.

Joseph and Mary, gathering themselves to their
little group of friends and neighbors, started for
home.

The boy was not by their side at the time ; but
when they inquired about him, some one of the
people, who answer any question anyhow, replied
that he was with So-and-so, — a relative or a neighbor, — and no further concern at the time was felt
about him. The company filed out of the city and
into the caravan route, reaching Beroth, where they
spent the first night.

With darkness the mother began to worry. The
child had not appeared. She and Joseph now in-
stituted a thorough hunt for him. The whole company was searched. Neighbors, friends, strangers,
Jews, Gentiles, all the accessible travelers, were
questioned. The boy was not to be found.

Broken with anxiety, Mary and Joseph turned
about the next day, and made all possible haste to
get back into Jerusalem.

With all the appliances of our civilization to help
us, a straying child is always one of the uttermost
catastrophes. Steam, telegraph, telephone, police,
detective, the press, shorten or lessen an agony
which is still, at its shortest or least, unbearable ;
and Mary had none of these assuagements. She
was spent with terror and fatigue, when, at the end
of the interminable hours by which she had plodded back to the capital, she and Joseph piteously
tramped the city over, seeking for the boy. For
three days not a trace of him could be found. The
anguish of Mary in those three days and nights !
How many millions of mothers since that Passover,
reading this chapter in her story, have in their very
hearts blamed her more or less ! How bitterly did

she blame herself! A little more anxiety a little
sooner, a little less sensitiveness to being called a
worrier by husband or friends, a little less " easi-
ness " or trusting to chance that the boy was safe,
and this terrible thing had never happened. She
thought of the mystery under which the child was
born, of his unknown future, of her own tremendous responsibility for it and for him.

It was no common child whom she had lost. If it
had been Jonas, or John, or Enoch, yonder there in
Nazareth, or even James or Andrew — but Jesus!

White with anguish, Mary tottered by her husband's side. They searched the Temple for who
knows how many times. How enormous the building! How endless the courts! How confusing the
gates! Oh, the wearisome glitter of gold, of gems,
of marble, of steps, of platforms, — the tiresome
crowds of dazzling costumes, the dreary chatter, the
sickening scent of the butchered lambs, the red-
handed priests!

The Temple rose, terrace by terrace, haughty and
splendid. The hot sky was clear. Some of the
rabbis were holding, as was their wont at these festivals, one of their interminable discussions, arguing
fine points of the Law. In one of the open porticos
of the Temple a crowd had thickened significantly.
Something of unusual interest was plainly happening there. Joseph and Mary hurried to the court,
pushed their way through the crowd. The people
were unusually still. A young, sweet, treble voice
was speaking: it was the boy's!

There in the covered cloister, in his little white

talith, with his head bare, the child stood, quite absorbed. The gorgeous Temple towered behind him. Gray doctors of the Law sat about him. Half amused, half respectful, surprise rested upon their venerable faces. The rabbis of Jerusalem were engaged in open discussion with the country lad ; the scholars of the Temple were talking theology with a Nazarene child. An audience of considerable size hung upon this remarkable debate.

When had it been known in Jewry that a child could argue with the rabbis ? And what an argument ! His questions were as astonishing as his answers. He talked like a man and a scholar. The expert controversialists by whom he was surrounded were hard put to it to keep pace with him. Such intellectual force and moral subtlety would have made the reputation of any gray scribe or rabbi in the land. These practiced polemicists regarded the twelve-year-old boy with perplexity and respect. The crowd became denser around the group. It grew silent. Only the young voice was heard ; — it rang on uninterrupted ; it took on unchildlike, priestly tones.

A low cry broke in upon the little preacher's exhortation ; but the child, absorbed in his theme, did not seem to hear it. Then the moving of heads and changes of expression in his audience distracted him, and turning, he saw his mother's face.

At this point Mary restrained herself, and, shrinking back in the crowd, awaited the boy's will. He finished his little discourse with dignity, and stepped down from the platform on which he stood.

The doctors of the Law looked after the lad soberly; the crowd murmured about him without laughter; he passed away from and through them all, and sought his parents' side.

Then the mother's distress broke out in natural, motherly passion of reproach:

"My son! Why hast thou left us so? Why hast thou dealt with us in this manner? Thy father and I have sought thee for these three days! We have sorrowed for thee! What didst thou mean? What hast thou done?"

She caught him to her, sobbing as she did so.

Joseph did not join in her reproofs; he stood silently by. Both parents were as much puzzled as they were troubled. Ought they to blame the lad? Ought they *not* to blame him?

Mary was not a scolding mother, and her gentle reproaches died away before the boy's quiet and abstracted mien. He looked at her with perfect self-possession. Nay, truly, the right of reproach seemed, strangely, to rest with him. He did not speak until he chose, then:

"How is it," he said slowly, "that ye sought me?"

Mary hastened to explain, to expostulate; but he regarded her steadily. Before his unboylike eyes her own dimmed with the pang that mothers know when they see the first signs of manly will and individualism in a growing son.

"Knew ye not," asked the boy, "that I must be in my Father's house? I must be," he said peremptorily, "about my Father's things."

CHRIST IN THE TEMPLE

His manner was as solemn, as mysterious, as his words. Mary and Joseph did not answer him. They did not know how. His look was high and unfamiliar. He glanced back at the rabbis, upward at the splendid background of the Temple, then downward on the tiles. Whatever his thoughts, he did not try to share them with any person. With the sigh of one awaking from a thrilling dream to a dull reality, he passed down the terraces and out from the Temple courts. His mother's hand held his anxiously. He suffered this, without childish fret or petulance. There seemed to be the decision of a man in the heart of a boy. It was as if he said to himself :

" I will trouble her no more. My time is not come. After all, I am but a lad! I will defer to my parents and be subject to them."

And this without protest or rebellion he did and was.

He went back with them to Nazareth like any other child ; and there, like any other child, he lived and grew, and did the things that he was told, and talked no more with the rabbis, and was not restless or fretful to go back to Jerusalem and have an audience in the Temple portico.

We have been told that he waxed strong in body and in spirit, and found favor with God and men. Beyond these quaint and beautiful words we know nothing more about the young life of Jesus Christ, until he was a man, and a man of thirty years.

Yet this period is, of all the unknown spaces on the map of his life, the easiest for the loving imagination to follow.

A boy who could deliberately abandon, after such a glimpse as he had received of it, the enticement of ecclesiastical eminence and active, public religious service, and take up again, unrebellious and uncomplaining, the duties of childhood, was not, from any point of view, an ordinary youth.

The little, exotic Christians of our own day, forced by steam-heated processes into the front of prayer-meetings and exhortations and conventions, would not have found the subjection and seclusion of Nazareth welcome. We may doubt if the young Jesus liked it any better. But he began life in a rare way, — by doing the unwelcome cordially. Think as we may about his resemblance to other children at this time, his lack of resemblance to them was early in evidence. A certain spiritual precocity showed itself beyond all question ; it had a finely dual nature. He could do, but he could refrain ; he could preach, but he could practice. He could lead his elders, but he could obey them.

The interest of centuries has centred around the Temple scene. But there was more individuality, more poetry, more beauty, more religion in his journey home with Mary's now too anxious hand on his, or her nervous fingers touching always at his talith ; in his patience with a mother's mournful, watchful eyes atoning for a temporary neglect by a permanent oversight ; in his deference to a father's orders, never before so frequent or so minute ; in his reserve when chattering neighbors pried him with questions about his truancy from the caravan ; in his silence at the Nazareth synagogue where the country rabbis droned. He listened meekly. He did not debate or defy or deny. A lad, he took his place among the lads, and awaited that majority of character which lagged so far behind the majority of law. How fair the vision of that one glowing hour in the Temple! Memory ran a gentle license in it.

Thrilling and mysterious experience ! What had he done? What should he do? Obey, renounce, retreat, observe, conform, delay, — so far clearly. But what more? What did it mean, — that flash of power, that jet of light upon the mistiness of a young and growing soul? What should he think? How act? How aspire, or how defer? *What was he?*

A boy; the son of Joseph and Mary; a country lad, shut into a mountain village ; put to a trade; about to become a carpenter.

A great writer has said that he who has seen the suffering of men and of women has seen nothing ; he must see the suffering of children. It may be said that the solitude of men and women is society beside the solitude of children, — immature, unreasoning, perplexed little beings, terrified at the opening mystery of life. The solitude of a child - genius stands quite by itself, " a garden walled." Who, never having trodden its silent and desolate short pathways, among its timid buds and premature thorns, can presume to comprehend that limited but passionate mental topography?

All children of genius suffer, and most of them acutely. The childhood of Christ was no exception to this law. The subjection of crude power, scarcely conscious of its own existence, to inferior but mature

minds; the dullness, coldness, criticism, discourage-
ment, or positive rebuke of parents who are cast in a
coarser or a different mould from their own offspring;
the push and jar of the wills of other children equal
in rank to the more gifted little one for whose peculiarities they have no respect (and they are seldom
taught it), such are the inevitable trials which mark
the lot of an unusual child.

The child Jesus was a religious genius, — of all
types of superiority the most refined, most sensitive,
most conscientious, and therefore least easily satisfied with itself, and least likely to recognize the real
mistakes of its elders. These, in his case, were less
than they might have been. Whatever her ideas of
the nature or the future of her mystical son, Mary
had a certain amount of faith in both. She was
thoughtful, observant, docile to "the signs" by
which it was natural for a Jewish mind to be governed in perplexing matters; herself a devotee, and
always an essentially womanly woman, — hence a
lovable mother. She was sympathetic, perceptive,
alert, not urgent with her own will against the de-
veloping will of her boy; yet not without opinions,
or dignity in expressing them.

Joseph, on the other hand, was a man of great
good sense. While the inevitable discipline of the
family fell upon his shoulders, it was not executed
with severity. He recognized to a certain extent
that he had the rearing of a remarkable boy. In
so far as he was prepared for the surprising in the
history of the lad, Joseph perceived that the education of the child could not be a thoughtless affair.

His own mind worked with slow but honorable con-
scientiousness about this problem. Too much freedom or too little, more restraint or less, and the boy
(he reasoned) might be spoiled either way. The
father accepted the responsibility thus singularly laid
upon him in no inferior manner. Too many a Jewish home, in which the childhood of Christ might
have been passed, would have cruelly intensified the
difficulties of his youth.

Even as it was, and taken at their best, these
were neither few nor light. The boy bent himself
to his parents' wishes without protest; but he had
his own thoughts and views of things. These he
neither obtruded nor avoided. His wide eyes, with
distance in them, watched the rabbis in the country
synagogue, and the neighbors at their theological
gossip. Early he learned that it was unnecessary
to say what one was thinking.

He went into the shop with Joseph as a matter of
course. Every respectable Jew was taught a trade.
This was the honorable thing. Jesus stood at the
bench and watched the shavings curl from the planes,
— strong oak, or shining pine, yellow like the sun
in the heavens ; or cedar, red as flesh and blood ; or
olive, rich as the fibre of life, — his delicate imagination fastening itself on fancies or on visions as he
worked.

Who shall say what these were ? whither they
tended ? what they portended ? The youth himself
knew not whence they came. Strange glimpses of
that which he might not reach and did not understand broke through the fog of his daily task, —

brightness, burning down. What was life? To be
a builder like his father; to do exact work honora-
bly; to receive a coin for drilling a hole straight or
setting a joist true; to go to the synagogue; to fast
and bathe and pray, and feast and fast again; to
commit an interminable Law to a wincing memory
and a troubled belief; to be a good son, a good carpenter, and a good Jew. Yet what was life?

Struggling with itself, with his surroundings, with
his lot, the soul of the child of genius and the child
of God felt about for its own significance.

Solitude was natural to such youth as his. There
was deep opportunity for it in the beautiful groves
of oak which gathered about Nazareth. His strong,
young feet sought them often and oftener; to be
alone was his luxury, as it is that of all thoughtful
and superior beings.

Years of boyish obedience to parents who were
wise enough not to insist that they understood him,
years of precise mechanical labor at a decent trade,
years of good scholarship in the ecclesiastical
schools, passed dreamily over his mind and heart.
His character was formed by two controlling and
conflicting forces, — law and independence.

He was expected to be like other young men;
conscientiously he tried to be so. Inwardly, like all
gifted and growing beings, he felt that he was not.
Yet how urge a difference which no one else seemed
to recognize? His personal modesty shrank from
this insistence. At times, to accept the estimate
formed of him by his neighbors seemed the only
reasonable thing to do.

He trembled away from over-valuing himself.
He tried to think he was like Aaron, or like Solomon, yonder across the village street. He blamed
himself for a kind of undue self-appreciation.
Gusts and gales against which no storm-signal gave
warning swept over him. They came from unexpected directions. The points of compass in his
soul seemed all awry. Yet the magnetic needle
pointed true. To turn to that was safe. He may
have found it natural, through the passionate weather of immaturity, to be an irreproachable youth;
but he did not find it easy. His nature was too fine,
too complex, for mere commonplace correctness.

Duty? What *was* duty? He sought it in his
own young heart, but conflict answered him. He
asked it — for he was a wakeful lad — of the blazing stars of the Eastern night; he looked down into
the red heart of the wild lily for it, and up through
the green arches of the mountain woods he peered in
search of it. But neither nature nor his own being
replied distinctly. There were long spaces when
even his mother's fine perception could not help him.
She admitted to herself that she did not always
know how to treat him. He felt that he was misunderstood. But he accepted the fact with a patience
not to be expected of his years or of his temperament. For he had now come to recognize that he
did not understand himself.

CHAPTER II

How docile, how silent the years! Eighteen of them lay between the visit of the lad to the Temple and the entrance of the young man upon public life.

It would be impossible to overestimate the self-repression required of any strong and gifted nature put through an apprenticeship of solitude and of patience like that to which Jesus was subjected before the opening of his career. In his case we have the added element of his mystical superiority. That which would have been a blossoming or a blighting experience for an ordinary being, — what did it mean to him?

Evidently, the subjection of a strong will to that of parental judgment; the power to live a village life without being narrowed by it; formation of the habits of a keen and quiet observer of men; the silent study of the religion and history of his people and times; intense love of Nature, and the learning of her more valuable lessons, — these Nazareth taught him, slowly and thoroughly; for nothing was forced in his training, nothing hurried, nothing skimmed. God took time enough to educate Jesus Christ. No half-taught, undeveloped character, no " self-made" mind, was thrust into the greatest career of history. And still beyond the obvious effects of Nazareth upon the young man, there was the something that we cannot weigh and may not measure, — the element of the incalculable, the touch of that which he who claims to understand and reduce to language shows thereby that he understands the least of any.

It would not be difficult to gauge the mental conditions of a young and ardent contemporary of Christ, whose preparation for public life lay also in retirement and renunciation; for such a nature speaks our language. That of Christ forever calls for interpretation. His first important interpreter was the young man of whom we speak. The two were related, their lives connected by strange prenatal history; yet their homes were far apart, one being in Galilee and one in Southern Judea; and they had nothing which could properly be called personal acquaintance with each other up to the time of the beautiful and dramatic hour which ushered in the public career of Christ.

It was a mild day [1] in the late autumn, or the early winter, of what we number as the year of Rome 780. The Jordan, a picturesque, and for its entire course a lonely river, — scarcely sixty miles from Gennesaret to the Dead Sea in a straight line, but two hundred by its windings, — had been for some months the scene of unusual activity. Everybody was talking of a recluse who had suddenly left his retirement, and was teaching upon the banks of the stream.

---

[1] The 6th or 10th of January. Tradition.

The forerunners of revolutions are among the most interesting men in history, but they are among the least understood ; nor do they easily understand themselves. Life, fate, the souls of men, their own natures, even the nature of the great movements which they represent, are liable to undergo a peculiar confusion of outline in their minds. They are not good judges of affairs ; almost always prejudiced; apt to be dreamy and not practical, or obstinate and short-sighted.

He who was called the Baptist was a person of extraordinary beauty of spirit. Few men who have been important to human affairs have sunk themselves so utterly in the depths of the cause to which they have offered dedication.

He did not so much as stop to think what men would think of him, or whether they would think of him at all. He was the servant of a great idea, and he did not offer it the discourtesy of any visible interest in himself.

The wilderness of Judea was the favorite resort at that time of recluses, — more or less miserable men, disgusted with the abominations and follies of their times, and taking to what they called philosophy as a substitute for faith, replacing happiness by solitude and superstition. These poor souls existed, and shivered, and starved, and quarreled in the ghastly clefts and caves of the great Judean deserts.

John began life like the rest of them, unnoticed, a solitary, a person of no consequence, a frequenter of the hills, the cliffs, the caves, and the gorges ; a man who could not live like other people, but must needs concern himself with impossible theories of more impossible practice; a person to be pitied, or ridiculed, or tolerated, or respected, according to one's temperament.

How or when he had become other or more, who knew? Where had he crossed the invisible line between obscurity and eminence? Long before the day of which we think, John had become a person of influence.

The region of the Jordan had been for some time, in fact, the scene of an extensive religious excitement; and the young solitary was the centre of it. Judea, Perea, Galilee, the people, the government, Jews, Gentiles, travelers, the hills, the hamlets, and the desert whispered to each other. For five hundred years the Hebrews had numbered no prophet among their great men. The rumor that one had come up out of the desert excited the keenest interest. Quickly and quietly the crowd began to thicken. John had now a regular audience.

This young man, spare with long fasting, with vigils, with prayers, weather-beaten and weather-colored, with the long, uncut hair and beard of a special vow, was a stern and sombre figure. He fortified himself for a day of hard public speaking by eating a few dried locusts (the food of beggars and of the squalid poor), and added the honey with which the multitudinous wild bees stored the wilderness of Judea. This religious enthusiast wore a single garment of the roughest weave of camel's-hair cloth; and his head-dress was the simplest possible arrangement of stuff, sufficient to protect from the

sun. He was tall and grave. He discoursed of
serious things. The dark-skinned faces lifted to his
grew sober. Fear sat upon many ; hope on others ;
attention on all.

John was not a flattering speaker ; he had no
adroitness, and little mind to trouble himself whether
he knocked a man's vanity flat with the bludgeon of
a condemnatory peroration ; but there was a secret
in his popularity. He was believed to handle a
political idea, the favorite of the Jews, and the impulse of the times.

The Messianic expectation was in the air of Palestine. The Temple and the market-place buzzed
with it, the caravans whispered of it, Roman rulers
feared it, and Jewish scribes consulted of it. Her-
mon, and Carmel, and Zion watched for it ; the
waves of the Galilean Sea repeated it, and Jordan
reflected it. John, like all forerunners of great
masters and great movements, was as much the
product of his times as the honey was the work of
the wild bee, or the gray-lined leaf the growth of the
olive bough, or the corn the consequence of the seed.
He preached what men wanted, expected, and were
ready for.

.   .   .   .

The horizon of Nazareth was past its warmth and
color, for winter was at hand. The mountains lifted
dark profiles against a thoughtful sky. The best
and burst of the blossom had dropped from the
landscape. The traveler thought of this as he
turned his face towards a ford in the Jordan, which
lay perhaps twenty miles away. Jesus had grown

to manhood in a world of flowers, the barren hills yielding more scarlet ranunculus and red anemone than pasturage; the rock-roses, white and pink, ran everywhere. His eyes were early trained to the tints of narcissus, iris, and the red tulip. He knew the pink convolvulus and daisy; he loved the cyclamen and asphodel.

But when he went out to the first act of his public life, he walked in the dying of the year. Responsive to signs and omens, like all his race, did he think of this, as he made his solitary way towards Jordan, gleaming below terraces of sycamore and tamarisk trees and lined by fringes of reeds? For he went alone, moved by the voices which speak only to separateness.

Behind him lay the assured past, — his youth, sheltered, peaceful; all the calm and cheerful years that precede responsibility; monotonous daily labor, respected and respectable, but safe; his gentle home; his mother, with the aureola in her eyes,— his mother, a widow now, for Joseph of the strong arm and great fatherly heart was dead; his mother, needing him.

Before him lay the future of a marked life; a future towards which he felt impelled, as one feels impelled to make a leap into the fog, for the sake of a motive blinder yet than the abyss into which one plunges.

Whither did his steps tend as he trod the path to the banks of Jordan? Whither did his purpose move? Beyond the investigation of a local religious revival, of which Nazareth talked like the rest of the world, what did that journey mean?

Had he been asked, he would have made no answer; it may be said that he did not distinctly know himself. Led by the first impulse of maturing character, he sought the thick of the spiritual battle nearest him. Yet he did not go sombrely, as a soldier enlisted for his death; rather happily, as a dreamer following his vision; or humbly, as a thinker asking a great question: let the answer, be it what it would, — for joy or for anguish, for success or for failure, — let the answer come!

Through the thick growth of the river banks he came out suddenly upon the glancing stream. The tall reeds, swaying to the light winds, parted and closed above his head. At some little distance above him, a crowd of Jews were drawing about a young ascetic. He of Nazareth, being unobserved, gathered himself against the shadow of the reeds, and, standing silently, looked and listened.

John had no velvet tongue, but his audience seemed to like him none the less for that. The adulations, nay, even the courtesies of oratory, were absent from his speech. He arraigned his times and his hearers. The banks of the river rang with tremendous exhortations.

"Repent! repent! Look to your sins! The time is short. The Kingdom is at hand. The Kingdom of Heaven cometh. Repent! confess!"

Gentler tones succeeded. There were persuasions to a better life. There were hints and more than hints of better public conditions and of brighter personal hopes. The great political yearnings and beliefs of the Jews were gathered into a form vague at first, then clearer, then definite, then positive. The speaker threatened, but he promised; he condemned, but he reassured. He scathed his hearers for their vices, but he flung before them the banner of their great National Hope, their long-cherished, proud, and splendid expectation: "Your Deliverer is within reach! Your Hero is here! He whom ye have trusted and awaited is close at hand. Behold, he cometh! Prepare the way for him!"

Now the people, hearing these stirring words, and wrought upon with the eloquence of the young speaker, took upon themselves a natural conclusion. Who should this man be who had troubled the waters of Jordan for so many a day? See Jerusalem, and Bethlehem, and Jericho, and the hill country, and the desert, thronging to follow this extraordinary recluse, who sought nothing, claimed nothing for himself! — this eloquent, self-forgetting being, burning in the flame of truth, and thinking no more of his own interest than the angels who talked with Abraham or wrestled with Jacob!

So his listeners pressed upon him. "Thou," they cried, "art He! Thou art no prophet, but He Himself! Thou art He whom we have sought so long!"

Then swiftly over the face of John there came the unconscious and the noble look of one who does not even recognize the high nature of the deed he does. In his hands at that moment he held the chance of such an attractive though delusive personal history as few men have had. The emotional Jews were ready to take him for his own Christ. He could have passed for their Messiah much more easily than he could persuade them just then that he was not the man.

The watcher by the river bank took a few steps forward and upward of the stream; so, drawing nearer, but still unnoticed, he could hear more plainly what took place between the speaker and the people. " Why should we look for another? Art thou not He? Thou art He! "

" Nay — nay, I am not He. I am not worthy to unloose the fastening of his sandal. He cometh after, but He is preferred before. He is before me and above me. I baptize you with this water."

As John spoke he gently drew one of the throng towards him into the ford, and moving to the shallow of the river baptized the penitent. This was done with the solemnity of one who believed in the sacredness of the act, and his own reverence therefor was seen to extend quickly to the people.

"There cometh One," he murmured, " He shall bathe you with fire, and with the Spirit which is Holy. Repent! for He is mightier than I! " As he spoke these last three words he perceived suddenly that he was observed by a stranger standing apart on the banks of the stream. The color fled quickly from the dark face of the young prophet. He ceased abruptly, and strode towards the figure.

The two young men stood for a moment face to face without speaking to each other. John was still pale, and the ragged fringe on the edge of his coarse garment trembled below his leathern girdle.

He of Nazareth, in a light talith, against the dark background of the reeds and river trees, took

on a strong relief. Their eyes — in both the solemn,
searching eyes of the devotee, undistracted by diversion, deepened by thought, undaunted by self-denial,
darkened by the unconscious shadow of coming
martyrdom — questioned each other. Those of the
one asked:

"Who art thou?"

And those of the other made strange answer, not
saying:

"I am He," but rather repeating, "Who am I?
Read me to myself." Words added little to that
instantaneous recognition of the spirit.

Neither could have put into language what that
moment meant to each. The face of John grew
rapt. But on that of the Nazarene a gentle trouble
lay. Possessed by who knew what thoughts, he had
sought the haunts of the popular teacher. Driven
by who could say what longing for recognition, of
which he sorely felt the need, he had come to his
unknown kinsman, this young man whose public
career had already so much the start of his own.
With the touching humility characteristic of his
whole life, he depended on his cousin for that encouragement without which he would not, perhaps
could not, have trusted the stirring of his own nature. On John fell the double responsibility of
recognition and of interpretation; he must identify
Christ to himself, as well as to the people. One
gesture did it, — one swift Oriental gesture of reverence, of worship. John's suffused eyes, bowed
head, outstretched hands, sinking body, prostrate
being, cried: "Thou art He!"

Still the face of the other, too gentle, too humble, to mistake the moment, regarded him perplexedly. "*Who* am I?" it said.

The people had now begun to press down the river bank towards the prophet, but John, by a motion which would have been impatient in a pettier man and at a lesser crisis of feeling, ordered them to keep their distance. The two were therefore still apart and undisturbed. The waters of the ford, deepening where they now stood, ran calmer and darker. The slender leaves of a willow on the banks dropped into the stream and floated down. Tree-tops were reflected brokenly in the river, — a palm, a red tamarisk, a clump of oleanders, and a few white-stemmed sycamores, beyond the fringe of reeds. Doves shimmered overhead. The sky was warm and deep. The Nazarene stepped down into the water.

Startled, incredulous, shocked, John perceived that Jesus was seeking the submission of baptism. The young man's whole nature rose in noble revolt against the situation in which he so unexpectedly found himself. He was destitute of the motives of ordinary forerunners of heroes: at the first intimation that his day was over, he was ready to drop the symbol and the substance of power; preëminence was nothing to him, the sweets of leadership, the fascination of oratory, — nothing and less! He longed only to be true to his one errand in the world, only to be the prologue to the drama, the herald before the king; only to be blotted, forgotten, obliterated in the glory and the story of the Wonderful!

THE BAPTISM OF CHRIST

"Nay, nay. Comest thou to *me?* Rather I to thee!"

But Jesus, smiling, had his will; and gently and enigmatically urging, "Suffer it to be, for now," he waded into the water and received from the awed and trembling hands of his kinsman the rite of dedication to a religious life. But when he came up out of the shining river the people had run down the banks of the stream, and many of them stood collected to see the newcomer, about whose baptism there seemed to be something of special interest which they had missed. They had scrambled along chattering, but a quietness fell on them when they reached the spot. For the look on the faces of the two young men was not a thing to gossip in the presence of, however much or long one might talk of it in after times.

And, while the whole group stood, thoughtful, a cream-white dove that had been flying to and fro across Jordan rose high in the heavens and swept out of sight. The stranger had fixed his gaze upon the flight of the dove; and, thus, dripping with gleaming water, with upraised face, he seemed entirely preoccupied with the movements of the bird. John, wondering at his absorption in this trifle, drew near to observe the other, and, seeing that he was at prayer, reverently drew back. The bird swept into sight again; graceful, snowy, palpitating like a thing half bird, half lily, pure as the film of the cloud, through which it descended slowly. The dove dipped toward the water, and with a few encircling movements settled gently upon the head of Jesus, whose uplifted countenance it seemed to study with that strange distance which the observation of a bird puts between itself and a human face, as if it came from a sphere too high to touch humanity. Almost before one could say that it had rested upon the man, it had ascended from him and melted into the sky.

A little murmur ran through the crowd at the beautiful sight; the people, who must always talk of whatever happens, turned to say something each to his neighbor. But Jesus and John, who did not speak, listened with held breath. Again their eyes met solemnly, each with a question in them.

"Didst thou hear aught?"

"Didst *thou?*" . . .

Afterwards a strange thing was said about the dove. It was reported that John, whose severe and honorable word was not to be doubted, had heard intelligible sounds from the heavens when the bird swept from the sky upon the head of the newly-baptized man; it was added that the other had himself heard them, and more than these, and that the words had a meaning which no man else could understand.

Some said that this was the Bath-qol, or Daughter Voice, common to the over-excited imagination of the Jews, by which those who were quite ready to believe in it found their affairs regulated, — business, marriage, travel, and the like.

But there were those who shook their heads and observed with significance that John was not a man to trouble himself about the Daughter Voice.

It was said that the stranger, standing in the Jordan
with the light of a fresh religious vow upon his
lifted face, with prayer in his eyes and the dove
circling to his brow, had been identified of Heaven
(John being witness to the fact) in mystical language:

"My beloved son!" What manner of words
were these? "I am well pleased with thee!" What
should be made of it?

There were not wanting philosophers and dreamers
as well as common folk, who claimed that John and
his kinsman had indeed heard that to which other
ears were deaf: for it was well known to Oriental
students that there are senses beyond the familiar
five whose culture is within a man's own control, and
whose grasp may reach strange facts, both of the
mind and of the body; and whose witness of the
marvelous no man less devout, less pure, less educated in higher truth than he who testifies thereof
has the right to dispute. At all events, it could
not be denied that the beautiful baptismal scene
on Jordan bade fair to become a public event of
marked importance.

The newly-baptized man was quickly made aware
that he had become the centre of observation. The
followers of the young prophet, half irresolute between the two, looked from one to the other with
their piercing Jewish eyes. Certain of the bolder
in the throng pressed curiously forward towards the
stranger: a Pharisee in full phylactery and a Hebrew merchant, both bent, it was clearly to be seen,
on a good bout of polemics; a Roman citizen and a

Greek traveler followed with the more nonchalant interest of men of the world in a passing episode.

But the Nazarene, stunned with the awful credentials which John had given over to him, and thrilling with the mystical experience of the past hour, turned abruptly away.

With bowed head he passed through the shivering river reeds in the direction of the desert.

CHAPTER III

THE WILDERNESS

From an early Jewish writer have come down to us these fine words: " The Holy One, blessed be His Name, does not elevate a man to dignity till He has first tried and searched him; and if he stands in temptation, then He raises him to dignity."

Overwhelmed with the events of the day, Jesus sought the solitude which it was his first and his second nature to love. There was nothing better to be done for the crowd at that moment than to gratify its curiosity, which he had no disposition to do; he escaped it, and, pushing through the reeds which grew above his tall height, left the river rapidly behind him.

The Judean desert was, of all the wildernesses to to be found in the vicinity of civilization, one of the most dreary and uncanny. The Jews, with grim succinctness, called it The Horror, The Appalling Desolation.

Jesus walked strongly and quickly. After a few hours he found himself at the foot of the western hills, in a more desolate region and quite alone. Day was declining; and the heads and shoulders of the bare chalk hills were at their kindest colors in the mellow before the sunset; but these were cold

enough. Flint-bound ridges looked icily at each
other, as if they intimated dark thoughts which they
were forbidden tò communicate. No sign of life
was visible except the birds of the desert, and now
and then one of its sly, wild animals. A few stray
thrushes uttered melancholy notes. A black grackle
with yellow wings flew over the traveler's head and
rose, vanishing. Vultures circled low in grim spots
about the landscape. An unseen fox, or desert par-
tridge, waiting for the dark, slipped stealthily among
the rocks.

Westward, valleys of tremendous depth already
held the night. Passage through them was not to
be thought of, they were so steep and deep, except
in their troughs below. Southward this grim country was impassable. Far away lay the only inhab-
ited spot in the desert, — a town, Engedi by name.
A few reservoirs, in hard limestone, held the only
water of the thirsty landscape. There were tales of
terrible torrents in winter and spring, and gorges of
incredible depth told the story of the rush of fresh-
ets from the heights. On the hills grew only the
plants that ask no water ; dry, sinister, with a skin
prickly to the touch. In the valleys a white broom
thickened courageously, but this bloomed in March.
In the summer the desert was a land of drought. In
the winter it held the chill and the repulsiveness of
the grave. In the night it had the outlines and the
shadows of sorcery, of the supernatural, of the ter-
rors that come after the grave.

Night was coming on. Jesus climbed to the front
of a high cliff, and looked about him. He saw the

chalk of the midland hills sloping from three thousand feet yonder, near Hebron, to half that height at the valley of the Dead Sea. He saw a country of caves and gorges, of secrecy, of shadow, of unclean and venomous creatures, of skulking things and hiding men. For he remembered that there were men who chose the desert for their only home ; hermits and philosophers, robbers and refugees from justice, and those weary of life; dwellers in caves and brooders upon mystery. One of these came out from a cavern that gaped black below the cliff on whose edge the Nazarene was standing, stared up at him sulkily for a moment with gaunt eyes, and flitted away like a bat. This momentary sign of human life served only to emphasize the sense of desolation hanging over the place.

The swift Oriental night swept on in large masses. The long lines of the gorges took on frightful proportions in the gloom. One came upon them unexpectedly. A false step might hurl a man to a tomb in which he would never be found. The solitary, feeling his way slowly through the twilight, oppressed by thought too tense to be aware of danger, suddenly drew back. His foot had struck the edge of a chasm, yawning thirty or forty feet across his way ; he peered over ; the bottom lay at the least a thousand feet down.

The sun was now quite set, and the chill of night was descending. Jesus, perceiving that it would be impracticable to continue his wanderings, sought such shelter for the night as the inhospitable place afforded, — a cleft in the rock, an uninhabited cave, a cushion of the dry plants that had no thirst, and that seemed when he touched them like an unnatural form of organism which shrank from him. The stars sprang out and the dew fell. Ravens croaked in some dismal distance. A rare viper, whose lair he had disturbed, hissed at his feet. The hills, in the darkness, took on portentous forms. The valleys sank away from the solid earth like bottomless pits. He had eaten nothing for some hours, and it did not occur to him to provide himself with food. His mind and heart were in a tumult which he found it difficult to understand or to calm.

The scenes and events of the day returned like doors folding upon themselves; through their apertures he passed and repassed. The long, dusty walk; vanished Nazareth; the watchful trees that guarded Jordan; the tall reeds; the gleaming river; the crowds lining the stream; the face and figure of the young prophet, his impassioned words, his burning eyes, his sudden recognition, his beautiful obeisance; the touch of the cool water; the emotions with which the sacred rite had been accepted, — followed fast in turn again. In the dead dark of the desert the shining of the white dove glimmered from the sky. From the silence of the wilderness throbbed up the echo of The Voice: "Thou — *thou* art My beloved Son."

The dull ear had not heard it, nor the deaf with pettiness and worldliness and vice. The senses of the pure spirit understood it, for to them it spoke. The perplexed and solitary man, pondering over all things, — life, death, truth, his own past, his own

THE JORDAN

future, his duty, and his fate, — could not doubt that
he had heard from the Invisible these to most men
inaudible words. The thrill of them was on him
yet. Whence did they come? WHO uttered them?
What did they mean? What did they involve in
him who had been chosen by their solemn articula-
tion? It were a deadly thing to mistake a syllable
of them. What depended upon their correct comprehension? The course of a whole life's history
must be decided in a few days and nights of thought
and solitude ; but that, to the watcher in the desert,
was the least of his problem. The fate of an ancient
people, the fulfillment of a great hope and of stately
prophecy, the outcry of humanity, the pitiable passion of the earth, crowded upon his consciousness.

" *Thou shalt carry the sins of the world.*"

These words pursued him. The scream of a night-
bird in the desert cried across them ; the howling of
a wolf, the barking of a jackal in the distance mingled with them ; the winds in the caves would have
drowned them, but they rang on. Where and when
had he heard them ? Were they the refrain of some
poem in the literature of his people ? The echo
of an ancient past ? Or were they the forecast of
an impending future ? Six weeks later these were
destined to be almost the first words which should
meet his ears when he returned to the habitations of
men. The voice of his young kinsman, he half commanding as a prophet should, would quiver with this
salutation. Jesus might have been astonished to
discover in himself, as he paced the wilderness, the
first, faint intimation of those extra senses which

men call preaudience or prevision; but he was too
far buried in greater and deeper thought and feeling
to dwell as yet upon the simpler signs of a new and
startling endowment. He who had but an hour
since heard the voice of God did not tarry with the
mystery of his own nature.

"*Thou shalt carry the sins of the world, . . . thou
Lamb of God.*"

.   .   .   .

Suddenly, bleating and piteous, flashed back the
face of a lamb that he had seen on that first time
when, a lad, he went to the Temple, — a white, tender thing, clinging to its butchers, bleeding! He
saw the entreaty in its dumb eyes, their last anguish; the red hands of the priest; smoke and fire
on the dripping altar. . . .

Day dawned without cheer. The outlines of the
great hill Quarantana, prominent because the last
peak of a western ridge, and ending in a sheer precipice, rose frowning. The watcher directed his steps
towards it, and, climbing to its front, looked off over
the dismal landscape which he had chosen as the
setting to the crisis of his life. The east broke
grayly with a sickly, purplish mock of sunrise. The
scorpions crawled into their hiding places sullenly,
and rooks croaked somewhere close at ear. A few
moving blots among the caves in the precipice indicated the presence of the miserable human beings
who knew no other homes than this jagged country;
they were seeking their morning meal. Even that
starving fare was not for the Nazarene; he found
himself already faint with the first distress of a hun-

ger that was not to be of short duration, and from which he shrank, as all men do from the opening stage of any form of long-continued suffering.

For that he *had* come to the crisis of his life his clear perception could not doubt. A threefold pressure crowded upon him and within him, — the views of other men, the movements of his own soul, and the voice of God.

The thought of his young kinsman was plain enough to read. John saw in Jesus the material for a great reformer, — of spotless personal character, to be sure, of positive religious fervor, of irreproachable motives; mysteriously (for who knew, when one came to this, just what John meant?) — mysteriously favored of Heaven, but a great leader of men; ordained to hold masses in his power, and fated to be an immense personal success, such a success as the devout mind of the young ascetic on the banks of Jordan would consider inseparable from the career of the chosen of God, the Messiah of a proud people.

Yet the views of John as to the nature and duties of the Jewish Messiah were as far in advance of those held by the majority of his hearers as his life was purer than a Roman gentleman's, or nobler than a Hebrew Pharisee's.

Jesus was too well-educated a man, too thoroughly learned in Hebrew literature, to be at all misled as to the kind of hero whom the Hebrews expected, awaited, and would honor.

In himself he did not find the material for any such ideal as his people passionately cherished. All the traditions of his race pointed one way. The instincts of his own nature drew him in another. Between them, gently as the dove had floated from the sky in the afternoon light on Jordan, descended the whisper of God. But saying what? . . .

His strong eye ran from the low-lying foreground to the heights of Moab and Gilead steadily. Who was he — a young man, unknown, unbefriended, inexperienced, a rustic from Nazareth — that he should take upon himself the most solemn claims possible to his people or his faith? What was he that he should parley with Jehovah? How should he presume to translate The Voice from Heaven?

"I will remain in this wilderness until I do." This resolve formed itself in his consciousness without explicit words, as one familiar with a foreign language translates it without transposition to his own tongue. Resolutely putting in the background of his mind his personal discomfort; his sharpening hunger, the gusts of sickening faintness that swept upon him, his suffering from the need of sleep, and the sense of loneliness so much more acute in a delicate than in a dull organization, — he held himself down among the creatures of the desert, like one of them. There he called on the genius of solitude and the angel of self-deprivation, as all men must who would approach God, to help him in the first great definite battle of a spiritual contest destined to last till his final breath should be drawn in agony, and his final prayer ascend in peace.

. . . .

Day succeeded night and week followed upon

week. With the natural respect of an Oriental and of a Hebrew for long-sustained fasts and seclusion, it did not occur to Jesus that he was subjecting himself to unreasonable rigors; in fact, his personal comfort was the last of all topics in his thoughts. His emotion far transcended all common interruptions to its current, whose depth and strength did but increase under bodily suffering.

A lesser man, acting under a meaner motive, might in the presence of admiring spectators have subjected himself to surprising feats in starvation, or burial, or physical contortion, or to the vagaries of voluntary and unnecessary martyrdom, seeking thereby personal glory enough to pay for the process. But this noble enthusiast, simply, without calculation, without witnesses, swept on the stream of a great impulse, suffered in solitude and in night, and in perplexity, — to what end? That his soul might know itself and its God; that he might learn his duty and do it. Yet was he no angel, but a man; and his human suffering encroached upon his strength. He weakened and sickened. Visions of food swam before his eyes. Pictures of home, of friends, of long-needed sleep, of his own rug in his mother's house, of her tender face, her gentle ministration, the evening meal prepared by her quiet hands, blurred against the dark background of the desert. He remembered that no one had sought him out in his solitude; half forgetting, as his physical distress extended upon him, that he himself had chosen to be alone. . . . Then the visions again! Cool fruit heaped up, dusky and rich of color in its own leaves, sprang out everywhere to his strained eye; the cliffs hung heavy with purpling grapes; and the mouth of the cave rioted with fig and olive, blazed with luscious melon, crimsoned with alluring pomegranate.

He put out his hand, and the teeth of the limestone bruised him. Fresh, unleavened bread hot from the oven, for the meal of a sacred day's use, stood smoking on the ground; . . . see! piled in loaves against the feet of the rock. He staggered up and stooped over to pick it up. . . . Stone! — stone as cold as the sepulchre, and as sharp as famine.

Night was coming on; the shadows of the desert took monstrous shapes; on the brain disordered by a fast already prolonged past the limits of torment, strange impressions were stamped. Uncanny tales came back to memory. Sorcery and witchcraft and demonology were allies to assault the intelligence and the self-possession of a starving man. Half-delirious dreams chased each other through a burning brain. The pains of hunger, which are outlived in the earlier stages of starvation, had scarcely received attention in their time; for the greatness of his emotion had not suffered them. Now the fatal and inexorable symptoms of the final failure of human strength within a famished body drew on. Delirium and syncope were close at hand. Food! food! He crept down the mountain to a cleft in the rock where water had collected and dashed it in his haggard face.

·   ·   ·   ·   ·   ·   ·   ·   ·   ·

Suddenly within him, like the groping, griping hands of a strong man fighting in the dark, uprose the movement of a something never felt before, — new forces in his soul; strange senses of the spirit, superinduced upon those of his fainting body; the shadows of coming gifts, of advancing possibilities, of unknown facilities of action and unguessed powers of will. What were these? Whence did they come? Whither would they lead him? What should he do with them?

He sat with his famished eyes fastened upon an oval, flat stone at his feet; it had the shape of shew-bread, such as the priests baked for their own food. He picked the stone up and handled it curiously. A thrill like the joy of feasting ran from his fingers through his whole sinking body. At that moment he perceived that he had but to open his lips and speak two words : " Become bread ! " for the rocks of the wilderness were his. The hard heart of the limestone would melt like dough beneath his touch. The resources of the desert would obey him. Starvation was his servant. The laws of human life were his slaves. He had but to speak. . . .

He did not speak. He laid the stone down — and it was but a stone. The famished man put his hands before his face and trembled, but not with physical anguish; and bowed himself to the earth in the dark, but not with bodily weakness. His whole being shook with the shock of a great moral escape.

It seemed to his delicate sense of spiritual honor that the exertion of a great and sacred gift to selfish ends were a heinous desecration. All the principalities and powers of the desert air might summon their cohorts against his starving weakness, but he who had heard The Voice from the sky above the river had other uses for his sense of power, — this new, thrilling, mystical power to do, to be, to dream, to act the Will of God Almighty; not his own. No, never his own; from this first moment in the knowledge that he was not like other men, to the last hour of his dedicated life, never his own will, for his own sake, for his own ends, for his own comfort.

There was another way. There was a nobler exercise for latent and mysterious strength.

The fasting solitary lifted his hands, his face, to the heavens. Food? Yes, a man must have food. But of what kind? It was easier for the starving body to be nourished by the mind and heart of God than for the starving soul to live on bread alone. In his great exaltation, this profound thought seemed to rest at his drawn and fevered lips like a chalice. Perishing, he drank life from it.

He had now reached that stage of physical exhaustion when the mind, nearly or quite freed from its usual dependence upon the senses, rules in a world of its own. Vision upon vision swam before him; these had the proportions of reality; sight, touch, hearing recognized them, and other faculties, unknown, unnamed, took hold of them. Yet his judgment curiously kept step with these. Bewildering, alluring panorama unfolded before him. It was as if they rolled and unrolled over the expanse of the whole desert. They extended so far that his eye could not compass them where he was, and, weakly crawling up, he managed to reach the nearest height above him, where bleak Quarantana looked down coldly on the darkening valleys. Here, solitary, observant, silent, he sank upon the rock.

Swarming below, he saw the people of his race, mad with hero-worship, but pugnacious to create their own hero, prostrating themselves at his feet. Their hot huzzas ascended to his ears. They were such a throng that their dark, bright, Oriental eyes rolled like the little waves of a great lake. Their spokesman held up a flashing thing, — a crown! Purple robes and sceptre, signets, jewels, flights of flashing marble steps, fountains, gardens, palisades, the ante-rooms of a palace, slaves, flowers, banquets, perfumes from behind the silken curtains of unentered, unseen apartments, swept trembling by. Stately emissaries of Gentile dignitaries awaited audience of him. Gentile nations, for his sake, honored his race. Persia, Egypt, Babylonia, bowed before the once scorned and captive Jews. Rome — ah, Rome! haughty, dreaded, and hated; Rome, afraid of her freed slaves, made terms with her equals; and he — *he*, Jesus of Nazareth, dictated and enforced those terms. To what end? His own glory, and the gratified prejudices and traditions of his people. At what price? At the cost of a political life; at the cost of feverish intrigue, petty restlessness, and deliberate emphasis of self; at the price of the lower motive, the personal greed, and indifference to best things which the politician may elect to pay, clothing personal aims in the diaphanous delusion of serving the public weal.

Was *that* what The Voice on Jordan meant to say? Did the white wing of The Dove brush his bowed and humble head for *that?*

Nay, nay. "Him only shalt thou serve!" The besieged man flung himself upon the visions of the night, of the desert, of his own powerful imagination and keen intellect, as if they had been spirits of the nether world, and as if it depended upon himself alone in all the universe to force the rebellion of moral guilt into subjection to imperial Good.

Ah, the Temple! Splendid, glittering, marble and gold; priests and altars; worshipers crowding up and down; the bleeding, burning lambs; the great and gorgeous sacred veil, stiff with embroidery of blue, of purple, of crimson, of white, with golden cherubim wrought thereon; the hidden ark; the Holy of Holies!

He passed through the Gate Beautiful, and wandered in and out. He reached the exquisite colonnade of Solomon's Porch, climbed the highest pinnacle, and there stood looking down and off. The gorge of Kedron yawned below him, — three hundred and fifty feet sheer down. The brook lay like a bubble below. What a leap! . . .

Yonder in the courts the people thronged. Some were looking up: they had caught sight of him above; they were speaking to one another about him. Jerusalem lay blazing in the sun; the heat of the day was breaking; people were coming from their houses; the markets were opening, the streets were filling, the whole world was there to see. What a

fall! What a feat! What a wonder! It were only
to leave this hideous den of death and night; to
break this mortal fast; to gather strength to make
the journey by the fire of his soul, to be in the
Sacred City. When? How? Perhaps by the willing of a wish, by the motion of a foot, by the out-
stretching of an arm. Who knew how the strange
powers within him, newly discovered, freshly lighted,
dulled only by famine and desolation, waiting for
their nourishment, crying for their exercise, would
bestir themselves?

He felt it in his thrilling consciousness that he
could have floated over that parapet, and descended
among the gaping crowd without a bruise. So great
was his exaltation, so mighty his sense of untried,
undeveloped faculties, at this moment, that the marvel seemed even small to him. It meant but the
ordering of a purpose; it meant but a turn of the
will. It meant that the allegiance, the adoration of
his race, were his, and his forever. It meant that
precious thing, — of all the ambitions of earth or
heaven most bewitching to a Jewish mind, — absolute recognition as their Messiah. It meant none
the less a devout life than this starvation in the
desert, nay, rather, meant it all the more. It meant
the most godlike, the holiest career of which the
Hebrew imagination could conceive. It meant the
use of a marvelous power. How? Not as God
directed; that was all. Simply not as the Author
of all Powers did ordain. It meant putting a great
gift to a doubtful exercise; superseding known laws
by the unknown, to gratify paltry curiosity and the

lowest form of superstition. It meant doing as he
chose, not as God had chosen. Searching in himself passionately for light and law, he found but
this: that, if a man wished to do the will of God, to
him it should be made known. Was it The Will
that he should capture Jerusalem by a great, dramatic exhibition of arts such as an Indian occultist
might claim to practise? To become the King of
the Jews, should he suffer himself to be thought the
king of sorcerers? God was mystery, but He was
not magic. The dignity in Christ's own nature revolted from this view of his position. In his reac-
tion from his momentary moral confusion, so near
did he come to the Invisible that it seemed to him
as if Jehovah himself had been assaulted in his own
being; and, rising to his full height, and crushing
the sharp stones beneath his bruised feet, he apos-
trophized the whole source and force of evil as if it
were one malicious intelligence:

" Thou shalt not try the Lord thy God! "

Every temptation needs its desert, and every
desert has its temptation. The true nature of his
moral trial now began to suggest itself to the Nazarene. What his race and his times would demand
of him — that he could not give. What he had the
power to achieve — that he might not do. It came
slowly to his awed and gentle thought to wonder if
he had been mistaken in daring to suppose that he
could be the Anointed, the Chosen of his people
and of his people's God.

The very opening indications of his mission took
on the character of an error into which he had

nearly fallen, an abyss into which he had all but slipped ; as he might slip into that fissure yonder below the mountains, fifteen hundred feet yawning down.

With his unapproachable humility, his royal carelessness of self, he put his splendid visions by. If he might not be the Messiah of the Jews, he could be not the less the Son of God. If not for him the sceptre and gems and the purple of life, he could still be a plain, good man, doing his duty in an obscure fashion as God bade him, and trusting Heaven to teach him what and where it was. With this simple and this grand resolve, he turned to leave the desert, and to seek the homely and natural presence of men.

But on the brow of the hill he fell fainting. He had come to the end of his strength, and unconsciousness compassionately found him out at last.

.   .   .   .

When he came to himself, he heard in the dark the movement of dim, strange forms, stately and merciful as his most cherished dreams of the strongest angel in the heavenly world. He heard inarticulate, brooding sounds of tenderness beyond the tenderness of earth. The grasp of unseen fingers touched his wasted hands. Vitality that had never known a pang or weakness flowed through the clasp. So the spent and famished man was comforted. And day dawned upon the wilderness.

CHAPTER IV

THE FIRST WONDERS

WITH the humility which is the marked feature of true greatness, Jesus came back from the wilderness into the world of self-seeking men. His heart was high, but his hope was low or lowered. His unique and solemn experience had not subdued his ideals, but had saddened his expectations. Solitude, vigil, hunger, and prayer spoke another tongue from the language of the people of affairs or the men of pleasure who looked at him with indifference or with curiosity and went their ways.

An impressive scene took place between himself and his kinsman, the prophet, who sought the earliest opportunity to reaffirm the first recognition of his favorite convert; but Jesus passed through this without apparent emotion. His mood was one of divine self-obliteration : like all exalted moods, it carried its own comfort with it ; but this was of the kind about which a man does not talk.

He became strangely incommunicative. With remoteness he approached the throbbing life of men. Gently he assumed the task which he had set himself, — to do the nearest duty in the noblest way, and trust God for the results.

To this simple purpose, this view of responsibility

so elemental that the weakest soul might overlook it, while the strongest needed all his strength to perceive in it the materials for a great theory of life, he began to adjust himself.

With extraordinary patience he sought and followed the leadings of his own heart, and of the heart of God as expressed to it in a manner incomprehensible to men less pure and docile than himself. These took him from experiment to experiment in the interpretation of the Divine purpose under which he had intelligently ranged the energies of his personal will.

He pursued at first, in great uncertainty, an apparently indecisive course. Those bleak weeks in the Judean desert had left him in what we may call a glorified perplexity. He had come out of it sure of little except of his own motives. These had escaped from trial as white as the wings of a flower set free by the wind from a whorl of thorns. He longed to justify in himself his own favorite appellation of the Son of God. This had become his one passionate purpose. He could bear it not to be the Messiah; apparently he was not the Messiah.

Nothing in his own apprehension of himself yet answered to the popular ideal of the Jewish hero. If it were the greatest of his moral struggles not to be deluded with this idea, he had achieved it. If it were the subtlest of his moral perils to mistake a call from Heaven for a delusion and a fantasy, he had not yet evaded it.

He found in himself no easier way to detect truth

than the old, plain way which common men with
uncommon consciences have always known and followed. He did the thing that he was sure was right,
and let the doubtful go. He could bear it not to be
the Messiah of his people. He could not bear it not
to be the Son of his God.

Pathetic at this time were the exaltations and de-
pressions of his mood, and the flickerings of his
illumination, — brighter to-day, darker to-morrow;
never quite steady enough to sustain in him a joyous
assurance that he was not mistaken. He entered
upon his career under the full human disability
which makes it the hardest thing in the early lives
of great men that they do not know whether they
are great or not.

Silent, pallid, wasted from famine, glorified by
prayer, he stood in his desert-stained garments
among the little group that, headed by his cousin,
met him when he strode back through the river-
reeds to the bank of Jordan. Dreamily he heard
the solemn apostrophe of John. Was his enthusi-
astic kinsman right? Was he wrong? How could
John — or Jesus — know? More perplexed than
elated, Jesus watched the movements of the young
prophet's favorite penitents, two or three of whom
left their old master and impulsively offered to himself their definite allegiance, after the manner of
Eastern pupils, or followers of a popular teacher.
But this humble man, thinking so little of himself
and so much of God, was more troubled than flattered when he saw those eager Hebrew faces lifted
to his own in the first light of personal idealization.

His surprise flushed delicately all over his noble countenance.

"Why?" he said with beautiful naïveté. "What seek ye?"

This was not the regal assumption which was expected of him, and significant looks of doubt and disapproval passed among the people. But the followers of John, who had been trained not to take the low or even the middling view of things, were not rebuffed by the honesty of a reply that might easily have cost Jesus his first friends, and hence perhaps. the rest of his coterie. This touched and pleased him.

Encouraged and stimulated by the little sign of public favor, or of heavenly preference (he found nothing yet to make it clear to him whether these two things were twain or one), he rose from his depression into a happy, hopeful mood. In its first energy he took heart to invite a few other men to add themselves to the small number of his friends. Out of these modest beginnings his following grew. In the fashion of the times, his personal adherents went by the name of disciples. They were plain men, many of them fishermen, men of the carpenter's own social rank, or somewhat below it. The upper classes did not concern themselves at this time with the young devotee.

.   .   .   .

A small Galilean town, quite unimportant in its day, scarcely more than a hamlet, has acquired immortal renown for one single entertainment in its local society. To one Jewish bride, — a mere girl,

almost a child let us think, a pretty, innocent creature, shrinking in her long betrothal veil, her little
head filled with the fit of her wreath of gilded
myrtle leaves, or the style of her wedding girdle,
— to that limited, childish mind, occupied with the
sole importance of getting married, did any power
whisper that hers should be the most famous wedding in history?

It was a Wednesday, the day of the week when
Jewish maidens might marry. It was a house of
some degree. The family were people of position.
Guests and gifts were many. The large reception-
room was full. The servants ran to and fro. All
the relatives were there, poor and well-to-do alike.
Great water-jars holding five and a half gallons
apiece, stood ranged by the door in the court, the
usual fresh leaves floating on the top. The guest,
taking off his sandals and bathing his feet, entered
the house barefooted, and stepping without sound
upon the large rugs which carpeted the dining-hall.
The couches and cushions were comfortable; the
feast was generous. Everything was, everything
must be provided with lavish Oriental hospitality.
The bride's heart throbbed with pride and fear and
joy.

A group of belated guests, coming up the dusty
pathway to the house, attracted her giddy and wavering attention. They were six in number, quite ordi-
nary-looking persons, unless one excepted their leader,
a young man with a fine mien, who approached the
courtyard with the manner of an invited guest, and
seemed to expect admission for his five companions.

The maiden recognized him for one of the kinsfolk
with whom she did not feel acquainted, and wondered why he had not arrived with his mother, who
was already among the company, or why, indeed,
he must needs appear in this extraordinary way,
with a following of unfashionable strangers. Dimly
through her thick veil she saw his face and figure ;
he seemed to swim a little before her gaze, like some
strange sight seen afar off, on clouds or in light, on
water or in mist. She watched him till he disappeared in the court among the wedding company,
and thought of him no more just then.

From the desert to the wedding party what a revolution of the horoscope! But that is life, and Jesus
lived. He had accepted the invitation to the marriage of his young kinswoman: his mother was to
be there, and his brothers ; it was the natural, social
duty of the week ; he was no hermit, and he performed it as a matter of course. His new friends
followed him, — fishermen from Bethsaida, and a
neighbor or acquaintance of theirs : he could not
turn them off ; they clung to him with the beautiful tenderness of a dawning affection. Already he
found himself in the attitude of a traveling rabbi :
the new dignities of the position must be respected ;
the new movements of his own nature made themselves not turbulently but timidly felt. A few
strange things had happened to him. Stranger
were whispered of him under the breath of a few
reflective and receptive persons. One man had addressed him impulsively in startling terms: " Thou
art the King of Israel ! " The soul of Jesus

vibrated like a too responsive harp beneath these
touches. What did they mean? He could not tell
himself, much less another. He could but seek the
duties of a conscientious man and do them. To
attend this wedding was plainly one of them. He
entered the boisterous Eastern marriage party quietly. Something in his appearance attracted attention. The rude jests, not uncommon at such merry-
makings, slunk away like vermin in his presence.
One fellow, who had spoken too freely, tried to meet
the eye of the Nazarene and brave it out, but could
not, and hung his head.

Jesus moved among the guests with a gentle cheerfulness. His mother was watching for him; she
took him apart for a moment with yearning eyes.
For seven weeks she had not seen him. Her heart
hungered for him, and his — did his for her? He
met her lovingly, but his mien was changed. How
haggard he was! She questioned him anxiously.
He looked like a man half-starved and wholly preoccupied. He did not talk about the desert, or of what
had happened there. He answered her troubled
look with one of reassuring peace. She sighed and
turned away. Mary was not the woman to nag a
grown son even with her tenderness. Yet was she
a mother, and one accustomed to be obeyed.

On a later day of the prolonged festivities she
sought him with some imperiousness of manner.
One of the servants followed her, for she had the
authority of a relative in charge of the occasion, and
respectfully awaited her orders. Mary called her
son aside, and revealed to him in troubled feminine

whispers the great disaster which had befallen the household. What could be worse than for the wine to give out before the entertainment was over? It was no less than a family scandal! She tried to impress it on his mind as such. Jesus looked at her with distant eyes. It seemed a small matter to him. But it was large to her, to the host, to the bride, to all those relatives whom a man must treat considerately, though they seem less kin to him than the red fox that had crept to his feet in the desert one stormy night, or the thrush that had sung to him one sleepless morning when he lay prone and famished on the rock. He listened to his mother deferentially.

With the candor of a mother she felt obliged to remind him of a circumstance which in his abstraction he was likely to overlook. The wine had given out, partly because five unexpected guests had arrived on the scene, — dusty, hearty, thirsty men, who had traveled for several days on foot; plain men who were not any too much accustomed to society like this, and who had taken their share of entertainment to do honor to it. In fact, was it a little questionable to have brought these fishermen at all into the presence of such a company? At all events, was Jesus personally wholly without responsibility for the family misfortune?

With his quick delicacy he perceived the force of the situation; he was no uncouth dreamer, obtuse to the courtesies of life: he readily acquiesced in his mother's view of the case up to a certain point. Beyond that, he drew suddenly and strangely apart from her and from it.

What did Mary expect or exact of him? What blind though adoring dreams drifted through her imagination? Did she dictate to unnamed gifts whose nature it was impossible for her to understand?

Did she require of him obedience as a son in a province where he owed obedience to no created being? Was he to enter upon a life of unknown possibilities fettered to the loving surveillance of a woman whose very love would thwart and perplex him at every step? The vague, rising sense of something in himself not like other men was vague in one respect at no time, either then or after. One Being, and one only, was or could be Law to him. Who was Mary, though the loveliest of mortal mothers, that she should obtrude upon him her own views of a mystery which rested between his Creator and himself?

Gently putting his mother aside, he said in Aramaic that here was a matter which was not a proper topic of discussion between them.

"I waive the subject. It is not for thee and me to dwell on. Let us not talk about the thing."

Then, troubled a little lest he might grieve the tenderest of women, — troubled more within himself as to the nature of his power or of his privilege, — half repenting, he offered her his confidence, as much of it as he could, with quick, beautiful filial trust.

"Mine hour," he whispered, "is not yet come. Leave me to myself till mine hour cometh."

He stepped apart, and brooded over the thing. What a little thing! What a petty use to which to put a great power! — if that *were* power which he felt within himself, stirring and struggling for embodiment in deeds. His eyes fastened themselves upon the water-jars, six of them, ranged by the doorway, tall and cool. The water in them was low, and the herbs hung limp at the bottom, like weeds, or the beginning of growth in damp places.

He thought of the long processes of nature, slow and still, secluded from the comprehension of humanity like other higher processes which were unrecognized by it; of the seed in the mould, the root in the earth, the sprout in the air, the dawn on the leaf, the pollen on the blossom, the sun on the fruit; and always the wet on all: mist, moisture, dew, gentle dropping, drenching storm, sudden shower, long, spring rain, — always water as the means of growth, and at the end, and as the end, the vine, the grape, the wine. There glittered before him the sparkle of the wine of life, the social joys of men, their love of wife and child and home, and their innocent happiness, common, warm, and good ; all the purer, better side of human rapture, — not for him, never for him.

To other men should come the joy of having happiness, to him the joy of giving it. Doomed, as he already felt himself, to be their critic, their teacher (to say no more), his loving heart rose easily to the opportunity of bestowing pleasure. Fated, as he early knew himself, to a solitary life, his delicate instincts floated like winged servitors at the threshold of wedded joy.

Then he remembered that there was a public view of this private, social deed.

His new friends stood looking anxiously at him. The lake fishermen whispered among themselves significantly.

His mother, standing in the background of the scene where he had placed her, watched him with luminous, trustful eyes. The servants buzzed about, officiously awaiting his orders. The chatter of the guests drove by in gusts. The bridesmaids were singing a Jewish bridal song:

> " Her eyelids are not stained with blue,
>   Her red cheeks are her own,
> Her hair hangs waving as it grew,
>   Her grace were wealth alone."

Was *this* the time, the place, the sufficient reason, for *that?* — for that strange indwelling, that mystical gift whose scope or depth as yet he could not guess? Would The Source of all Power be troubled with such a matter? Was it The Will? . . . Try! Put forth the hand, the heart, the mind, the prayer, the being!

" Fill the water-pots with fresh water. Carry it, and offer it to drink."

These words they heard who stood near the young Rabbi, and they saw that he trembled as he spoke them, as a man might who stood partly in doubt, or partly in fear of his own audacity in an untried direction. There were unspoken words that no man heard.

" Thou water, that art the source of life, the secret of growth, the food of the blossom and the fruit, the essence of earth and sea and sky, the matrix of creation, thou purer and mightier than the blood of the vine, return upon the steps of law! Omit, be haste, be force, be season, be blossom, be vine, be sap, be grape; be wine! Such is The Will. Obey."

Everybody was talking of the marvel. But he, being overstrained with it, tried to take himself away. He seemed, indeed, more exhausted than it was easy to explain.

The literal imaginations of his friends followed him with dull admiration. The fishermen clung to him, and refused him a moment's solitude. It was impossible to understand that a man who could do the deed could need recuperation after it! His mother revently kissed the edge of his talith. She had never touched him so in all her life before. The servants pointed at him, gossiping volubly. The host and the chief officer of the feast jested about the wine. The guests drank deeply of it.

The bride, among her maidens, tasted it, wondering as she heard the story. Strangers crowded up to ask, to doubt, or to believe. Important functionaries of the church scowled over the thing. A hubbub set in upon the wedding party. For an hour it seemed quite doubtful whether the young Rabbi were likely to be most popular or most unpopular because of it.

He did not wait to see, but resolutely turned away. His own soul was as much perturbed as elated. So it was true, — it was real; he could never say to himself again that those were the hallucinations of a starving brain which mocked him in the desert. Some one had brought him a cup and he tremulously put his lips to it.

"It *was* water. It *is* wine." The fact gave him almost as much trouble as pleasure for that first hour. What should he do with it? Where would it end?

He longed exceedingly to be alone. But the fishermen followed him closely, chatting as their large feet dragged the sand clumsily over · his slenderer footprints.

.   .   .   .

Broken, experimental, anxious, patient, the months of that year succeeded each other humbly. For nearly half of it, no record tells us how this invaluable time in the opening of a great career was passed. It has well been called The Year of Obscurity. Jesus had the rare power of happily accepting obscurity when he felt himself capable of eminence. Whether to be distinguished or to be unknown, — that was not important to his view of life. His mind lay like a burning-glass scorching beneath one thought: "I will find out what and who I am; I will learn what I am to do, and how I am to do it."

In rays illumination visited him. At moments his soul smoked and took fire with its sense of blinding light. The power in him would not always down.

All his touching gentleness, his modest estimate of himself, could not extinguish it. It flashed up in jets of brief, passionate scenes, now and then burning through the dull lens of that year of preparation for a broader and more positive life.

.   .   .   .

It was Jerusalem and the Temple; and he stood, in the first thoughtfulness of his young manhood, among the phantasmagoria of Passover week, for he seemed to himself, in such a panorama, but a phantom among the shades of a mad world. Half of what he saw distressed him, and the rest inspired. He shrank, as he had always done, from the sacred butchery of worship. He pitied the lambs so, that he could not bear to look upon the priests.

The fishermen and the strangers who clung to him were clamoring for what they called miracles (for the thing that he had done at Cana had followed him like his disciples ever since), but he distanced them by an appeal of his hand, and moved away alone. He approached the sacred veil with the emotion of a devout worshiper. Tears sprang to his eyes when he bowed before the Ark; for the Holy of Holies lay within his own heart, and all his nature was a prayer.

Crowding about him, his people slew dumb things to pay Heaven a price for their sins. He sought for guilt in himself. What was it? What did it mean? How should a man sin? How could a child of God distress his Father? It was impossible to grasp the consciousness of it! He slaughtered no lamb to burn upon any altar, — he could not do it. But at that solemn Passover, the first of his sad, grand manhood, he offered and consumed himself.

" I shall be the Sacrifice," he thought.

Filled with incommunicable emotion, he passed out of the inner Temple, and came suddenly upon a

raving scene. The brokers! — they had possession
of the outer courts, and the air resounded with their
greedy roars. People from all parts of the world
crowded up, gesticulating, haranguing, bargaining,
changing the coin of all nations for the currency
that might be accepted in the Jewish Temple, haggling for the sheep, the oxen, and the doves to slay.
The sacred spot rang with the rage of a wild exchange. The vulgarity, the desecration, the hideous-
ness, were more than the Nazarene could bear. The
whole sight flared like blasphemy before his blazing
eyes, yet moist as they were with the dew of prayer
and consecration. Instantly the meek worshiper
towered into an outraged God. A little, unnoticed
cord (it had been used to bind some butchered
thing) was lying near by; it twisted for a moment
in his nervous fingers, then it uncoiled from his
hand, like a snake, and leaped. He rose to a majestic height. His mien was something for that moment awful to look upon. Lashing and pursuing,
he strode down. The swish of the cord hissed in
the air, but sharper the accents of his scorn.

"God's house — your *den!* Ye *thieves!*"
Thus rang from the lips of Jesus his first protest
against the ecclesiastical abuses of his day. And
then was born against him the demon of a grudge, one
of those silent, venomous hatreds which bring down
a day of inevitable reckoning upon any man who
arouses them. From the Temple booths the High
Priest's family is said to have received enormous
revenues, and from that hour the sullen eye of
Annas singled out the Nazarene.

But, for the moment, the brokers slunk away like beaten curs. Not a hand was raised against him; they so many, he but one. The scattered coins lay trampled under fleeing feet. No man stayed to pick up the money.

He stood alone, quivering. There ran from him a medley of scattering animals and cringing men. The look of his eyes sprang after them, like flames of holy fire.

He stood untroubled, undefiled, as God might stand behind the judgment bar, — as fearless and as solitary. At that moment his sense of power flooded his being.

The great Temple rose behind him, gorgeous, intricate, a marvel of architecture, forty and six years in building.

" Destroy it ! " he cried, carried on a wave of glorified assurance stronger than he had ever known; " I will build it in three days ! "

. . . .

It was in Samaria, and he was traveling. He spent the dull intervals between the few brilliant moments of that year in the commonplace duties of an itinerant teacher. A preacher he had not yet presumed to be.

With characteristic modesty he had refrained from any appearance of rivalry with the career of the prophet from whom he had accepted religious initiation. He had gone on quietly, for the most part practicing the methods of John as he had studied them. To his few followers he delegated certain important religious functions; among others, that of performing the rite of baptism.

He taught and prayed and exhorted. Now and then into the routine of his obscure service something wonderful crept. There were tales and rumors of bountiful movements of his heart resulting in strange consequences. But chiefly he had been leading the ordinary life of a humble evangelist. His methods were intensely practical. He denounced sin and urged repentance; he gave himself up for this year to the most unwelcome of human tasks, — that of starting in a community or a people the consciousness of their moral degradation without taking advantage of it to place himself in a position of very great prominence or spiritual ascendency over them. His own soul at this time was a sleeping mine. He had the great forces of reserve, of self-abeyance, of that which can bide its time. His future, the fate of his nation, the hope of the world, lay staked upon his silence, his submission, his willingness to be unknown and unsuccessful, his power to exchange a warm and splendid dream for a chill and gray reality.

.   .   .   .

The cool of the day was coming on. He was very tired. His friends had left him for a while; they were seeking food for him and for themselves in the town chosen for their night's lodging, — Sychar by name. Grateful to be alone, as he always seemed, or was, he sank wearily by the deep rock-cut well, and lifted his face to the west. It was a historic well, famous from ancient times as the property of a distinguished family; no less a one than that of the founders of the race.

The sunset was falling from glory to tenderness, and all its colors were mild. Something soothing in their tone crept from the sky to his heart.

The interrogation of his own nature which went on in him steadily through depression and elation, receiving uneven replies, but never abandoned because these might be faint or discouraging, spoke to him then with the movement of a rising cry.

His head was turned in the attitude of one who listens to that which no man else can hear. His large eyes were fastened upon the dying day, whose luminousness seemed to have entered into and remained in them after it had left the clouds.

He was so absorbed that the movement of a woman's robe near him did not arouse his attention, or did not seem to do so.

She glanced up lightly, then quite gravely looked at him. The tinkling of a bangle on her brow seemed to embarrass her, as if it were an obtrusion on a silence meant for better things, and impulsively she drew her hand over the clanking coins of gold and silver and hushed the flippant sound. She had set down her water-jar to do this, and stood at the edge of the well with both beautiful arms free. They were bared and she was unveiled.

The traveler did not look at her, and she bent to draw the water with which to fill her jar. The silence was not oppressive to her, for it was natural and expected. The stranger was plainly a Jew, and with her people the Jews were not on social terms. To women of her kind (as she perceived with the keenness and swiftness of her class), this man per-

sonally was not in any event liable to lower himself
by passing the commonest salutation of the day.
That he should ignore her was a matter of course.
Her astonishment began when he spoke.

"Give me to drink," he said gently. His voice
sounded far removed from her, though he was so
near. He did not turn his head, nor detain his eyes
from the darkening sky, but the words flowed out
like the current of an unseen river bathing the
shores of an unknown world.

She stood staring. Then he turned and looked
her full in the eye. She was a voluble creature, and
exclamations, amazement, questions, tumbled over
each other. He continued to look at her silently.
Then her own eyes dropped. When he saw this,
he began to talk with her.

As they conversed affably and earnestly — he a
young Rabbi with a position to maintain, she a woman to have speech with whom was enough to cost
him his reputation — the emotion in his own heart
rose high. Carried upon it, he floated above her
low history. He confronted her with its episodes,
necessarily unknown to him, a stranger. He rebuked her for them boldly. Yet did he take the
pains to reason with her, and allure her to a better
view of life. With the respect for womanhood
which was marked in him, he ingeniously aroused
her own lost sense of modesty. It was a delicate
task — not a great one, as the world looks at moral
achievements — to restore self-respect to a woman
who had thought herself below it; but the soul of
Jesus climbed on this rude pathway to a far, fine

height. His breath came fast, like that of a mountain traveler in an altitude too high for ordinary respiration. Vision and prayer blended and separated and met again. His eye glowed gravely. His pale, dark cheek lost its faint tinge of color. His troubled consciousness, for months past surging to and fro within him like a tide whose moon did not reveal herself by fixed expression, took to itself one of the movements which surpassed all common laws.

"I know, sir, that when the Messiah comes" — The word, over which his mind and heart had grown so sore and anxious for so long, fell low from the lips of the woman, spoken softly between her sobs.

But Jesus, when he heard it, rose to his feet. His full height stood against the west. His soul's height rose with it. The truth which so often eluded him radiated from his eye, his smile, his brow, his outstretched hands.

"I," he said, "am He."

His exaltation had not departed from him when his friends returned. It so shone upon him that no man of them dared trouble him. They stared at the woman with dismay, but no one obtruded a question on his breach of etiquette. He seemed grand enough to be the master of all customs, the maker of all laws. Every petty thought or foolish query went down before his look. Affectionately they begged him to take food, for a man may not live on ecstasy.

But he motioned them away with these to them mysterious, and to all men matchless, words: "I

have meat to eat. Ye know not of it. . . . My meat
is to do His Will."

Then, for his heart and his lips were freed, he
broke into a strain of commanding address, assuming for that hour his oratorical and his spiritual
rank. It captured the village. Hospitality was
pressed upon him. Gratified, he accepted it for a
few days. He was startled when it was reported
to him that the citizens, gathering about the poor
woman and treating her with the respect due to a
despised person who had been suddenly subject to
the notice of a revered one, had called him by the
most solemn appellation that the lip of man could
utter, or the mind of man conceive:

" The Christ; the Saviour of the World."

CHAPTER V

KNOWLEDGE of disaster then, as ever, found wings. In spite of the leisurely movement of news which our electric civilization lacks the imagination to appreciate, the fact of a great public and personal trouble quickly reached the ears of Jesus.

John, the prophet and preacher, had met his natural fate. This young zealot had followed his grand sense of duty one step too far. He had meddled with the vices of the throne, and the throne had replied. For the sake of denouncing a royal *amour*, dignified by the illegal name of marriage, John had sacrificed his liberty and was to sacrifice his life. It may seem doubtful to us if this fearless deed were quite worth while, but it did not seem doubtful to him who did it. The brave man, the freest of all his class, an out-of-door philosopher, accustomed to the weather and the sky, to sleeping on the ground, to eating with the wild bees at their own carved tables; a strong and steady walker, dependent on exercise and air, and on the liberty of his own mental and muscular moods, languished in the dungeons of Herod — to any man an unspeakable fate; to him, of all men, one of the worst.

How far did the prophetic gift accompany him in that dark and noisome suspense? One may hope that it mercifully failed him a little then and there. Did the windows of the approaching future open and show him the dizzy scene of a splendid entertainment in the palace one hot, bright night? the whispering of women royal only in name? the revenge of an adulteress upon a man of God? the hesitation of a girl young, beautiful, vain, good-natured, but used to obeying an imperious mother? Did he hear the cymbal in her long brown fingers, the tinkling of the bracelets on her arms? Did he see the other burden, displacing the cymbal, which her beautiful hands bore, dripping, through the horror of the dancers beneath the wavering of the palace lamps, — the scintillation of silver, the color of wet red, the look of eyes surprised by assassination in the fitful, early slumber of a dungeon night?

Or did the curtain fall upon the casement of his mind, and were his last days muffled in hopes of life, in visions of the desert where bird and beast and man arose and slept and moved at will? in dreams of Jordan shining among her reeds, of the faces of his converts, of the water glittering on them; of one on which the dove had rested; of the life for which his own was spent, like baptismal water fallen, forgotten, a drop in the stream? He was content to be spent, and more than content! For that was John; the greatest of forerunners, a self-obliterated, a man glad to be defeated, so that a greater might succeed.

Shocked beyond expression at the news of his cousin's incarceration, Jesus hastened to the refuge into which he carried all his difficulties. His familiar friend the desert received him, and in the strong society of solitude he sought comfort for his sorrow. As is always true of a man who knows how to value and when to cultivate solitude, he found more than he sought. He found the immediate direction of his own life. His trouble became his guide. From the foreground of his grief the mists of his habitual perplexity began to clear away. Excepting the death of Joseph, — a gentle sorrow dating years back, — he had known no personal bereavement up to this time. The loss of John took on something of such a character.

To his delicate mind the fate which had overtaken the man who had sacrificed everything for him seemed peculiarly distressing. John's future thus blackly quenched, appealed to a certain chivalry always easily uppermost in the nature of Christ. John's work lay at his feet, a splendid wreck. No sense of courtesy to his early religious leader now withheld Jesus from the full exercise of his own vocation. Rather, every voice of loyalty and gratitude summoned him to expression. He began at once to preach.

Glowing with sacred indignation, and consumed with dread for the fate of his friend, he cast himself now into the furnace of a life distinctly to be henceforth classed as that of a religious orator.

Deeply absorbed, he came back from Judea and Samaria into Galilee. There he uttered himself.

The wayside, the country, the town, received and
listened to him. His fame as a worker of wonders,
dating back to his last visit to Jerusalem, preceded
him, but a greater followed him. Assuming the
full authority of a rabbi, he exhorted freely; and,
without any of the diffidence which had heretofore
restrained him. At first his discourses were brief
and modest in the extreme. He felt his way, as all
young preachers must, to the interest of audiences,
if not to the measurement of his own powers. The
nature and extent of these he learned by experience,
like other men. He developed at the very outset of
his career an intensely human, well-balanced mind;
it was always attentive to practical affairs; he did
not waste himself in speculation,. or lose himself in
aimless Oriental reverie. He sat on no stone pillar
with crossed and idle feet, a figure given over to
dreams and desolation, a spectacle for curiosity, a
scarecrow for common men. He withdrew into no
useless trance, no remote psychical experimentation.
He entered into no Nirvâna. A plain man among
men, he took his few friends and trod the country
over in search of the most useful thing that he
could do or say whereby to startle vice or comfort
misery.

These two thoughts, these two purposes, from the
beginning strode out into the foreground of his
mind; and there they remained, like strong figures
wrestling with all lesser preoccupation. The ideal
man of God has always united in one personality
the functions of priest and philanthropist. Jesus
carried on the two preëminently.

On this tour through Galilee, when the novelty of his newly-assumed position as a preacher sat upon him with such a young and sparkling enthusiasm that he might easily have been pardoned if he had overlooked the simpler calls upon him, he showed the evenness and breadth of an old and experienced missionary. At this early point in his story he developed almost immediately one of the most prominent traits in his character, — instinctive, abounding sympathy with the sick.

It was in Cana, where the wedding was. Following some natural impulse to retrace his steps to the spot where he had first learned that his personal gifts had a practical scope, he revisited the village; now with the stronger step and the manlier brow of one who feels that he is acquiring a position, and has some right to its recognition.

He was met by an officer of Herod Antipas, a distracted father whose heart was breaking and whose boy was dying. The courtier begged the young Rabbi to hurry to a stricken home in Capernaum, some twenty miles away; he raised the old, piteous cry which grief has sent up to the healers of the world from the beginning of time till now: "Come down! come down, ere he die!"

"He liveth," replied the Nazarene without hesitation, "go thy way to him."

The prompt and bold reply astounded the town; it may have surprised the speaker himself. The words leaped from his lips. There was no recalling them, if he had wished. He had staked his reputation on one great inward movement of trust in himself.   Would the facts verify or refute his venture?

The young, inexperienced healer and the agitated father looked at each other silently.   The Rabbi's eye did not quail; that of the father grew calmer; the trust which precedes hope softened its feverish depth; the look which one man gives to another when he recognizes superiority and hangs his heart's desire upon its pledges, passed over his face.   It was the seventh hour of the day, and growing dark. The two men parted without further words; the one to seek a living or a dying child, the other to test a living or a dying power on whose genuineness his whole future, his faith in himself, his faith in God, might depend.   Jesus passed the next few days in a condition which hovered between unrest and assurance.   Most of his little group of disciples had scattered to their homes in neighboring villages, and his acquaintances did not suspect the nature of his thoughts, for his mien was quiet, and his eye content.

The people of the village talked enough to make up for this reticence.   Doubt, derision, respect, and belief battled from lip to lip.   The story of the water-jars at the wedding was repeated and re-echoed.

When the news came slowly up from the villa by the lakeshore, it was received with less talk and more thoughtfulness.   The credulous father, wearily coming towards home, — afraid to delay, afraid to hasten, not daring to enter the door of his stricken house, and not daring to stay away from the sick-room with such encouragement as he bore, — suddenly lifting his eyes, saw that the servants were running to meet him, tumbling over each other, gesticulating with Oriental excessiveness, voluble, smiling. . . .

Capernaum and Cana nodded and whispered: " The fever turned at the seventh hour, and it was to the child as the Nazarene had said." When they hurried with the tale to Jesus he smiled quietly, wondering and blaming himself if there had been any hour in which he had expected otherwise. But if there had or had not been, he told no man.

A little, petted boy in a luxurious lakeside mansion, with the laughter of convalescence in his eyes, cuddled against the throbbing heart of a father whose dark cheeks blazed with joy. But on the face of the young healer, pondering in the inland town, there shone another happiness. He had tested himself. He had tried his own mystery. Its great and sacred source had answered to his summons. How hesitate? why doubt? He had asked. God had replied. That hour sprang up to meet him like a herald; a smiling future trod beyond it. Jesus knew just then a respite of hope. There now began to grow in him a sense of something rooted below hope, beneath moods and dreams and longings: the consciousness of Power.

Every public teacher has two especial problems before him: that of himself and that of his times. In the life of Christ, both of these had unusual features. In proportion as a man is above his fellows, he finds it difficult to understand his own

nature and to adjust it to common conditions. In
proportion as his times are extraordinary, his work
is more interesting, but his responsibility for it less
clear. There is something in the sweep and force
of great current events which, while it tends to create heroes, tends also to create humility. A man
may hesitate to take the helm of his times precisely
because they are so urgent that they seem to be the
lord rather than the subject of destiny. A modest
soul may well question its own impulse to assume
control of forces so masterful that the very essence
of fate itself appears to be in them.

Jesus Christ lived in an age which was desperate
enough and dark enough to confound any human
intelligence, and to confuse any human conscience.

Haughty, vicious, and decaying Rome was mistress of the world. Her destinies were in the hands
of one man, the commander of a standing army of
three hundred and forty thousand. Her conquests
had reached their mathematical limit, and could go
no farther. Her morals were unutterable, and her
religion was undecipherable. The apotheosis of the
emperor was the climax of worship. Prayer was
chiefly the expression of corruption or of greed.
A man prayed for the death of a rich relative, or
for the gratification of wishes such as civilization
declines to name. When such petitions were unanswered, he dropped into blasphemy as a creditable
sequence. Marriage had almost ceased to be respected, and, if still respectable, it was only by
courtesy to a dying tradition. Family life abounded
in abominations at which modern thought does not

glance, and public indecency was too black to recall. Philosophers themselves were known to practise the vices which they professed to scorn. The population of the empire was estimated at one hundred and twenty millions ; of these one half were slaves. To be a sick slave or an old one was to be cast off to perish. The cruelties inflicted on slaves were monstrous, merciless, and a matter of course. New-born children were murdered whenever it was convenient, and the law made no account of so small a matter.

The fashionable theory of charity took the ground that it was hardly worth while to give alms ; better to let the beggars die, and out of the way with them! Such a thing as a hospital was unknown. Life was a deification of corruption, and death but an exasperating interruption of vice. Among the epitaphs of such an age we long remember an outcry like this over the grave of a child : " To the unjust gods who robbed me of life." Or this, carved in memory of a girl of twenty years : " I lift my hands against the god who took me away, innocent as I am." Such arraignment of Heaven rang from the world as has never been exceeded in its history.

Latin authors longed for some assuagement of the wide and deep despair. Men whose great names are familiar to us in ancient literature revolted from hope, and dreamed of virtue as a lost ideal, and looked on at human life as a pitiable play, scarcely up to the proportions of a farce.

The Hebrews, the captives of this ripe but decaying empire, were not unaffected by the taint of their masters. One of their greatest teachers and writers thought so lightly of marriage that he sanctioned divorce if a wife burned her husband's dinner. The easy sin of a religious people abounded, and the hypocrite was everywhere. Long prayers, long faces, and short virtues went arm in arm.

Theology had ousted religion, and ecclesiasticism had strangled devotion in temples and in synagogues. The people were helpless, fierce, and rebellious ; but they had the vices of despair, and the errors of a religiosity which has so long taken the place of faith that men have ceased to know the difference.

Jesus was profoundly moved by the condition of his people and the vices of his times. No philosopher could have studied them more carefully. He had known some opportunities to do so in Nazareth, where men from all parts of the world poured by upon the caravan routes. He had seen the culture of the Greek, the luxury of the Roman, the manners and characteristics of the Phœnicians, Persians, Arabians, Chaldeans, and the corruption of all. His pure and secluded youth had strongly and silently observed, reflected, and stored up material for a mature view of the condition of his age. He had also stored up sensitiveness all his own.

Quivering with recoil from the moral horrors by which he was surrounded, he flung his whole nature deliberately and determinedly upon them. He was no Roman gentleman turning with a dilettante indifference from the degradation of his times ; he was a Hebrew mechanic, an itinerant missionary, pouring the pure energies of a devotee into the polluted current by which he refused to be stirred.

In the first fire of his enthusiasm as a preacher, he made one apparent mistake. He went to Nazareth. What minister of any times and of any people recalls without wincing his first sermon in his native place, or in the village of his childhood? The tenderness for old associations, the innocent pleasure in appearing before old friends, the inexperienced belief that they would be more glad to hear him preach than other people, — how reluctantly these have given place to the surprised pain, the slow suspicion, the smarting realization of the truth! In his oldest acquaintances the young exhorter finds his severest critics, his coldest hearers, unwilling appreciation. It is the way of the world, — not one of its noble ways, — and Jesus, like other leaders of men, must needs take the world as he found it.

He arrived in Nazareth, let us think, on a Friday afternoon. The sun was about to set. The Seventh Day was at hand. Already the signs of preparation for the Jewish Sabbath stirred across the village. Domestic and field work, trade and travel, hurried to cessation. The women indoors and the men without ran to and fro with busy interest. The little town, occupied along the length of its rough highway, turned indifferent eyes to the mountains which were blazing in the dying day, and paid scant attention to the appearance of the young citizen who had left a while ago, unknown, and was returning famous. Jesus looked

at the familiar hills, — grand, silent, these in solemn
shadow, those transfigured with color, all carrying
the thoughts up; but the villagers scarcely looked
at Jesus. Their eyes were on the level earth, his
on the heights. What wonder that they could not
meet?

He had scarcely arrived when there broke upon
the evening air the clear, strong call of a trumpet uttering itself authoritatively, — a double blast.
The synagogue minister stood on the roof of his
house with his face towards Jerusalem. He an-
nounced the arrival of the Sabbath. He summoned
every Hebrew soul within reach of his official cry
to cease labor and to begin worship. The trumpet
called three times. When it ceased, the trumpeter
laid it reverently down by his side, that he might
not profane the sacred day by carrying the instru-
ment. Now, all over the darkening village, from
every house, there sprang out a gentle spark. The
Sabbath lamp had been lighted. A sense of fes-
tivity glittered with it. The Sabbath was the
pledge of affection between God and Israel, and
every home was arrayed to meet it, like a bride or a
queen. Every one wore his best clothes. Every
table held its best meal. Benedictions were spoken
over the wine and water. The suspension of labor,
the coming on of rest, the glory of worship, made
holiday of holyday. The traveler shared the general happiness.

Sleeping with the peacefulness which comes with
return from more stirring scenes and noisier loca-
tions to a country home, he awoke refreshed and

NAZARETH

vigorous.   The day rose bright and warm.   The
early hour of worship approached.   Jesus anticipated it gladly.   He walked rapidly (for such was
Jewish law) to the sombre place where he had worshiped since he could remember, — the old, stiff
building, dreaded and loved, wherein to laugh or
joke, or eat or sleep, was sinful, and wherein no
man but a rabbi might seek shelter from a storm.

The rustic synagogue was crowded.   Jesus modestly took his accustomed seat among his old neighbors.   His heart was full of thoughts and feelings
which he wished he could share with them.   He
was so loving, so gentle a man!   He felt tenderly
towards all these people, among whom he had lived
so many humble years.   He watched for their well-
known forms and faces as they came in and took
their seats, — the men by themselves, lordly, as
Jewish men were wont, putting the women apart in
a gallery of their own.   The elders of the meeting
pompously took their places on the raised platform;
behind, stood the movable chest, representative of
the great Ark of the Temple, and itself containing
the rolls of the sacred writings.   A curtain hung
across it, and the holy lamp burned before it.

While he sat there, lost in reverie, modest, gentle, thinking not of himself, the chief ruler of the
synagogue came up and spoke to Jesus, formally
asking him to act for that day as the conductor of
the services.   This request was not unexpected to
him, as it might have been an act of courtesy or of
curiosity on the part of his neighbors to extend the
invitation : due certainly to any rabbi with much

less than the fame already gathered about the name and personality of their townsman. At all events, the politeness was paid him. Trusting in the sincerity of his old friends, believing with his secret instincts in their better motives, he confidingly accepted their invitation, and rising, stepped to his place at the lectern.

He began the service of the morning in the formulated manner by repeating the Jewish liturgy. This was one of the prayers with which he opened that Sabbath meeting in the Nazareth Synagogue:

"Blessed be Thou, O Lord, King of the world, who formest the lights and createst the darkness, who makest peace and createst everything; who in mercy givest light to the earth, and to those who dwell upon it, and in Thy goodness day by day and every day renewest the works of creation. Blessed be the Lord our God for the glory of his handiworks and for the light-giving lights which He has made for our praise. Selah. Blessed be the Lord our God who has formed the lights."

The invocation sounds a little cold or dull to our ears. The young preacher of that summer morning was accustomed to do it reverence; it was the liturgy of his church, and of his childhood; yet, certain public prayers of his own, uttered later in the course of his ministry, and immortal to human needs and worship, indicate something of the distance of his nature from the formality to which he deferred.

He deferred, however, and he conformed to the

customs of his church, like a man of acquaintance with life, up to a certain point. When he reached that point he departed promptly and thoroughly. He followed the usual order of exercise; another prayer and a better one succeeding the first; then came the repetition of the creed, another prayer and six eulogies or benedictions; at their close a distinguished rabbi was at liberty to add certain prayers of his own which might be fixed or free. At last the time for his discourse arrived. The sacred roll was taken from the ark and handed to him by the chazzan or minister.

On this occasion the lesson for the day was from one of the greatest of Jewish prophets. Jesus selected as his text from Isaiah these impressive words:

" The spirit of the Lord is upon me because He hath anointed me to preach the good tidings to the poor; . . . to preach release to the captives, and recovering of sight to the blind, to set at liberty them that are bruised, to proclaim the acceptable year of the Lord."

Having read the text in Hebrew, translating as he went into the common tongue, he gave the roll back to the minister, and according to the custom of his church sat down to preach.

He looked for a moment silently over his audience. Familiar faces answered his gaze with curiosity or with that doubt of his ability to give them a remarkable sermon, natural to a man's fellow-townsmen who have known him since he was a little boy among them. " He is just like us. What can *he* have to say? There must be some mistake about this ado people are making over him in other places. They do not know him as well as we do." Polite attention could not hide this inevitable mental attitude from so keen a perception as his who now addressed them.

His face was quite steady and strong; his eyes large and luminous; not a line about his mouth wavered. His high brow, soft, curling, unshaven beard and hair, and clear brown pallor were relieved like a medallion from the background of the curtain and the ark and the plain limestone finish of the country synagogue. He had the beautiful, oval contour of the face, like his mother's. His robe was that of the Jewish rabbi; he wore a blue talith on that Sabbath; with a white and hyacinth fringe. Nothing about his dress was *outré;* there was no effort to be eccentric. Nothing was remarkable about his appearance before the congregation of his own village — nothing but his beauty, his dignity and that air to which we apply the word high-mindedness. There were crises in his history when this look reached a quality requiring a much larger word. But at this moment it was a simple, natural, noble expression, not too far above the comprehension of his hearers, and not so far apart from their standards in the estimation of character as to be lost upon them.

His first words startled them disagreeably.

"This day is this Scripture fulfilled in your ears," he boldly said. Then, his lips being unloosed, he poured out his heart.

He maintained the astonishing intimation of his opening sentence with a firmness not to be ignored for whatever it meant in so unobtrusive a man. He gave his audience to understand that the most precious tradition and hope of their people was about to be verified. The great messianic expectation in which they all believed, was to become a fact. In a word, he himself was the fact.

This daring assumption, firmly suggested, was received with mixed emotion by his townsfolk. Some thought: How gracious his mien! How melodious his voice! How agreeable his thought! For the Jews were experts in the criticism of religious oratory.

Their ideas of a popular preacher were peremptory. He must be suave, persuasive, attractive in appearance, manner, and style, polished, and altogether pleasant. He must be a good story-teller, witty at some times, eloquent at all. He must keep unwelcome truths to himself, or clothe them in the fine raiment of metaphor, so that they met a man politely. An audience was not to be hit between the eyes. The popular preacher must abound in tact; he must be a religious diplomat; it must be amusing or moving to listen to him; a hearer could not be bored, or made uncomfortable with truths that he did not like or accept.

These things might do for wandering evangelists, wild as the reeds among which they exhorted. They were not for the rabbi, accepted in the synagogue. The orthodox preacher, working in the orthodox channels, would not mistake his business.

But the congregation in the synagogue at Nazareth that Sabbath morning was not wholly satisfied
from the outset, and, as the young preacher progressed in his discourse, their dissatisfaction grew.
With the customary freedom by which Jewish audiences were allowed to question their teachers, they
interrupted him, cynically requiring proof of his
tremendous claim.   Having heard the rumors of
unusual gifts vaguely associated with his name, with
the vulgar love of a show, and the common Jewish
fancy of a "sign," they raised the usual popular
demand for miracles.   Here, to their annoyance,
they were met by a flat refusal.   This came in the
form of a reply which has become one of the most
famous epigrams of literature, and a favorite maxim
of all nations.   A prophet, he caustically said, has
no honor in his own country.   The dexterity of this
rejoinder was reinforced by a fearless defense of his
own ground.   They might naturally ask him, he
admitted, to repeat in Nazareth what he had done in
Capernaum.   But of the advisability of that, they
must allow him to be the only and the proper judge.
Ingeniously turning to their sacred writings for support, he illustrated his position.   Thus and so had
taken place.   Israel, in the days of ancient famine,
had not lacked for widows ; but to only one starving woman, and she in a foreign town, had Elijah
been sent with relief.   Israel, in the time of Elisha,
had abounded with lepers ; but a Syrian was the
only wretched creature cleansed.

Jesus was about to continue the discourse of
which we have only a fragment reported.   Plainly,

he had more to say.   His introduction had but parried with the discontent of his hearers; he was seeking, perhaps, to swerve it from the deeper purpose
of his address; or conscious, possibly, that he could
achieve little or nothing against it.   Still, the things
he would have said, the truths that Nazareth needed,
surged to his lips.   His brain throbbed with them.
His heart was inundated with them.   His outstretched hands pleaded eloquently and silently for
opportunity to explain and to apply the unwelcome
candor of his opening words.

But hubbub had already set in.   Displeasure
grew to anger; anger mounted into rage.   The pro-
nounced Jewish features of the congregation were
contorted with spite.   Whispers rose into audible
comments: " Who is this fellow, after all, that we
should sit here and take insolence from him ?   Why,
nobody but Jesus — little Jesus, the carpenter's
boy — we have seen him around, ever since he could
walk.   He used to play with my boy.   He came
to our house on errands.   He has been to school
with our children.   I gave him an order once to
make me a table.   His father sent him to mend
our chest.   He has sat all these years in this very
synagogue, and known his place, and kept it. . . .
How came he out of it ?   Teach it to him !   Show
it to him !

" Nazareth is not good enough for him.   Jerusalem
was, and Capernaum; even little Cana.   We are
not grand enough for him to show off his signs and
wonders, and other eccentricities.   Get rid of him,
and his airs !   We are used to preachers, not char-

latans, in this synagogue.   Turn him out of it! . . .
Shall this carpenter sit there and talk to us as if we
were lepers and Gentiles ? "

The young preacher tried once or twice to hush
the clamor; but it had swollen to a stream in which,
before one might know what had happened, he was
borne along like a broken bough.   Convulsed with
quick Oriental passion, his townsfolk tore him from
the lectern — they were many and determined —
and dragged him along down the aisle, and out of
the synagogue.   The outer air of the hot summer
Sabbath morning smote scorching on his grieved
face.   Whether from sheer surprise, helplessness, or
prudence, he tried to make no useless resistance.
Immediately he found himself near the edge of a
considerable crowd of pushing, scowling, howling
men.   They urged him along virulently.   In a very
short time, looking straight ahead with wide astonished eyes, he perceived that he was rapidly approaching the mountainous boundary of the town.
He remembered the nearest precipice — no mean
gulf.   Was it probable ? was it *possible ?*

Turning to guage the intention of the village mob,
he felt himself pushed along the faster for this
momentary negligence.   The truth now began to
be evident.   It was the purpose of his neighbors —
not to commit open murder, not to hurl him over,
distinctly, but imperceptibly, as it might appear un-
knowingly, to *crowd* him over the edge of the gorge.
It would be easy to say, afterwards, that his foot
slipped, that he struggled in the wrong spot against
the deep religious displeasure of an outraged con-

gregation; and so fell. Half a dozen explanations of this ghastly accident would be possible.

When the real purpose of the rioters became manifest, the unpopular preacher suddenly turned and withstood them; not by blow, or buffet; he did not wrestle or strike out upon them as an angry and imprudent man might have done. He defied them by the finer resistance of a look. He stood back to the hills, whose rounded heads and shoulders rose high above the shameful scene, and whose bare faces, unveiled in the hot light, seemed to try to turn away from the sight they saw. The terraces of Nazareth overflowed with summer colors; every little street marked by lines of vegetation rich and ripe. The woods where he had walked and dreamed and prayed all his quiet, unoffensive youth stood still in the windless heat, like a phalanx on duty, awaiting orders in a martial crisis. All the familiar scenery had a friendly look.

Only the familiar people wore this other — what a glare of hate! He glanced from face to face — his old neighbors! All his life his friends! Here and here and everywhere a dogged murderous rage! With this man he used to walk home from the synagogue, pleasantly talking. To that one he had offered many neighborly favors. These — they were lads with him, they had studied the law with him in school hours, and roamed the fields and forests with him at play together. Had he ever done them a wrong — any one of them all? Had he ever failed to do them a kindness, and that, how gladly, when he could? He thought of the things that he had meant to say to them in the synagogue that morning; how his heart had yearned over them; how lovingly he would have led them to a nobler view of life! How tenderly he had longed to teach them broader truth. How his soul had poured itself out to serve them!

Before that gesture his old neighbors began to move back from him; not a man of them could have said why. He stood still, defenseless among them all, there on the edge of the rock. The chasm gaped below; a step would carry a man over. He glanced down, then back at the people, then began slowly to advance upon them.

What was that startling change upon his gentle countenance? Only a few times in his life was it witnessed and noted: but no man who ever saw it ever withstood it or forgot it to his last hour. As if they had been smitten of God the Nazarenes fled before that look. The crowd wavered, broke, and melted. Jesus continued to advance steadily upon it; passed through it; and went his way, down the hot village street. No man ventured to molest him — nay, nor to address him. He passed on silent, and protected in the unutterable scorn which the highest may put between itself and the lowest soul.

He passed on, and out from Nazareth; wherein from that day he never made his home again. The wound had gone too deep.

CHAPTER VI

THE HEALER

THE rest of the summer passed in quiet excitement. He spent much of it alone. His career developed by gradual and beautiful stages. His first step was to make for himself a new home, removed from the village which had insulted him; for this purpose he chose Capernaum, a busy, central town, in which he had already spent more or less time, and in that place he remained a legal citizen during the remnant of his life. His mother and brothers also took up their residence there, but his sisters, having married, stayed on in Nazareth, not anxious to mix themselves further with the affairs of a family which had acquired so unpleasant a notoriety. His brothers, on the other hand, for that very reason, preferred not to return to the village; they showed no especial sympathy with him in any of his successes or failures. It need not be said that they were, necessarily, among the number of his friends who publicly expressed doubts of his sanity. But, for whatever reason, they did not make him any too welcome under his mother's roof.

It is impossible to say how much of the suffering of his sad life came from the condition of his family affairs, — a tragedy in itself to a sensitive heart longing to be loved, and itself the essence of love. Popular comment always reserves a sharp hit for the genius who is not appreciated at home, and a special fling for the religious leader whose relatives do not seem to believe in him. Jesus had the full smart of this to bear. His mother's home was not made so happy to him that he cared to stay there with any regularity. He turned rather to his fishermen friends for shelter and companionship. He spoke pathetically once, in his short and troubled career, upon this point, contrasting the wild things of the desert and of the night with his own un-cherished life. Between himself and his mother, however, no family differences were suffered to in-sert themselves. Their mutual sympathy remained sweet and strong, and later she often followed him upon his preaching tours, with a few other thoughtful and gentle women not of the ordinary type. But he lacked the power to make a home of his own for Mary; he was too poor a man to maintain one, and too busy to provide the means to do so. He was reared to a trade; he had entered a profession. Like many another man who has taken a step of such a kind, he had abandoned a comfortable income for an uncertain support. He and his small group of immediate friends lived upon such money as they earned among them, or upon the contributions of the public, — a scanty source of maintenance of which he made the best, with cheer-ful patience; though it meant fewer comforts and more hardships than he had been accustomed to in his parents' home in his earlier life.

No sudden access to ease padded his opening prospects. To luxury he was always an indifferent
stranger. He never made money. He did not
handle money. The treasurer of the little society of
twelve, which he soon found it necessary formally to
organize, looked after his wants. They were not
many, and simple enough. He must have a few in-
expensive, decent robes, such as a rabbi ought to
wear, — the red and gray striped tunic, or what we
might call jersey undergarment, covered from sight
by the talith, which was usually of hyacinth blue,
and always fringed, with the tasseled corners of
blue and white, indicating his ecclesiastical position ;
the girdle, the head-dress, or white sudar, performing the office of a turban, but a little differently
constructed; the sandals and staff. He must have
a plain meal when he was too faint to live without
it any longer; a shelter at night; a spot to bathe
his dusty, aching feet after a hot day's march; a
rug on a friend's floor; a door to shut between him
and the clamoring people when he was too far spent
to do anything more for them ; the merest protection from crowds which a public man requires at the
hands of some affectionate friend, if his own family
do not give it to him. These comprised his modest
daily needs. He lived the life of a poor man, with
the consistency and simplicity of a gentleman. Vulgar poverty, aping affluence and quarreling with its
limitations, found it as hard to understand him as
position and wealth.

This educated mechanic, this heretic preacher,
this humble leader of men presented from the very

outset an annoying social puzzle to his countrymen and to his times.

In spite of his bitter experience at Nazareth, and of his more than usually lonely summer, he was happier at this time than often — perhaps than ever — in his life. Of his public life, this was distinctly the most cheerful year. Now, he began to know the pleasantness of growing popularity. Now, he began to feel that his great sense of moral truth was really communicable to a certain proportion of minds. Now, his spiritual force gathered itself to encouraging action. Now, he knew what it was to hope for more than the space of a mood. Now, his consciousness of power grew upon something more solid than dreams, and more tangible than prayer.

Having, for many practical reasons, selected Capernaum, he made that thriving port his headquarters. Here he recalled to his side the four fishermen friends who were pursuing their calling on the Galilean lake. Up to this time their service and society had been irregular, but he now summoned them to new and definite obligations in his behalf. This downright act of authority — a new assumption on his part — he enfolded in such a warm outburst of sympathy with their practical affairs that he became in a half hour the most popular of men among the Galilean fishermen.

The men had been out since the day before, and the capricious lake whose abundant shoals of fish sometimes choked and sometimes evaded the most skillful net, had yielded nothing to an all night's hard work. Sleepless, hungry, uncomfortable, wet, and discouraged, the fishermen had rowed ashore, sullenly washed their nets, and put out again at the request of Jesus, who expressed a wish to use one of their boats as a temporary pulpit wherefrom to finish one of his brief discourses. At the surprising order of the preacher that they set their nets in such and such a spot, the cross and disheartened men smiled with respectful doubt. A superior rabbi does not make a good fisherman. The lectern, not the deck, was the place for the landsman. When, however, they hopelessly followed his suggestion, and the richest haul of fish taken on Gennesaret that night broke the nets and all but sank the boat, the moral effect was such as only poor men can appreciate. Here was no common rabbi who would stick to his synagogue and let a man starve. Here was a wonder and a wonderworker, caring for a poor fellow and the catch; concerning himself about your affairs, not above your troubles. The most warm-hearted man in the crew dropped to his knees among the leaping fish, and impulsively offered to Jesus the service of his life.

From the fishing town the Nazarene made circuits, taking preaching tours here and there about Galilee and back again, whenever and wherever the occasion seemed to demand. His gift in religious oratory quickly developed itself, and grew with marked effect to the point of public influence. But he gave less attention to preaching at this time than to the practice of the truths which he preached. His methods were intensely practical, and showed extraordinary wisdom.

On the Sabbath and on the special synagogue days of the week, Monday and Thursday, he took his proper position as a rabbi of eminence in whatever synagogue was inclined to receive him, and gradually opened the gates of his belief to outsiders. But on every day he gave himself to the daily needs of every class of society; whether of his own or other races, whether of his audiences or not, never made the slightest difference. He had no parish; he confined himself to no ecclesiastical ties; he swung wide of every parochial as much as of every theological tradition. He gave his growing fame to those who needed him most. That was his simple rule; from it he never deviated, though by it he was often embarrassed.

First, last, always, from the beginning to the end, Jesus Christ sought and received into his great heart one class of people, — the most miserable. Foremost among these he rated the sick. No person who has himself known the deeps below the lowest which underlie the desolations of an invalid life, can ever, in the dreariest dungeon of his incarcerated powers and joys, forget the preferred attention given by the greatest Master of human sympathy to the prisoners of pain. It is not possible for the well and active, the superficially gay, the physically comfortable, to rate this instinct in the nature of the Nazarene at its value.

It was the more remarkable because he himself was a well man. The healthy mind in the healthy body dowered him. He had the poise of true nerve in wholesome tissue. He inherited no taint, no

CHRIST THE HEALER

disorders. A pure life, simple and free, passed
in manual labor, out-of-door exercise, and close
thought had wrought its ends. The carpenter had
been a man of mental application ; the student had
been a mechanic. Mind and body were so in equi-
poise that the overwrought soul whose sensibilities,
as life went on, quivered under the most terrible of
strains, did not make havoc of his physical system.
His organization was a harmony, strong because spotless, sweet because strong, wonderful in any aspect.

Rare is the healthy person who is patient with —
rarer if he understands — the sick. Jesus showed
an almost incredible comprehension of the conditions
of disease ; he distinguished with amazing skill between the true and the false claims on sympathy ;
he never confounded controllable hypochondria with
anything more serious, nor mistook the more serious for the manageable delusion. He had no medical education, and relied upon his own divination
in diagnosis, and his own personality in treatment.
Almost immediately he entered upon the difficult
and dangerous life of a people's healer. Often his
cures were made in private, or even in secret ; but
one of his first was a wholly public affair.

One summer morning, soon after he had come to
Capernaum, a maniac happened in the synagogue,
pushing in with the crowd to hear the new Rabbi.
The poor wretch, moved by who knew what psychical
irritation at the sight of the pure face and calm
demeanor of the young preacher, created a disturbance in the congregation, and made himself so
annoying that it became necessary to put him out

unless he could be controlled. A thrill ran through the audience when the madman, raving at Jesus, hurled at him this unexpected and awful recognition : " I know thee, Thou Holy One of God ! " The excitement was not lessened when the Rabbi by a few remarkable words quieted the maniac, and restored him suddenly to sanity.

Belief in demonic possession was as much a feature of the times as the wearing of sandals or travel by caravan. The spectators and the lunatic shared this theory of his condition as a matter of course. The healer did not combat the popular idea ; whether he shared it or not, he did not choose to explain. The event itself aroused a wide curiosity. That same day occurred another incident of no less public interest. The healer's gift was put to the test in the family of a favorite disciple ; an elderly woman being dangerously ill with one of the poisonous fevers peculiar to the Jordan valley.

When the woman got up from her bed, and, with true Jewish feminine meekness, immediately prepared the supper and served the masculine members of the household, the effect on the minds of those who witnessed the cure was not as complex as it would be in our time, but it was sufficiently startling. In a few hours the lakeport town buzzed with it. The well told the sick, the sick told each other ; the news was discussed in society and markets, on deck and on shore, and received on solitary pallets by sufferers who had been cheated of hope too often to be easily roused to exertion or trust. The tide of patients, which had already set in, advanced rapidly. He did not obtrude his healing power, but rather would have preferred to shelter it for a time, like an altar fire which must not be rudely fanned too soon.

But the demands upon his skill and sympathy grew like a conflagration. In twenty-four hours he had relieved too much misery for his own comfort. That Sabbath evening he was besieged. Half the coast and country flung themselves upon his sympathy and vitality. Either or both might have given way; neither did. There now began one of the greatest conflicts of history, and one that has never received its due of attention, — the wrestle between the woe of humanity and the organization of one merciful man.

At this early stage in the struggle, while his vigor was unimpaired and his enthusiasm fresh and strong, a sparkling success gave joy to his achievements. His patients were of all classes, all disorders, all varieties of gratitude or ingratitude, all shades of faith in the healer on whose skill they massed themselves without pity. Of the immense number it was simply recorded that "he laid his hands on every one of them and healed them."

The fishing town was in a tumult of excitement. With the natural selfishness of the sick, the petulant demand arose that Capernaum should claim and control the full benefit of his skill. He was troubled by this appeal. Forcibly to tear asunder the ties formed between relieving health and dependent disease is one of the hardest of tasks for any sympathetic nature. Such ties may spring up in an hour, but their roots strike down as deep as time.

When Jesus retired to rest on the evening of that crowded day whose cries of misery and whose murmured blessings reëchoed in his ears, his brain throbbed and his heart ached. He had now at once to meet on a great scale the perplexity which all agents of mercy must meet on a small one ; he must choose between the suffering ; he must seem to neglect for the sake of remembering ; he must omit so much misery for the sake of so much more.

Worn as he was with excessive drains upon his strength, which only the demanding sick can make, he slept but little. Before the gray of the dawn, while yet it was quite dark, he stole out and away by the shore. The water lay before him a dull and oval map ; the outlines of the surrounding hills through whose black gorges swept down the gusts that made the lake so dangerous, rose frowning. No sign of human life presented itself. Nature wore the remoteness and bore the chill of the grim hour between the night and the dawning, when the strong weaken and the weak sink, and the sick die, and the soul faints. Nature did not offer to help him. He turned to God.

When his friends, missing him, long after daybreak, searched and found him, — in the shelter of groves, with his face to the lake and his eyes on the rose-lit skies, and his delicate lips moving, the young healer was at prayer.

.   .   .   .

" They demand thee," said Simon, when his sense of decorum would allow the fisherman to speak. " There is a great crowd coming on behind us. All

had sought to bring their piteous lot to his attention. What a brilliant deed to have recalled one
of these outcast wretches by a look, and cured him
in the presence of a couple of thousand witnesses!
Jesus had seen fit to do nothing of the kind.

Now, in the silence, the remoteness, the solitude,
unseen of any other eye, he chose for the first time
to test his power upon the malignant contagion.
Had he any secret doubts about his ability to control it? He had now acquired an unavoidable confidence in himself; it acted on his power, and his
power reacted on his confidence. Acute sickness
had proved itself his servant, and hereditary disease
his slave. Still — a leper!

The repulsive being, tortured out of all semblance
to fair human form and flesh, suddenly shuffled like
an image of some demonic dream ahead of the
Rabbi, and desperately barred the path. He lifted
his mutilated arms and hands. A hoarse wail came
from his hideous lips:

" Cure me, — even *me!*"

Jesus stopped, and gently regarded the leper.
His fathomless pity arose and flooded his face.

" Thou canst if thou wilt," observed the miserable
creature half reproachfully.

By all the laws of church and state, the two were
forbidden to approach each other, and the leper did
not further defy the law.

The healer, on the contrary, did not recognize it.
He advanced directly, and put out his hand. He
seemed deeply touched by this cry of mingled reproach and entreaty, as if he could not bear to be
misunderstood by so wretched a man.

Such desolation of suffering acted upon him like a law of mechanics. Whatever the cost, he had to relieve; whatever the consequence, he could not refuse. Such was the government of his nature.

Without a gesture of repugnance, he laid his cool, clean touch upon the other's crumbling flesh. The outcast of contagion looked in vain for the expression of disgust that he was used to seeing on the faces of well and blessed men. Not a shadow crossed the eyes of the Nazarene : they were like stars become human; ineffable compassion rayed from them, — only that.

" I will," he said heartily, as one man speaks to another when he means kindly by him; " I will ! " Then rang out the vibrant tone of command peculiar to himself, and familiar now to half the sick of Galilee :

" Be clean ! "

.   .   .   .

Was it moments ? Was it hours ? Was it weeks ? The leper could not have told. He had fallen prostrate in the dust. He arose slowly. Where was the horror of all those years, — half a lifetime of loathsomeness to himself and to all humankind, — whither had it betaken itself ? What had become of the shame, the anguish, the defilement ? The infected man looked for one revolting sign and another of his acquaintance with disgrace. Was he gone blind, or maniac, that he could not find them ? Gently through his body, that had been the den of torments, the sense of freedom from pain and from impurity, strange as the laws of a foreign organism, began to stir.

. . . .

The Nazarene stood smiling. He seemed to be charged with joy. The happiness of the other looked a faint thing beside his own. It was as if he himself had suffered everything that went before, — as if all that history of woe had been his own. So exquisite his sympathy that the very thrill of being healed seemed to run through him. The delight of healing was but a portion of his beautiful pleasure. He felt every pang that he had removed, and all the bliss that he had given. Gladness like the gladness of a God shone all over him. It was one of the happiest moments of his life.

"Go," he said with a low and joyous laugh. "Find the priest and be purified."

Now he who had defied in this act of mercy every ecclesiastical law relating to contagious diseases which as a Jew and a rabbi he was bound to respect, loyally enough deferred to the statutes of his church and of his land.

A stranger thing he did, for he added the peremptory and totally unexpected order that the manner of the cure should be kept a secret between the patient and the healer.

With every intention to obey the Rabbi, the cleansed man went his ways. But joy and the curiosity of his friends was too much for him. His head was turned with delight. The novelty of health bounded through his nerves like delirium. Leaping, laughing, praying, singing as he ran, he babbled of his good fortune. He had no more power to keep the name of the Nazarene out of the affair than a child to keep a secret from his mother, and the whole town knew it before nightfall.

The consequence was precisely what Jesus had foreseen, and what he had especially tried to avoid. Before he could evade the popular excitement, it had rolled up against him, — a wave of suffering, vast and dark. He was immediately overwhelmed with the entreaties of the incurable and disfigured sick, who, if they could not reach him in any other way, crawled upon the sands to his feet, and lay there, piteous and hideous, until he considered their plight.

The state of medical education in the East at that time was such as to emboss the methods of Christ in strong relief upon a background of almost incredible folly and charlatanry.

The heads of mice, the brains of an owl, the eyes of a crab, the fat of a viper, a bat, a grasshopper, might be among the popular remedies. If a man had a cold in the head, his physician ordered him to kiss the nose of a mule. For certain disorders one carried about a peculiar species of small snake reported to possess the accomplishment of traveling backwards. The cuttings of vines not four years old, burned in seven ditches, were believed to contain peculiar therapeutic virtues, provided one sat in the smoke of the seven ditches, each in turn.

Such a materia medica was the offering of the regular schools to suffering humanity. At such a stage and into such a phase of medical science, the

healing gift of the Nazarene entered quietly. Its
simplicity, its good sense, its delicacy, its efficacy,
its amazing results threatened to overturn the therapeutics of his time. The physicians were derisive,
then disgruntled, then alarmed. Their consultations
were neglected; their *clientèles* thinned out; their
patients deserted them for the new healer. The
danger was that the sick public would go over *en
masse* to the courageous and singular man whose
prescriptions required of his patients only clean
lives and faith in himself. The most learned and
fashionable physicians in Palestine were set at
naught. A growing uneasiness ran through their
ranks. Before he had aroused the serious opposi-
tion of the clergy to which the heretic preacher was
inevitably fated, the humane and gentle man who
began his life's work by such a love of the sick and
such a sorrow for their sufferings as has never been
equaled in the records of human sympathy, brought
down upon himself the enmity of one of the most
jealous classes in society. He had to meet the an-
tagonism of the whole medical profession.

The absence of superstition in the nature of
Jesus was something that never ceases to astonish.
Simply reared in a mountain village, in a secluded
youth, in a devout family, how easy for him to have
conformed, to have believed, like other men! But
freedom of thought was the condition of existence to
him. Far above his contemporaries, looking off and
away at an altitude in which they could not breathe,
he quickly took the broadest view of any practical
question. He never did an ignorant thing.

Against the medical superstitions of his times he directed himself with a progressive independence which commands the keenest admiration. Perceiving that the people who appealed to him suffered more from the abuses of the profession than from the effects of disease, he took high ground. He antedated by two thousand years the efforts of modern science to reduce the abominations of a benighted past in the practice of medicine. He threw away all drugs, all nostrums, all nauseous traditions, all the disgusting superstitions of the age, and brought his patients up to pure living and high thinking as his simple code of therapeutics.

It is never to be forgotten that he added to these principles in the control of disease the forces of a personality that stands apart, beyond reduplication. The wisest and most courageous of the modern schools does not hope for a similar professional success; only the purest dwells upon it. But he who studies that supreme achievement learns his subtle formula, if he will, from the " irregular " Hebrew physician whose manly faith in God was the first and last condition of curing, and whose patients found that something not unlike it was the inexorable condition of cure.

An opportunity presented itself for an interesting thrust at a favorite popular superstition involving both medicine and theology, and requiring a double amount of courage on the part of him who dared to attack it.

The successes of many healers are largely confined to disorders of the nervous system. The cures of Jesus were not limited at all to these, but he had performed his share of such. An impressive and dramatic scene had taken place in Galilee, at the home of his friend Peter, a man in comfortable circumstances, whose house was of some size, and accommodated both audiences and patients in considerable numbers. The Rabbi had preached in the house, under the gallery, and the crowd overflowed into the street. Suddenly, in the middle of his sermon, there descended at his feet, mysteriously let down from overhead, a paralyzed person, whose muscular and ingenious friends had carried him up the outside stairs of the house, or had taken " the road of the roofs " from a neighbor's ; so they stole a march upon the healer's attention, perhaps by tearing up the earth and the brush from the gallery roof, and forcing a space large enough for their purpose. As this image of woe fell flat at his feet, the preacher's voice hushed. Only the eyes of the patient could move, and these clasped the person of the most merciful man whom Galilee had ever known or heard of. The entreaty was so piteous that the lip of Jesus trembled. He could not go on with his discourse till he had cured the patient.

The memory of this scene occurred to him poignantly one Sabbath, when, being in Jerusalem at an ecclesiastical feast, he walked out alone to one of the " wells of healing " in which the East abounded. This spot was not far from the market, and easily accessible. It was eminent for its legendary cures, and sure to be frequented by people suffering from those forms of nervous disease which

forbid a patient to get too far from home, but
are sure to take him somewhere in a whimsical
search for health. The place went by the name of
Bethesda, and was a pretty pool, picturesquely
guarded by porches. It was one of the intermit-
tent springs whose rise and fall was attributed by
the ignorance of the times to supernatural agency.
The waters were disturbed at irregular intervals,
and only the poor wretch who pushed his way in at
the expense of his weaker companions, and at the
precise moment when the spring began to swell, had
any chance.

Jesus stood beside Bethesda, and it was the Sabbath, — the awful Sabbath, in which a man was
forbidden to carry fuel, a rug, a bundle, or to lift
the sick upon their beds. Only the dying could
be carried by good Jews. A medical cure was forbidden. Jesus stood watching the mass of misery
that had accumulated at the pool. His now practiced eye perceived among those wretched people a
large proportion of nervous patients, and among
them he readily recognized the worst and most
genuine case. A helpless man, disabled for thirty-
eight years, and deserted by his friends who had
grown tired of taking care of him, lay sadly in one
of the porches by himself. The ruder and more
restless sick complained and quarreled around him.
He alone lay quite still and acquiescent. The patience born from long-accepted despair had settled
upon him. His drawn face demanded nothing ; his
wasted hands made no appeal. His eyes were dull
with endurance that had passed the stage of fever-

ishness, hope, or fear. He lay waiting for the
chance which had never come, — which would never
come. This was the sickest man at the spring, and
the only one sure to receive no attention.

Jesus went directly to him. The two were apart.
No one noticed the Rabbi who came to see Bethesda,
a common resort for country folk visiting Jerusalem
and anxious to see the sights. Jesus entered at
once into conversation with the disabled man, who
had attracted his interest. He did not insult the
nervous patient by expressing doubts as to the reality of his disorder. He did not prejudge hysterical
symptoms, or underestimate the nature of a suffering only too evident to his refined perception. An
ordinary physician might easily have turned this
case off as one of the Bethesda hypochondriacs.

The Galilean healer was too sensitive for that.
His mind was too keen to make this blunder, because it was too fine. Gently drawing from the
poor man his story, which was not altogether that
of an innocent sufferer, he sorrowed for the patient
more than he blamed. His heart ached at the plaintive and uncomplaining, —

" Sir, all the others can get into the water, but
there is nobody to help me. Before I can get
down " —

But there the stranger interrupted him. The
morbid, motionless man clinging to his superstition
because he had nothing better, looked, startled, up.
What words were these? What face was that?
What fire, half of indignation, half of pity, played
across those gentle features? Why did the Rabbi
shake his head?

What? Not believe in the waters — not in the
Bethesda waters, — after all?   Believe only in this
face, this voice, this sweetest sympathy ever found
in all a lonely, miserable life? With a rush of emotion, it suddenly seemed to the neglected invalid
that if he had been dead he could have lived had
this man spoken to him, had he looked at him so.

" Take it up ! " cried the stranger, pointing to the
bed.   "Carry it.   Walk ! "

With this authoritative order he dismissed the
case, and took himself hurriedly away.

Later in the day Jesus met his cured patient
accidentally, and exchanged with him a few words.
But these were not many, for the story was now
public property, and a curious crowd crushed upon
the two.

A sullen excitement had set in over the case.
Both had defied the law ; the healer had wrought
a cure, and the invalid had carried a bed upon the
Sabbath day.

Ecclesiastical feeling ran high. A timid man
would have retreated from it.   Jesus, on the contrary, went straight to the Temple, where he was
sure to meet the full brunt of it. His object in
coming to Jerusalem at that time had been no light
one. He was no mere traveler, no comfortable
worshiper.   Strange and strong as the story of his
career had been for the last few months, the movement of his own nature had been stranger and
stronger.   He felt the imperious need of a broader
scope. Braver deeds beckoned him. Deeper dangers called him. Beautiful Galilee with her listen-

ing synagogues and her happy convalescents was
not the world. Problems of church and state troubled him.

The character of his own peculiar mission asked
him awful questions. These gave him no rest. He
came, and he came alone, definitely to test the
attitude of the capital towards himself. His method
of doing this was entirely his own.

In the cause of humanity he had boldly broken
the Sabbath laws, ancient as Moses, precious as
Israel, rigid as death. In the cause of common
sense he had treated a superstition dear to Jerusalem with unpardonable contempt. Could he not
have cured his man on any other of six days out of
seven? Could he not have done it at some time
when the spring *did* rise? All ecclesiastical laws
and pathological precedents he had simply ignored.
The clergy, the people, and the government were
equally offended. Not fully prepared for the consequences, Jesus calmly awaited them. If he felt
any agitation, he did not show it. In the Temple
he serenely defended himself. A mob was the
result.

The very madness of joy looked at him from the
eyes of one adoring man, — the escaped prisoner of
thirty-eight years of misery. He could see his Bethesda patient excitedly arguing the case with scribe
and priest and Pharisee. But the church frowned
on the heretic. The people imitated the church.
His own discourse in the Temple, a powerful and
fearless address, had made everything worse. The
country Rabbi became in an hour dangerously un-

popular.   With hurt surprise, with pathetic wonder
that left no room for fear, Jesus perceived that he
stood in the Temple of his race, in the holy city of
his heart, in actual peril of his life.

He had come up from the country filled with no
man knew what secret hopes, with what growing
exaltations and exultations too pure for comprehension by his nearest friends.   He had come up trust-
fully, looking for some cheerful signs of the popular
feeling under which he might map out the plan of
his work.   But Jerusalem met him with a malicious
rebuff, and dismissed him with a murderous threat.

His independence of conviction soon brought more
trouble upon him.   Having heartily allowed his
hungry disciples to pick corn on the Seventh Day,
he found that he had committed an unpardonable
offense.   Jesus defended his innovation warmly and
authoritatively.   "I am Lord of the Sabbath," he
said.

CHAPTER VII

THE PREACHER ; AND THE DEAD

WHATEVER had been his disappointment in the
results of his experiment at Jerusalem, Jesus did
not express or cultivate it. He came back thoughtfully to Galilee, — impulsive, fickle, lovable Galilee,
where he was affectionately trusted and perplexedly
admired, — and drowned himself again in his work.
With that noticeable good sense which characterized
all his public movements, and with his habit of
following the clear duty instead of urging the doubtful, he resumed his opportunity among the warm-
hearted lake-people and their inland neighbors.
Their welcome was genuine enough, and encouraged
him, but it never flattered him. He was now
approaching the height of his fame. He had not
fully realized its proportions before he left home.
His return from the capital to the country revealed
to him some new and pleasant aspects of his growing
hold upon the people. He accepted his popularity
with unapproachable simplicity, serenity, and modesty. He gave no evidence of one dizzy hour. The
moral vertigo which confuses many great men at
the whirl of their success did not perceptibly affect
him. If he ever felt it, he gave no sign of doing
so. The giddiness was conquered before it reached
the poise.

This was the more to be noticed because he had a kind of temptation to lose his balance, which is only to be measured by some appreciation of the eminence that he refused himself.   Beside it, that which he allowed himself was a lowly success.   This fact, which time enunciated with a terrible distinctness, began now to murmur to his consciousness.

Galilee was at his feet.   Just then he could have done anything with Galilee.   The neighboring provinces overflowed on the lake side for his sake ; Judea sought him and studied him ; and even Jerusalem had her delegates at his mass meetings. The clergy and officers of his church had begun to observe him.   His audiences were numbered by thousands.   His patients were never numbered. Sickness, misery, sin, and shame swept against his heart as the winds swept Gennesaret, whose shape was like a harp.   Both audiences and patients were increasing with appalling force.   He could get little sleep.   Rest was impossible.   He had scarcely time to eat, and his nervous vigor was so taxed that food was taken with difficulty.   It had become necessary for him to own or to control a boat for his frequent trips across the lake, and that he might push out into the water and so use the deck as a pulpit, putting a space between himself and the masses which would otherwise have disabled him from addressing them. Wherever he went, he took and left crowds.   He was trampled by humanity.   He was almost crushed by its near proximity.   The pressure of its woe closed upon him till he could have cried out for agony from his delicate perception of what that meant. The sense of its taint bruised against his exquisite purity till he could have shrunk away forever, from sheer moral recoil, out of repulsive contact. He never did. He had not an atom of false sensitiveness. His delicacy had not a morbid nerve in it. He took the world as he found it. But he did not, he would not, he could not leave it so. Where he was, vice hung its head. Where he trod, virtue was the only comfortable thing. Misery crept like a child to his arms. Assuagement was in his touch, because pity and power held the balance of his impulses. His life was as foreign to every conception of life held by the people of his times as the unknown continents of the western hemisphere. He passed through Palestine like a new law of moral science, which men obeyed without understanding.

He had been but a short time at home again when he found his work so grown upon his hands that it was impossible to continue it without responsible assistants and more of them.

The selection of these cost him much thought and care. More depended upon it than was perceived by any spectator. He had already given offense by numbering among his especial friends a collector of the Roman government. With his fearless independence he had never paid the least attention to the feeling caused by this expression of indifference to Jewish prejudices, and the collector proved to be one of his most valuable men. He chose the subordinates he preferred for qualities best appreciated by himself. Out of them all there was but one failure. An unhappy choice could hardly be called a mistake, which was plainly as necessary to the action of the mighty drama in which he moved as treason, death, or heart-break to the motion of a Greek tragedy.

The night before he completed the organization which was the nucleus of the great faith that bears his name, he spent in that solitary, solemn manner which marked all the critical decisions or events of his life. Northward of Capernaum, in the hilly region, he knew and loved many lonely haunts. Thither he went, and there he wandered. In thought and prayer he wore the whole night out. The lake that he loved was at his feet; the stars, acquaintances to other men, but comrades to him, were marshaled above his head; the stillness that he craved, and could never command by day, stole to his nerves.

Darkness without hid those hours of darkness within, of which he told no man. What doubts, that he knew not whether to acknowledge or to ignore, beset him! What fearful questions catechized him! What forebodings tortured him! How often did he ask himself if he had mistaken himself, — if he were deluded about it all, — if his own consciousness rang true! Had he misread the signs of mere popularity for the will of heaven? Did he hear in the clamor of men the voice of God? The first trouble in the wilderness by Jordan, the first moral emergency, — was it his next and next, and always his until the last? Was it the cruelest difficulty of his solitary mission that he was never quite sure, without interruption in his own conviction, of his

CHRIST BY THE SEA

commission from God? Then was it the grandest
achievement of his life that he went straight on
doing the one thing of which he was sure, and leaving the nature of his mission to take care of itself.
There was no doubt that the sick were wretched,
and that he could heal them. There was no doubt
that men were evil, and that he could make them
better. There was no doubt that he could comfort
the unhappy. There was no more doubt that he
could preach and teach and heal than there was that
he suffered and was misunderstood. Was he the
Chosen, the Wonderful, the Anointed, the Messiah
of his people? Was he the Son of his God? The
answer to this awful question lay in the lips of
Jehovah. There were black hours when those lips
seemed sealed for him who hung upon their motion
for the breath of his being. There were bright
hours when whispers inarticulate to common ears
inexpressibly comforted the lonely man.

When he came down from the heights at dawn,
his friends, accustomed to read the changes of his
dear and noble face, — and that with some affectionate skill, as they read the weather on the Galilean
lake, — were moved by his appearance. Plainly
this had been one of the nights when he had prayed
almost to exhaustion. Lines of sleeplessness and
intense feeling were cut upon his face. Yet he
did not look unhappy. Wan as he was, he smiled
warmly. Joy came down the hillsides with him.

The plain men, who loved him better than they
understood him, connected in their own minds this
night of vigil and of prayer with the solemn cere-

mony through which he immediately called them to lifelong allegiance to himself. It was a tremendous occasion to them. It was a serious one to him. But they soon perceived that he had needed extra strength for another purpose. That night of solemn preparation was the prelude to a great public address.

He and his twelve friends had scarcely turned their grave faces from one another, each awed with his own share in the important compact through which they had just passed, when the people, crowding up and on, crushed to the Rabbi's feet. He was so encompassed by them that he could not have been heard or seen ; and, after protesting gently but in vain, he withdrew from them and climbed to an elevation that commanded the crowd.

It now contained a vast number of persons, — how many no one cared to count. For an undiverted interest centred upon the preacher. He did not always follow the custom of the Jewish rabbi, who sat while he instructed. On certain occasions his impulse drew him to his feet. But this was not one of them. At the height on which he was, it was quite possible to assume the usual ministerial posture, and still control his audience. This was now so large that he needed to make some effort to be heard in the open air. Yet he seemed to make none. His enunciation was remarkably distinct, and was understood by the uttermost straggler on the edge of the crowd.

His voice was carried to a surprising distance. It had a clear, vibrant quality, and rang; its vowel

sounds were exquisite ; it was music articulate.   It
was a voice to love, to long for, to follow, to obey,
to recall long after it had ceased, as one recalls
indescribable pleasure; it was the organ only to be
commanded by a pure, high soul united to a powerful intellect.

Yet, though it could hold an audience of thousands of restless people, the voice of Jesus was not
loud.   Its timbre was one of marvelous delicacy.
Its lowest tone — and he preferred the low tones —
could be heard where a coarser man would have
been obliged to strain all the functions of the throat
and lungs.   He spoke with perfect ease; as if he
were not obliged to think how he spoke.

He began that morning in a low, penetrating
voice.   It was music, pity, and power in one.   The
lightest listener in the audience sobered before the
sound, and the lowest shriveled; but the most miserable wept for very comfort.   Before their slow
minds had begun to grasp the significance of what
he said, his hearers were fascinated by the way in
which he said it.   It was one of the voices that
predestine the career of an orator.   It took but a
few moments for a cultivated observer of the throng,
reflecting dispassionately as he studied the scene, to
decide that a man with that voice, and that presence,
was created to be the most famous religious orator
of his times.   How could the imagination of any
Hebrew or Roman, Greek or Persian, of that day,
compass the knowledge that he was listening to the
greatest preacher of history ?   Such the Rabbi from
Nazareth has proved himself to be.   His discourse

that morning on the rocks outside of Capernaum
has gone far to give him the claim to this title.

It was and remains, seen across the span of civilization, and judged by the standards of the severest
modern criticism, the great masterpiece of religious
address.

Contrasted with his first youthful and interrupted
sermon in the Nazareth synagogue, this discourse indicated a natural but obvious growth in the preacher.
All hesitation, experimentation, were behind him.
He preached like a man sure of himself and of his
subject.   His facility of expression had become
more marked.   His increased intellectual force had
an iron grip.   His logic closed like lock and key.
His style had become polished and brilliant.   His
persuasive power was irresistible.   Who, reading
the Sermon on the Mount with anything like attention, wonders at the exhausting night of study that
preceded it?

Jesus was what we call an extemporaneous
speaker; but, strictly speaking, this was no extem-
pore effort.   The evidences of careful construction
and finish abound in the discourse itself.   He was
destitute of tricks of speech.   His methods were
never sensational.   He used the best of grammar.
His rhetoric was a model.   He did not cater to the
ignorant by an appearance of ignorance.   He
avoided vulgarisms.   He spoke like a gentleman.
This educated mechanic was a polished orator.   He
was and is the great instance of the eternal truth
that a superior mind never need abase itself to reach
an inferior.   His simplicity, directness, force, per-

suasiveness, were a compliment to the most ignorant person among his hearers, who responded to them without knowing why ; and the most cultivated, who knew why, could no more help responding than the ignorant. The sermons of Jesus indicate that he was an habitual student, and this of no easy type. Days and nights of severe application marked his career as a preacher. He was no half-taught, half-ready, popular talker trusting to his emotions to take him through the hour. He was thoroughly equipped.

On the occasion of which we speak, he addressed himself particularly to twelve men. Twelve hundred, or twice or thrice that number, were in the audience; but his disciples, with their fresh vows scarcely parted from their lips, were in the foreground. He placed and retained them in close proximity to himself, while he made of the private ceremony through which he had but just initiated them a solemn public event. He had now reached a stage in his life when organization was necessary to the advancement of his principles, and when he began to feel their advancement an urgent thing. This conviction he wished, if possible, to share with the witnesses of the scene. Formality, as a rule, he avoided. No other great leader of men has scorned it as he did. His methods were simple and modest ; he was incapable of display ; he always acted like a man who did not know the use of it, or who forgot that it had any, in human affairs. This was one of the very few occasions of his life when he took advantage of a ceremony to achieve an end.

The beautiful and impressive formalities of the morning were not lost upon the crowd; the dullest minds in it understood that Jesus regarded the organization of his disciples as a matter of profound importance to himself, to them, to the Jewish race, and to the world.

The Jews, being a people born and trained to severity, took it as a matter of course. Of mercy they knew little. Commandments carved in stone by the greatest of legislators grimly cut their ancient laws into the Hebrew instinct. Jehovah had not wasted words with the people. It was: Thou shalt not, and Thou shalt. With explanation, or appeal, or promise He had never concerned himself. Moses was not a tender man. The fiat and its consequences were as unornamented as Sinai, and as hard.

Jesus, too, came down from a mountain on the day when the principles of the Christian faith were first publicly laid down. Introducing a reverent reference to the ancient laws of his race, — which in a less sincere man would have been a marvel of dexterity, — he succeeded, by a wonderful mingling of oratorical tact and genuineness of feeling, in unfolding his theories of life and of religion. These were so startling and original that they took the breath away from his audience.

Instead of commandments, Jesus offered beatitudes. Instead of thunder, there was music. Threats were replaced by promises. Punishments interested him less than rewards. After a thousand years of law, who could understand love? Amazement which amounted almost to stupefaction listened to him.

He spoke of incredible things.   He treated them in an astounding way.   Something in his manner was more than priestly; it was more than royal.   He tore down old, solid, respectable errors of church and society with the assurance of a God tossing aside human affairs.   In his audience were a certain number of ecclesiastical delegates and pompous pietists of the established belief.   He paid no court to their position.   He did not on their account soften by an adjective anything which he had to say.   He singled them out, in fact, as he did on more than one other occasion, by one of the severest rebukes ever known to fall from his gentle lips.   He added to his enemies on that morning.   Conservatives did not understand him, and hypocrites feared him.   Silent and secret jealousies and aversions grew in his audience alongside of the admiration, affection, and trust which it was impossible for him not to inspire.

For he spoke of strange thoughts in a strange way.   He offered great things to small people.   He selected the overlooked, the despised, those who were of no consequence.   He made extraordinary promises for ultimate preëminence to men without what is called "spirit;" to those not quick to take provocation, — patient people, the gentle, the humble; to those weakened by too much grief; to the tender; to those whose longing for what he called righteousness, or rightness of heart, was a spiritual starvation.   The unhappy, the slandered; those who loved peace and tried to preserve it; those who suffered hardship for a good cause; all the obscure and unfortunate whom it was not the fashion to notice, — these he preferred.

To one class of men he reserved the most solemn and most tender of all his affectionate pledges: "The pure in heart," he said, "are blessed. They shall see God." His voice sank with these words; it was audible only because it was so clear and sweet; thousands held the breath to catch the falling tone; hundreds hung their heads like children, when they understood what the Rabbi said. No person looked at his neighbor. Every one was busy with his own soul. On the face of the preacher crept such a look as an unclean man, beholding, might have died of, for very shame. Then dazzling brightness smote his countenance. Many in his audience covered their eyes before its radiance, — these as if they had seen, those as if they should never see something too precious to speak of; something dearer than life, more inexorable than death.

.   .   .   .

The preacher paused at this point, but only to gather strength to proceed with his remarkable discourse. The sermon was not a brief one, and its beautiful opening was followed by a train of thought whose power and originality were no less great than his introduction. What he said was as fearless as the lightning, yet as practical as any statute of the ancient law.

He spoke as the maker of a new system, the legislator of a higher law. He treated of many moral offenses. The list ranged from murder to rash judgment, from immorality to excessive anxiety. He dealt with many virtues ; their names were new to his audience.   Each watched to see how his neighbor took these confusing things ; rich travelers and poor rustics, philosophers and women, listened with a common bewilderment.   The few plain men who had given their lives to his service lifted trustful and affectionate faces to Jesus while he spoke, but they experienced their share of the general perplexity.   The preacher stood among his doctrines as if he were the creator of a new world.

In an age when human life was held as cheap as the fish in the nets at Galilee, or the ants crushed by the hoofs of camels in the caravan, he taught that one venomous wish makes a man before God guilty of murder.   In an age when common decency was so defied that the pen refuses to write of the immorality of the times, he taught that one coarse look or low thought broke the seventh commandment.

In an age when private revenge was sweet and fashionable, " Forgive thine enemy ! " rang from his firm lips like a military command spoken in a language unknown to the rank and file.   To a people whose habits of thought were stiff with the selfishness of a race to which self-protection has been for generations foremost in mind, he flung down the incredible demand that they should love their neighbors as they loved themselves.

In an age when a slave had not as many rights as a pauper dog in our streets to-day, and when a prince or a priest treated a poor man as he chose and no help for it, when rank and wealth were never asked for their credentials if they trampled obscurity and poverty into bruises and blood, he taught the equality of man, the rights of the wronged, the value of the slighted. In a society of sham he scorned worldliness by an epigram which has remained superb and final from his day to ours.

To a church dying of ceremony, rotten with hypocrisy, and dark with distrust of himself, he gently offered an ideal of worship which defied every ecclesiastical conception of his race and times. An immortal prayer distinguished and hallowed the great discourse. It was the most exquisite episode in the morning's service. The Lord's Prayer has never been approached as a model for public worship. All times and all people have appropriated that matchless petition. The perplexity of the audience which listened to Jesus that summer morning did not decrease as the sermon proceeded.

Were they Gentiles, that foreign ideas like these should be offered them without apology? Were they angels, that virtues never heard of in human character should be expected of them? Who and what was this Rabbi? His air of authority was unimpeachable. Whence did he get it? What did he mean by it? The most willful skeptic in the throng felt it. There was no such thing as escaping it; and when were authority and persuasion ever so mingled in one address? How could so regal a man be so winning? how could so gentle a man be so imperial, commanding?

And now, indeed, a few thoughtful persons recalled those recent rumors about the Wonderful.

Was this he who once or twice, in his religious enthusiasm, was said to have claimed the awful personality of the Messiah? But the preacher that day had said nothing on the subject.

We like to think that he passed the night succeeding this great sermon in sleep, for he was worn with his recent vigil, and the strain of the day had been very heavy. The mere intellectual exercise of such an address was no light matter. Add the spiritual energy, which was of such a sort as no mind not in sympathy with it can appreciate. And he was destined soon to undergo a still greater ordeal, one of the supreme experiences of his life. He needed all his strength.

He found it, — only God and he knew how. His strange consciousness that he stood in some exceptional relation to the Deity came to him at times in mighty form and force. There were crises when he leaned upon it as on an infinite Heart beating behind his own, as nothing but the heart of fatherhood ever beats, whether in divine or human being.

Fortified by prayer, encouraged by achievement, and calmed by sleep, he left Capernaum and proceeded on one of his preaching circuits. His followers were with him, much impressed by recent events, and fired with new enthusiasm in his service. They cast at him frequent glances of admiration touched with reverence. He was unusually silent. They wondered why. But they were used to wondering where their Master was concerned. It was their habitual state of mind. He was not like other men;

he did not act as other persons did. His personality, his conduct, his motives were all so much above those of common people that at times the affection which his twelve friends had for him mounted into awe. Yet they loved him too much to feel altogether afraid of him.

They were traveling towards a little Galilean town (its name was Nain; "The Delightful"), — he still silent, and the whole company quieter than usual, — when they saw before them, as evening came on, the sombre movement of a funeral procession, preceded by women, a custom peculiar to Galilee. Hired mourners were chanting:

> "*Alas, the hero!*
> *Alas, alas, the lion!*"

The air was so still that the sound of the dirge came mournfully to a distant ear.

By the impressive Oriental custom, courtesy required each traveler to stop his journey and join the mourners. The dead and the bereaved might be strangers, but grief was the awful acquaintance of all humanity. Jesus and his followers, obeying the etiquette of the occasion, moved up to attach themselves to the cortége which was slowly winding its way to the burial. One of the beautiful but hopeless names given by the Hebrews to the grave was, The House of Eternity. Some of them had but little if any hope of life beyond, and the dreariness of their funerals had not much to relieve it.

But what was the Rabbi doing? Etiquette did

not call upon him to give orders to the burial procession. Custom did not allow him to stop the
bearers. Yet they had stopped. Jesus himself
pushed forward to the wicker bier, and stood resolutely beside it. The spectators were somewhat
shocked when they saw the Rabbi, who was neither
a natural nor a hired mourner, so concerning himself with this funeral.

The face of the dead was uncovered. It was
that of a man and young. He had endured a wasting disease, and his features were much emaciated.
He had been a comely lad; there was something
more appealing than revolting about his appearance even now: he had the look of the dead who
have died in their patience; who have bravely borne
the worst, and given little trouble, and left more
grief than relief in the hearts of those who loved
them least; and have left in the lives of those who
loved them most a loss and woe unutterable. Jesus
seemed to be somehow drawn to the youth, as if he
might have cared for him living, — as if he could
have found it easy to mourn this stranger, dead.
There are lost friendships in every life; never,
perhaps, met by the roadside until too late. Was
this one of his? Or was there nothing more in the
scene than the natural movement of his great heart
towards the anguish of a great sorrow? He stood
looking down, close beside the bier.

.   .   .   .

An elderly woman was the chief mourner. She
was weeping piteously. Years upon years — it
seemed to her lifetime upon lifetime — ago, she had

followed the boy's father, like this, to the swift
Eastern burial that snatches the precious dead
out of sight within a few hours. They had been
married lovers, and this child was their only one.
The widow had reared the lad with the blind adoration which lonely womanhood offers to the only
thing it has to love and live for. She had nothing
left. She had not thought it possible that Jehovah
could crush her so a second time. She had saved
that unreasoning faith in fate which the least hopeful of us do sometimes. She had thought to keep
the boy. She was beginning to grow old. . . .

"Be not weeping!"

A low voice quite near her surprised her misery
with these words, spoken with what ineffable sympathy! In all her life she had never heard any
one speak like that. She looked up dully. The
sky, soft as it was with the approaching night,
smote and dazzled her. The mourners looked
small, and seemed to reel. Pinched, gray, cold, lay
the precious face. That little, dreadful thing
seemed to blot out the whole world. She stirred
towards it and swayed. She heard some one say:

"She faints!"

But she had not fainted. Misery was not so
merciful. She was quite conscious of everything.
She saw the stranger standing tall and erect. Ah,
what a look! What a face! What pity! What
fathoms of compassion in his eyes!

She had heard of this look of his. She perceived, indeed, that it was the Nazarene. She
knew the deeds he did, for their fame was in every

tongue. If her son had been born deaf, or born
blind, or had been bedridden this dozen years, or
had never walked at all, or if he had been a leper,
— and alive! Or if she had met this man a few
weeks, a few days ago! — But the boy was dead.
This might be a great healer. But the boy was
dead.

She turned away indifferently from the Rabbi,
and mechanically began to cover the face of the
dead with her shaking hands. But Jesus gently
deterred her.

.   .   .   .

Two crowds had met, — that which followed the
funeral procession, and the other, larger one which
followed the Nazarene. The witnesses of this scene
were now of a very great number. The mass
pressed up and closed around the mourners. But
at a look from him it fell back.

With a gesture clearing a little space for himself,
so that he might be free from contact with humanity, Jesus lifted his face towards the sky. Yet he
did not seem to see the sky. His gaze pierced
beyond it, untroubled, undazzled, but deep with
interrogation. He remained in this attitude some
moments. Then his color slightly changed.

. . . Stooping over the bier, he regarded the face
of the dead with majestic intentness. His hands —
delicate, veined, nervous, but instinct with life —
hovered over but did not touch the brow of the
corpse. So he stood quite still, thrilling with vigor,
shining with purity of soul and body, a man ideal
with the halo of heaven on him and the pity of earth

within him, glorious to look upon, defiant life confronting monarch death.

The awe of the scene had now extended itself to the lightest spectator in the crowd. The mourners had stopped chanting. Honest silence shamed the hired wailings. Only the mother's sobs broke the stillness.

The countenance of Jesus had become quite pale. What awful concentration of will, of prayer, of faith, of energy grasped through his being? He seemed for an instant to gasp under it, as if its grip were more than mortal frame could bear. . . . Then, stooping so that his warm breath touched the dead man's cheek, he commanded the body, as one commands a living thing that can obey :

"Young man, arise! I say, arise!" Now, swelling from all the people, accidental and awed witnesses of this tremendous scene, there surged cries and murmurs, fright and worship battling :

"Nay, nay! Spare us! Flee! Pray! Jehovah have mercy upon us! Lord God of Israel, what kind of man is this?"

For the frozen arms of the dead had clasped the Nazarene around the neck; and the icy lips, which an hour hence would have been shut down forever beneath the earth, had melted into broken words.

A woman's cry rang to the very footstool of God. When the weak or the aged die of joy they cry like that.

But the Nazarene solemnly put the young man into his mother's arms and turned away. His own agitation was now plainly visible.

Many of the people had fled in terror from this sight ; but some remained, and those who did fell flat upon the ground in homage.

When the throng could find their senses, Jesus was nowhere to be seen.

CHAPTER VIII

THE RABBI, AND THE WOMAN

THE East was always palpitating with mysticism, and the Jews, we cannot too often remind ourselves, were a wonder-loving nation. The strange things that had been recorded of their ancient prophets were naturally recalled; many remarkable deeds which Jesus did were subject to explanation such as it was easy for the growing party of his opponents to proffer. A few slighting words cast at a noble act, a few illustrations of other wonders done by other persons prominent in Jewish history, might, for the moment, make an impression. But the steady progress of the facts made a stronger and a longer. The people always find out, in the long run, who is their friend. The mass of the people were not to be deterred from their belief in a man who made their interests so utterly his own; who threw himself into the pit of their miseries and struggled there with them; to whom their bereavements and their famines, their debts, their terrible poverty, their revolting diseases, were as important as if they had been his own.

They gave to the marvels attendant upon his career the natural trust of witnesses who had been the benefited party. But those who were inclined

to believe in him, and those who were not, had now
come up against a momentous event. Doubt and
cavil could not do much with it. Sneer and innu-
endo and the thrust of medical jealousy, ecclesiastical dogmatism, or political taunt, slid away silent,
like snakes in the grass. There was a young man
in Nain, — known of his neighbors, visible to his
friends, — a breathing, stirring, smiling man. A
radiant mother clasped him to her heart. Thoughtful, he trod among the anemones in the resurrection of the year. The witnesses of the fact numbered thousands of sane and sensible people. It
created a stir as tremendous as was to be expected.
In a short time Palestine thrilled with the story. It
ran from the shore to the capital; the mountains
and the plains discussed it with respect amounting
to awe.

It penetrated to the dungeon of Herod; and from
that fastness of night and woe there issued to the
ears of the Nazarene one piercing appeal. It came
from his poor kinsman; the only cry uttered by
John in all his courageous martyrdom. Trustworthy
agents dexterously brought the question from the
prisoner to the Rabbi:

"Art thou the man, — the coming one? Must
we look beyond thee? Or art thou *He?*" — a magnificent message, quite like John; there was not a
word of complaint of his own pitiable condition; no
reaching out in the fear of his now closely approaching death, after sympathy, after some expression of
the love of the man whom he loved above all the
world besides; not a word about himself. Still, to

the end, quenched in the fire of his one noble duty
in life, John could think, could speak of nothing
but the great personality in which he had absorbed
his own. The prophet was worthy of his lord.

Jesus was inexpressibly touched by this message.
Its supreme unselfishness appealed powerfully to
him; and its pathos stirred freshly in his heart the
grief and affection always burning there and ready
to blaze at every thought of his kinsman John.

He was surrounded at the moment by a large
crowd. It comprised the usual proportion of patients, waiting their turns at his attention. These
were of all varieties, from the mild disorders to the
incurable and loathsome cases. They were clamoring for him.

Jesus stood a little apart, listening to the messengers of John: he could not conceal his emotion;
why, then, did he not reply? Why this discourtesy
to the disciples of his friend? Yet he stood quite
silent. Troubled, they repeated their question; its
solemnity was enough to have challenged attention
in the lightest nature. What then? Was this irre-
sponsiveness political caution? The dungeons of
Herod had many lips, and the palaces a thousand
ears. Was the Nazarene *afraid* to answer the dying cry of his kinsman?

The messengers of John looked on to see themselves apparently slighted by a silence so enigmatical
that they knew not what to make of it. For Jesus
turned abruptly away from them and went on with
his morning's business.

Precisely as if nothing had happened, and no vis-

itors were there, he proceeded as usual to attend to
his patients. They crawled and crowded to his feet.
He gave to each case his habitual attention, patiently
individualizing, as he always did (for this was one
of the minor secrets of his success in healing), and
following one cure by another with an enthusiasm
which no form of disease and no accumulation of its
drain upon his strength seemed ever to check. When
the healer had finished his work for the day, the
preacher began his. The morning's cures were followed by one of his impassioned religious addresses.
The friends of the prisoner, who had been using
their eyes to the utmost, now began to use their ears.
Their momentary resentment at his apparent refusal
to answer them had long since died away ; they were
swept into the common stream of feeling; they
could have knelt at his feet with the rest.

When he had completed his discourse the preacher
turned with a swift, commanding motion to the messengers of John. Upon his face the tense changes
in his mood had cut deep marks. Now he gave his
emotion rein. Ah, how for a moment had they
thought he did not *care !*

It needed no words now to tell the dullest of men
how the Rabbi's heart melted for his kinsman's sake.
Then, and not till then, he spoke. And then he
delivered one of the most remarkable replies ever
made by one public man to another concerning the
movement of large affairs.

" Go," he said, " tell John what ye behold. There
were the blind, — they see ; the deaf, — they hear.
You saw those lame men ; they walk.   Lepers are

cleansed. There was a dead man. The dead are raised."

To this list of marvels he added, with a significance as easy to understand in his times as it is difficult in ours, this impressive climax:

" To the *poor* the Gospel is preached."

These were his credentials. Without comment, he sent them to the dungeon. John would understand.

Was this the Messiah? Was he not? Here was the profoundest question possible to the age in which these two men lived! Let incarceration and martyrdom answer; solitude and the shadow of hurrying death might reply, when the free and the comfortable and the light of heart could not.

It was in one of the pauses of this missionary journey, — it was autumn, — and he had been invited to the house of a prominent citizen. This man was a Pharisee.

The real aristocrats among the Jews at this time were the Sadducees, a cold and polished intellectual sect, remembered in the history of philosophy as cultivating a pugnacious disbelief in immortality; and the Herodians, who were the courtiers and free-thinkers. From some of those subtle causes which fashion creates but does not explain, the priests, the scribes, and the Pharisees never socially outranked, perhaps did not quite rank, the exclusive skeptics; but they remained the leading classes of the people, a powerful and pretentious body of men.

They corresponded in position somewhat to our

clergy and important laymen, and were of goodly numerical size, about six thousand. The Pharisees were the fussy formalists of Palestine.

As a class, they did not love the Nazarene, who did not hesitate publicly to rebuke them when they deserved it.

They were the inconsistent church officers and church members who in all times do so much mischief. Men of the world without religious convictions had in that age no more patience with the religious pretension which was not backed by character than they have in this.

There was a certain coldness of heart combined with pettiness of ceremonial in these ecclesiastical autocrats, which has made the name of their sect a synonym for pious sham from their day to ours. Jesus had no patience with shams. He never failed to denounce one when it came in his way, if he thought it of any use to do so. The spiritual rottenness of these religious pretenders was peculiarly abhorrent to him.

His host, on the occasion of which we speak, was one of the better specimens of the sect ; a man not without some sincerity, or even that tendency to earnestness which, falling a little short of the quality itself, makes a man uncomfortable in a wrong position, without forcing him into a right one. This man had been observing the career of Jesus with some candor, and, on the entrance of the itinerant Rabbi to his town, took advantage of the opportunity to obtain some acquaintance with him. Simon the Pharisee was a man of position both in church and in society; and social attention on his part to the heretic Nazarene indicated some independence of thought; for a Pharisee was, in his own way, as exclusive as a Brahman in his social life. Possibly Simon was a little fond of lionizing strangers; at all events, it was not without a certain sense of patronage, curiously mingled with deference, that he extended the invitation.

Jesus accepted it. He was never anything of a recluse. While he had no interest in what could be called society, and no time for it, yet he never obviously shunned it. He believed thoroughly in the culture of the human relations. As a means to his high ends, he would use the smallest avenue of approach to hearts. One striking thing about his history as a preacher is that, while he gave so much time and study to his discourses, he did not shut himself in to what we should call the pulpit. He never fell back on his public position, on his immense and exhausting public responsibilities, to excuse him from any reasonable form of private usefulness. He relied much upon personal influence, — very much upon the personal interview. Nineteen such private interviews are said to be recorded of him, and these were but the fraction of the facts. It was quite according to his method to accept a social invitation in a circle where he was not altogether sure of a sympathetic atmosphere. He went to dine with the Pharisee.

It was a house of some degree, and the interior indicated ease, if not large wealth. The Rabbi was received politely, but not with intimacy. Some

little ceremonies, such as the offer of the host himself to kiss the cheek or anoint the hair of a cherished friend or very distinguished guest, on entering,
were absent from the occasion. Still there was no
default of a certain sort of cordiality; and apparently the guest was satisfied with his reception. A
rustic Rabbi, not too familiar with the best society,
— why should he be conscious of any deficit in
etiquette? It seemed he was not. The banquet
opened amiably.

Jesus, as the guest of honor, bore his part in the
entertainment with that brilliant self - possession
which always surprised men of the world in this
itinerant missionary. His air of conscious superiority restrained by modesty was very attractive. It
was the essence of good-breeding. People of polite
life wondered where he acquired it. Was he not a
carpenter, and, if one were correctly informed, a
Nazarene? The gay world had now begun to give
some attention to this extraordinary zealot. The
church was watching him keenly, and that with
growing disfavor. Society would have liked to take
him up, but his dignity was too marked for this; it
was unapproachable. He responded only to a certain element of sincerity. Without seeming to do
so, he really exacted a given amount of deference.

As the Pharisee's dinner progressed, this deference became more obvious. The conversation of
Jesus was so remarkable, his mien so high, that
mere social ease wilted before him. Position suddenly seemed a paltry thing. Birth and ease,
money and fashion and ecclesiastical eminence lost

their usual proportions. The host and his friends grew thoughtful before this courtly democrat. Profound respect replaced the polite curiosity with which the guest had been at first received.

The company were reclining on their comfortable couches in the fashion which had crept into Palestine from the far East, — each leaning on his left elbow, leaving the right hand free for use at the table, — when a little disturbance occurred.

It was a very easy thing to obtain access to an Eastern house, and a slight noise without the dining-hall, as of servants parleying with some unwelcome person, aroused the quick ear of the host. He looked up anxiously. The sight which he saw sent the color flushing to his forehead. He glanced at his eminent guest with evident trepidation. He might have entertained many a visitor whom the incident would not have especially repelled ; or at most it could have been passed off with a light apology and a laugh, and the servants would have taken care of the intruder. But *this* man ! — what would he think of it? The man of the world tried to frame an apology suitable to the character of his guest, but the words failed on his lips. He would have given rough orders to clear the room of the objectionable person, but a look from the Nazarene deterred him.

The intruder was a woman. She stood just within the entrance to the dining-hall, half determined, half disheartened, and wholly uncomfortable. The long, silk curtain of red purple which she had pushed aside hung about her ; her arm was still

lifted to hold it; the gold and silk fringe vibrated
on her shoulders, for there was a light draught and
the curtain answered to it. The woman was young
and beautiful. She was daintily dressed. One
hand had closed over a small, carved alabastron
which she wore suspended from her neck by a gold
chain. Her black hair was loose and very long: it
wrapped her modestly, and fell forward over her
burning cheeks. She did not try to push it back.
She was painfully embarrassed, and seemed to cling
to this natural veil. Wrapped in it, she took a few
steps forward, and stood uncertain. The room had
grown quite still. Suddenly a sad, little sound
broke the quiet. It was a sob. The woman was
weeping.

The gaze of every guest at the table was now
upon her, but the Nazarene had not turned his
head. She seemed disturbed at this, for, from the
moment of her entrance, the poor girl had fastened
her large, mournful eyes upon the guest of honor;
she had no power of vision in her for any other
person in the room. He ignored her so completely
that she seemed to be half crushed by his indifference, and for a moment, though she was now so
near him that she could have touched him, she
seemed inclined to turn and fly from the house.

But, although he neither spoke nor glanced at
her, something in the attitude and expression of
the Rabbi restrained her. Half retreating as she
was, she turned again, and, overcome with emotion,
bent above his feet. Her hair, in this position, fell
forward, and completely covered them and her own

face from sight.   Within that dark and gentle protection she could cry as she would.   Indeed, the
woman was weeping sorely.   She was not a hard-
ened creature who did not feel the true nature of
her position.   She felt it acutely, — the discomfi-
ture of her reception in the dining-hall, the cold
anger of the host, the manner of the other guests,
the sneers, the scorn, the indignation, the smile that
was worst of all.   These trifles had started the
tears, but their springs were far below all trifles ;
and they flowed on; as a woman's tears will flow,
called up by any very little thing, but answering
to the deepest miseries of her life.

The life of this woman had been a fathomless
misery until but now, a short while ago ; until the
day when, lightly joining the great crowd that had
crushed to hear the wonderful Rabbi preach, she
had come away astonished with the moral astonishment which he so often sent shaking through the
soul.   She could never forget that evening, — how
tired he looked, but how grand, as the people came
clamoring about him, after he had done preaching ;
nor how she felt, — like a grub to which a God had
in one moment given wings.   She went with the
crowd lightly, as the flippant do, but she came away
never able to think lightly again ; turned grave forever ; a woman persuaded out of her past by the
sight of such purity as she had never dreamed of.
One word, one look of his was enough.   She could
not be in the same world with him and do wrong.
His spotlessness seemed to her something relentless,
like a law that must include herself, like some-

thing in the presence of which, or even in the memory of which, guilt could not draw a breath. And then his pity! Oh, his pity! If she had only had the chance to try what *that* would do for her!

It was trusting to that unknown quantity that she had come to this house. She had tried other times, when he was preaching, to speak to the Rabbi, as she saw the others do, but there were so many others! And people had pushed her back, saying: "You are not fit to talk to such as he!" And one said: "He would not like it. He would not want to see you." She was used to such repulses. So she had accepted them meekly and gone away, and had never exchanged one word with him, though she would have died for it. And now he would not speak it! Perhaps he was offended with her for forcing her way into the dining-hall. Perhaps he could not bring himself to overlook her history, or was afraid of the effect on his own reputation if he defied the customs of virtuous society and noticed the presence of a woman like herself. Her tears flowed faster at the thought; but, with the gentleness of true sorrow for error repented, she meekly refused to be discouraged by the wound to her timid and dawning self-respect. Her feeling towards the Rabbi was too deep; her heart melted with the touching idealization which can be given only by the tainted to the pure. She was so grateful to him for living in the world, she loved him so for being what he was, that she could have thrown her life down in an ecstasy of torture for his sake.

The poor woman would not accept his rebuff, if rebuff it were. If she might not see his face, she could worship at his feet; those patient, tired, but never-resting feet which trod the dust of Palestine over in search of unhappy people whom he could comfort.

The storm of her tears became a deluge, and drenched the bare feet of the Rabbi where they lay upon the low cushions of his couch. She was half frightened at this, and, seeing what she had done, she hurriedly wiped away the wetness with her thick long hair. She tried to stop crying, but could not. Suddenly he felt a strange thing. The lips of the woman had touched his feet; timid and reverent and delicate kisses fell one upon another, — an outburst of humiliation and adoration such as the lowest soul on earth might offer to the highest God in heaven. The woman had reached one of those moments of spiritual exaltation when one neither knows nor cares what may happen next. Until she saw and heard the prophet, she had not understood what disgrace meant. Now, at the very crisis when she first had knowledge of the nature of shame, she had her first experience of a communication between God and the soul, — we give it different names : repentance, or forgiveness, or some word which is all too definite to hold it; but the most that we know is, that there is a beautiful mystery which extinguishes shame and never tells us how.

She forgot the angry host, the sneering company; even the silence of the Rabbi himself ceased to

trouble her. She had forgotten herself, her misery,
and her error. She remembered nothing in the
world but him.

The little, white alabastron had fallen from her
trembling hand and hung forward by its chain. She
took it up and unsealed it. One of the powerful
perfumes of the East flowed out pungently and filled
the air of the dining-hall. The alabaster vial contained a precious, scented unguent, much favored by
all classes of society that could afford it. The woman poured it out lavishly, covering her hands and
the feet of the Nazarene with it, while she humbly
anointed them. She asked for nothing; not even
a sign that would give her a breath of confidence
in the new feeling which she had begun to dare to
call respect for herself. She only offered all she
had or could. She was sorry, and happy, and different. She wanted the Rabbi to understand. She
longed that he should know how she felt about him.

Up to this time the Nazarene had not spoken; but
his delicate features had shown many varying and
fine emotions during the progress of this touching
scene. Now, unexpectedly, he spoke. But he spoke
to his host, who, restrained by politeness from inter-
fering with the conduct of his guest during this
unprecedented episode, had taken no pains to conceal either his displeasure or his personal skepticism
in the matter.

" Simon," observed Jesus suddenly, " if this man
were a prophet, he would have known what kind of
a woman she is who touched him."

The face of the Pharisee crimsoned with embarrassment, for in these precise words his thought had been at that moment cast. The Nazarene read him as if he had been a Hebrew scroll. Simon flung out his hands in Oriental deprecation, but his eyes dropped. With a quiet sarcasm, all the more cutting because perfectly courteous, Jesus proceeded to suggest the number and variety of social attentions omitted in his own case by his host. No one had anointed the visitor's head when he came in. He had observed the absence of the Oriental kiss of greeting. Nay, even the usual courtesy, the commonest one of all, had been overlooked by careless servants whom a none too careful master had not rebuked for their neglect. This country Rabbi had not been so ignorant of the world, after all! He had noted the slight of every little lapse of etiquette. And, worst of all, he had detected his host in the very breach of it most galling to a Pharisee. For Simon belonged to the sect whose god was an incessant lavation. A Pharisee might cheat, or lie, or oppress, or evict his tenants, or slander, or do as he pleased about the moral law; but he knew which way every drop of water ought to run, and fully expected to bathe his soul into the kingdom of Heaven. An eminent Sadducee once said of a distinguished Pharisee that he would wash the sun itself, if he could get at it.

The woman was still weeping. She could not altogether follow the conversation which now took place at the table, partly because she was crying so, partly because it was so foreign to her habit of mind that it was not easy for her to understand it. But she soon perceived that it concerned herself, and began to concentrate her attention upon it. Was the Rabbi saying a kind thing of her — *her?* Incredible!

"Thou, Simon, didst not kiss me, nor anoint, nor give me any water for my feet. But *she* has washed my feet with her tears, . . . wiped them with her hair, . . . anointed them; . . . she has not yet ceased to kiss my feet."

The words were said in a low tone, but the humiliated woman heard them with broken distinctness. For very joy and awe she stopped weeping; suddenly, like a comforted child. Impossible! Did she hear correctly? Was she deaf, or dazed?

"She has loved much. . . . Much is forgiven her."

Did the Rabbi, could the Rabbi, say *that?*

She raised her tear-stained face, pushed her hair back from it, and courageously lifted her head.

Oh, wonderful! He had turned to her at last. His glorious eyes, like altar fires, were lighted for her. His grave lip, fine with feeling, moved for her. His pity, — now she knew what his pity was! His own heart seemed to ache or break with it. It gave her a bewildering feeling, — she a creature scorned and stained, — as if, for his sake, because he pitied her she must have value, she must be worth what it cost him to think of her as he did.

His exquisite compassion, tenderer than woman's, stronger than man's, a quality undreamed of before in the world, seemed to lift her from the dust to the stars.   Jesus regarded the woman for some

minutes in one of the profound silences for which
his manner was distinguished. He seemed to be
gauging her nature, taking careful account of her
genuineness, whether it would hold or not. His
next words were the result of careful reflection, and,
when they came, no one in the room wondered that
they were uttered with the solemnity of a man who
weighs the full force and consequence of what he
says.

" Thy sins," he slowly said, " are forgiven thee."

" Are forgiven me ! " she repeated with pathetic
incredulity, — " forgiven *me?* "   She had fallen
upon the floor before his blinding face. Now she
raised herself awkwardly to her feet. He did not
extend his hand to help her. She felt that it depended on herself from this hour how she stood
before the world. She walked tottering but erect.
His look was as if it would dismiss her ; perhaps as
if he would spare her the inevitable consequences
of this scene, and shelter her from rude comment,
in solitude, and in white thoughts.

" Go," he added gently, " and in peace."   With
lifted head and shining eyes she went. Not a sneer
from the coldest lip in the company followed her out.
No one smiled. The servants made way for her
without a glance of disrespect. She did not even
look back at the Rabbi, for she felt that he would
not wish it. The silken curtain parted and fell ;
and in the thrilling echo of his last great words she
was gone.

The woman had gone, but the fact remained. The
Rabbi had done a wholly reprehensible and danger-

ous thing. He had put on record before influential ecclesiastical witnesses the boldest heresy of his life. He had dared, — and the heavens had not opened to smite the blasphemer, — he had presumed to take upon himself the remission of sins. This was a doc-· trine dear to the Jewish theocracy, and protected by ages of formalism and of awe.

Jesus, a rustic from Nazareth, a carpenter-rabbi, had dared to forgive a sinner, and she the lowest of her kind.

The banquet broke up in displeasure and disorder. Who was this person who arrogated to himself the power of Jehovah? Who could forgive sin but God Almighty?

That scene in the dining-hall at the house of Simon proved an epoch in the story of the Nazarene. One of the kindest and manliest deeds of his life became one of the strongest links in the unseen chains which were already dragging him to his doom. Palestine soon resounded with the impiety of the great heretic ; and behind dark, ecclesiastical curtains and in grim, political corners his name was marked.

One of his offenses in this act of lofty chivalry was the attitude which he took towards womanhood. This was, and remained throughout his life, so far in advance of his age, that it was nothing less than stupefying to his contemporaries. It was one of the most original, as it was one of the most noble elements in his philosophy and in his practice. The position of women among the Jews was far beyond

that which other Oriental nations gave them.   Still,
men who refused to sit beside the ladies of their
families in the synagogue were exasperated by the
social code of the Nazarene.   Races which thought
it degrading for a man to allude to the existence of
his own wife outside of his home, races whose favorite proverb taught that " the threshold weeps for
forty days when a girl is born," were perplexed by
his estimate of the nature and position of woman.
He paid no attention to the bitterness which he
aroused in this respect.   He advocated a startling
reform as calmly as if it were as old as Sarah, Princess of Abraham.   He seemed almost unconscious
of the social revolution of which he was laying the
foundations.   He went straight on with serene and
beautiful indifference, always treating women with
respect, always recognizing their fettered individualism, their force of character if they had it,
their undeveloped powers, their terrible capacity for
suffering, their superiority in spiritual vigor.   He
boldly took, from the beginning to the end of his
history, the stand that he had taken in the Pharisee's dining-room : that the restoration to a respected
future of a woman who had repented her past was
to be made a matter of course ; that men and women
stood before God upon the same moral plane, and
that they ought so to stand before human society.
This was a thing hard to understand, and harder to
forgive.   Men with holy faces and unholy lives
rebelled at it.   Men with haughty hearts, bad tem-
pers and self-indulgent habits, — all the domestic
tyrants whose yoke women were meekly and hope-

lessly enduring, — resented it. Even the kind men,
the loyal, the loving, of whom in all ages, thank
God, the world has had her happy share, were more
perplexed than enlightened by this social heresy.

But there is not a single instance in the life of
Jesus in which for a moment he seemed inclined to
weaken on this point. Every incident in which a
woman figures finds him as fearless and as chivalrous in his treatment of her as if he had held the
ruling of society in his own hands. With men he
was sometimes severe; with women never. Men he
could scathe with scorn; women never. For men
he could reserve a rebuke amounting to denunciation; for women his impulse of forgiveness came
uppermost.

A little later in his story, a beautiful incident
is related of him, in which he compassionately saved
from sentence of death a woman who perhaps deserved it. But the moral lesson, which has lasted
from that day to this, was worth the pardon.
The exquisite modesty and delicacy of the man who
[1] could not bear even so much contact with so much
shame, and who, from obvious embarrassment, wrote
upon the ground with his finger, and with downcast
eyes, while he gave the case the consideration that
he must, have dropped upon our lives like petals
from the very flower of chivalry, the blossom of
purity, manliness, and godlikeness.

While his success in Galilee was at its height,
Jesus was forming the deepest friendships of his life.
At the time when life was at its summit, he, like
other men of eminence, found these easy to select.

[1] *Ecce Homo.*

He had, among the twelve chosen, one preferred.
This man, John, has acquired for all time the
enviable reputation of being the dearest disciple of
Jesus Christ. John was a Galilean fisherman, like
several of the others; but he far surpassed his birth
and training in a refinement which won him a precious
place in the heart of his Rabbi. Jesus was deeply
drawn to John, and it is one of the noble things
about the others in the little band that none of them
showed any jealousy of this preference, but treated
the friendship with rugged generosity, memorable
when we think how they all loved and honored their
Master; all but one dark soul. That man, the treasurer of the association, like other men born traitors
but posing friends, hidden in protestations, awaited
the time when the movement of the drama should
betray him to the world; perhaps — who knows? —
first reveal him to himself.

There were other friendships peculiarly dear to
Jesus, but chiefly cultivated a little later in the story.
Their central figure was a young man living in the
suburbs of Jerusalem; but there were grouped about
him the women of his family, sisters, who had their
share in a tenderness which always centred loyally
about their hospitable home. Jesus was such a
lonely man that an attractive home, where he could
feel himself one of the household, had a pathetic
charm for him.

At the time of which we speak, and in Galilee,
the devotion of several high-minded women had
already been offered to his cause and personality;
and he had accepted it with the fine discernment in

CHRIST AND THE FISHERMEN

such matters which never failed him.   No sentimen-
talists, no gushing, giddy heads were admitted to his
circle.   Extraordinary as it might be for irreproachable women to march Galilee over among the converts to this Rabbi, in whom the meanest mind in
Palestine could find no blame, the thing was done
and done with dignity.   One of these ladies was the
wife of the steward of Herod Antipas.   Another
was in high social position.   The group was soon
joined by a joyous woman known as Mary of Magdala whom the healer had cured of a violent mania,
and freed from a terrible past, and whose gratitude,
too real for words, forced itself into deeds.

Mary, the mother of Jesus, the most eminent
matron of the company, received the position which
belonged to her.   This was the happiest time in
Mary's later life.   Perplexity and trouble lay behind her.   Anguish ineffable lay before her.   But
for the moment she knew a little comfort.   Family
friction no longer annoyed her in her relations to
her son.   In this respect she had asserted herself.
She no longer brought to him or suffered to be
brought to him any criticisms upon his judgment or
his conduct.   She was convinced that he was not to
be interfered with.   She bowed to his superiority
with more than usual maternal adoration.   The
thought of his mystical birth, the belief in his mystical mission, for so many years submerged in her
mind, had now come uppermost.   Feeling a little
as if she had wronged him by having ever listened
to what the other children thought or said about
him ; filled with a noble sadness for any hour in

which she had ever wondered or questioned whether he were fated to grow into a grand destiny, she plunged herself into the beautiful devotion which only a woman may know and show, and only for a great son.

The presence of his mother was an inexpressible comfort to Jesus in his homeless and wandering life. With starting tears we thank God that he had it, and had it just when he did. For he stood trembling on the height of his success; filled with the perplexing weariness, with the vague portents slowly assuming distincter outlines, that besieged him in the last days before the decline of his fortunes set in. He moved apart from his dearest friendships in the inexorable loneliness which nothing but utter love could approach; and the love of a mother who does not ask to understand, only to give, was at times the only one which his hurt and patient heart could bear.

CHAPTER IX

ACROSS THE LAKE

THE happiest year of his life was almost over. Galilee had known her one great opportunity, had interested herself in it for a dramatic twelvemonth, and was ready to drop it idly through her fickle fingers.

Jesus observed the fluctuations in the popular mood with an eye now keen with experience in public life, and with an inward illumination fed from sources unknown to other men, and not always consciously available to himself. He was in the position of a man whom success has seemed to decoy to an unperceived doom, but whose own foresight was not in reality deceived, and who, considering only greatness of character and purity of conduct, had gone straight on, ignoring the advance of fate. Whatever knowledge of the outcome of it all he possessed never deterred him for an hour from doing the plain, right thing. The simplicity of his moral purpose in face of his complex and tragic story is the very essence of grandeur. He did not vacillate. He did not trim or veer. What he feared, he endured in silence. If he trembled, no one knew it. He pursued his course with the indifference of a star in which, all the while, the heart and pulses of a too sensitive organism are beating painfully.

That year pressed hard upon his physical strength. The demands upon the healer, the duties of the preacher, encroached upon his endurance to the point of an exhaustion which never overcame him, though it seemed sometimes to threaten to do so. There were nights of vigil and prayer, in forests or on the lakeshore, when the trees, the hills, or the waves were the only companions whom he could bear, for he was so spent. There were mornings when those who loved him, seeing him sitting in his pulpit-boat, with the people moving after him on the beach and cliffs, felt the pang at the heart which we have at sight of the suffering of one dear to us whom we know we do not understand ; for he looked so wasted. Yet he never sank. Exactions that would have crushed an ordinary man he met, not without signs that he suffered from them, but serenely. Strains which would have killed a lesser being he endured, — who knew how ?

The simple people who followed and watched him did not understand, as well as we who read his story now, the laws of the highly-strung organization ; those terrible laws which make the very physique qualified to do a certain deed the more liable to surrender to the effects of it. One of the simplest and sincerest healers of modern times — a man who received his thousands of patients a day for a few weeks — found himself unable to continue the strain on body or brain, and suddenly retreated from the clamor which he had created ; disappearing to isolation or to death. Jesus did not retreat. He did not disappear. He did not yield. He endured with the delicate sturdiness peculiar to himself.

What was the secret? He stood and withstood, giving out always of his fathomless pity, urging his trained and powerful will. Any man in the professions which depend upon the concentration of will-power on human conditions or character can form some pale idea of the mental and emotional energy required of Jesus Christ. The expenditure of life in him at its least daily estimate was tremendous. His splendid vigor refunded it all. How? His glowing vitality never ran in debt. Why? Yet was there something significant in his continued inability to bear too great or too close human proximity. Just the little span of water, put between himself and the throng upon the shore, saved him for his day's work. Something in his nature could not, even after all this experience of crowds, endure the thoughtless pressure of them without that odic space.

What became of his boat, so dear to the fishermen for his sake? Did they keep it safely moored on Gennesaret, putting out in it now and then, with tears which they did not try to hide from each other, and talking in low voices of him? Though they had starved, not a man of them would have sold it. Was it ever used for a fishing-trip again? Did any of the thousands of people whom he had comforted care enough to treat it as a sacred thing? Did it find its way into mourning homes, carved into relics

and treasured for generations? Or did the little
craft meet, in age and honor, the end that a boat
loves? Was it wrecked or sunken on the sea that
had known and carried it and him?

One of the favorite homiletic methods of Jesus he
used very much at this time. He preached by the
parable ; and some of these most famous addresses
were delivered from the thwarts of his boat.

The parable was a peculiarly Oriental form of
teaching, and one of which he made a valuable use.
It was, in fact, a species of self-protection to him.
Beset, as he was, by masses of people who cared little for the truth, but much for the excitement of a
novelty, he had to deal with them somehow ; and he
would not waste his highest thought upon his lowest
hearers. If they gave any evidence of capacity or
wish to understand it, no one ever lived so free as
he from intellectual aristocracy. He would offer all
he could. He would share his best with the worst.
But, with sheer shallowness and with mental vulgarity, which could not or would not grasp a sacred
idea, Jesus was ingenious. He did not refuse to
speak, but he adapted himself to his audience. People who came begging for stories, and incapable of
listening to anything else, got them.

The use of the illustration came to a brilliant finish in his discourses. But he was never deceived in
an audience if it could not go beyond that.

His reserve in the expression of truth, always so
marked in him, became at times massive. He had
so much in thought which he might not dare to say,
— he believed so much which he could not induce

others to believe, — that he put great skill into the construction of his sermons.

Once, being puzzled by one of these intensely popular discourses, one of his friends asked him in private what it meant, and why he preached as he did. The reply of Jesus was a significant one, and not much easier to understand than the sermon.

He intimated that, as a certain sort of audience could not comprehend the whole truth if he gave it to them, he purposely gave them what he thought fit, and did not, indeed, always think it necessary to make what he chose to say perfectly clear to them. Truth was always something royal to him; something to be treated with deference. He once spoke of it as a pearl, and warned his followers against wasting it on creatures of the trough and the mire. In this superb democrat, who counted no treasure of brain or heart too costly to share with the humblest being that valued it, such intellectual reticence is very striking.

The parables of Jesus were a succession of homely stories, the homeliest that he could select. A search for a lost sheep, a laborer working in a vineyard, an episode in the relations of servant and master, the bursting of a leathern wine-bottle, the blossoming of a wild lily, a commercial anecdote, any such trifling incident in common life, was enough. It gave him his illustration, and one that was sure to attract the attention of his audience. The noticeable thing was that he packed it so tightly with the truth which he desired to convey. The lightest story was heavy with thought. The illustration

never slipped. Any mind capable of thinking beyond the silken cover of fiction could find more than
enough to keep it busy in the parables of the Rabbi.

He was preaching in this picturesque way, on the
western side of the lake, on a day eventful even in
the rush of incident with which his life was at this
time crowded.

The people had over-wearied him that day, and
pressed upon him till he could bear no more. With
one of the peremptory decisions which he knew so
well when to make, he determined to escape from
this human torrent, from which, at its full, an
angel's vitality might have fled; the current was so
insistent, so thoughtless, so tainted. Longing for
that which only the wave and the shore can give to
the heart that loves them, he turned to his dear
lake. It was towards evening. Beautiful Gennesaret,
throbbing among her smiling hills, where even the
rocks were turned to leaf and blossom by terraces;
the mobile lake, where the colors painted by flaws
and sudden foam — the metallic green, the blazing
blue, the stately purple, the silver white — chased
gayly over the water; Gennesaret, sinking to exquisite
calms when every mountain-top was let into the depths
from the heights, each in its own hue and fine outline, and when the silken sails of the belated pleasure
boats crossed the bows of the fishermen rowing
home, — Gennesaret was at her loveliest. The sun
was sinking. The moon was rising. The wind was
light and steady upon the little sea. Clouds hung
upon the opposite hills, but they looked innocent
enough. Jesus took to his boat with his friends and

gave the order to cross the lake. He sat for a few moments thoughtfully watching the disappointed throng which he had left ashore, as it slowly dispersed in the growing shadow. He drew a sigh of relief touched with regret. The strain had been severe that day. It was one of the prominent lineaments of his character that he knew how far he could go in endurance, and that he never hesitated to stop at the right point. He had none of the short-sighted senti-mentalism in philanthropy which pushes the moment to the ruin of the year, or sacrifices the ultimate scope of a great work to a temporary call upon the sympathies. His that day had been sorely taxed. He withdrew from the draft upon them.

He was very tired, so tired that he did not try to talk, but went aft and lay down, thinking to rest if he could. His most thoughtful disciple had put a pillow there for him upon the stern seat. His friends, respecting his mood as they always meant to do, even if they did not always succeed (for the Master had strange hours, hard for fishermen to understand), left him undisturbed. The management of the boat soon occupied their attention, for there was more wind than one would have thought. Jesus fell asleep; he was so completely worn out that nature insisted, and he slept long and deeply.

What were his dreams? A man so sad, so lonely, so spotless in motive, so wrapped in purposes which no one understood, so shrouded in fate which no one could defy, — what would his dreams be like? Did they drag him under the dome of martyrdom, that dark vault whose great circumference was already descending upon his life? Did they intimate failure, shame, torture, to his shrinking nerve? Even in sleep, did trouble pursue him? Those who have suffered much know how difficult it is for misery to let the victim go, in dreams. Was the anguish of his lot more merciful to him? Did the machinery of endurance go spinning on? Or did he know a little respite? Did visions of the great joy which kept him up gently visit him? Did he dream of the most precious possession of his consciousness, in life or death always foremost to his mind, — his faith in his God? Did his Father Invisible comfort the wornout man?

We like to think so, for he slept well. The moonlight, painting his quiet face, softened its lines of care and deepened its expression of peace. The nobility of his brow, the beauty of his delicate lips, the pathos that speaks in the closed eyelids of a man acquainted with grief and bearing it patiently, — to these unconsciousness lent the grave charm which would have moved an indifferent spectator, and which was touching to those who loved him.

But they who loved him were not watching him now. Suddenly, startled from a deep slumber, rested and refreshed, he was aware that there was an unusual commotion on the boat. The little craft was laboring painfully in the trough of a heavy sea. One of the sudden squalls for which capricious Gennesaret was famous had struck the lake. The wind drew down from the gorges of the hills in dangerous flaws and gusts. The water was smitten to madness. The full moon had gone under a thick cloud. The light was gray and wan. Foam flew. The bow plunged too deep. Water was rushing over the rails. The experienced crew were thoroughly frightened, and that with good reason. The boat was in danger of swamping.

The fishermen had lost their heads. The lateen sail was already down; they were in too great depth to anchor; they had not been able to keep head to the wind; their rudder refused to do its duty; and the boat was at the mercy of the sea. They clambered aft in terror. One of them had roughly awakened the Rabbi, and they were all crying out together:

"Master! Master! We are perishing!" He rose to his feet quietly. The fishermen, all their lives used to the tricks of Gennesaret, were altogether demoralized. Their rude voices rang above the roar of the storm: "Save us! save us! save us!" In fact, the boat was practically sinking. And they were far from either shore, too far for swimming. The situation was serious enough.

A strange expression crossed the countenance of Jesus. He seemed more surprised at the fears of his friends than disturbed at the common danger.

But he turned his attention at once to the storm. He seemed to study it as a subject which he must grasp, — intensely, because it must be grasped in a moment. Indeed, there were no moments to lose; for the water was dashing over bow and stern, and was filling the boat rapidly.

He seemed to make a curiously fine distinction between the wind, which was the offender in the

trouble, and the passive sea, which was only the
helpless agent. Suddenly there shot from his lips
a severe rebuke; as if the wind were a conscious
and a guilty thing, and as if he were lord of it; as
if he and nature understood each other better than
he and man. As if it acknowledged the order, the
wind went down meekly. There fell upon the air
one of the sudden calms, quite possible on the lake,
but which there was no evident reason to expect just
then. The moon swept out from the cloud. In the
reviving light, the crew saw one another's terror-
stricken faces, and his who showed no fear. He
stood serene, smiling, with one upraised hand and
arm, a statue of strength and assurance. In a very
low tone they heard him speaking to the water; not
as he had addressed the wind, authoritatively and
like a master calling to account, but in a sweet,
persuasive voice, such as one might use to a nervous
woman or a frenzied child: "Hush! peace! peace,
and be still!"

The noisy sea trembled; the choppy waves sank;
the lake began to ripple; the ripple wasted away;
then such a calm took the water as lay like a sheen
of silk from shore to shore. On it there fell a
strange silence. The keel was even. The fishermen
began to bail out the water from the boat. They
did not speak. But the Rabbi watched them with
a kind of astonished sadness.

"How is it?" he said slowly, — "how is it that
ye have not any faith? _Why_ are ye so afraid?"

His voice had a wistful accent to it, as if his
heart ached more than any one of them could know;

as if he had expected to be trusted, and they had disappointed him. He did not blame them. He went back to the stern and lay down again quietly upon his pillow.

But the fishermen did not answer him. They did not dare. Each man of them looked at the other, quailing. They hung their heads, half in shame and half in fright. They were more afraid of the Rabbi at that moment than they had been of the storm.

"What manner of man is this?" they muttered; "why, the wind and the sea obey him!" It was the sailors' supreme tribute. They could not go beyond it.

The boat came to land in the night on the shore of Gergesa, — a populous coast. Throughout the whole region the cliffs adjacent to the towns were burrowed with caves and tombs, the shelter of the dead, and of certain of the living who were less fortunate than the dead. Flocks and herds lay in dim blots over the pasturage of this hilly locality. Occasionally some wretched human figure flitted across the landscape, emerging from blackness and becoming quickly submerged therein. As the Rabbi and his friends landed, two of these human wraiths followed them with ghostly silence and pertinacity. Peter and the others pointed them out to Jesus, whispering. The bravest man in the twelve looked over his shoulder at the uncanny sight; the weird figures, the feeling that only midnight gives, were startling to every nerve. One of the disciples instinctively took up a stone in self-protection, but it fell harmlessly. One look from the Rabbi seemed to thrust it out of his hand.

Jesus did not join in the repugnance of his friends to the dreary spectacle. Indeed, he expressed neither distaste nor surprise when the bolder and madder of the two maniacs flung himself in the way of the party and addressed the Rabbi with all the ingenuity of an insane vocabulary, appealing for protection against the delusions of his disease.

These were acute. We are not yet wise enough in the finer psychology to pronounce dogmatically upon much easier questions in alienism than that involved in the particular hallucination so common to the East, to that age, and those people. The lunatics wholly believed themselves to be possessed of devils. Jesus, like expert physicians much less successful than himself, did not in the least antagonize a deranged patient by fighting his whim. Whatever view he personally held of the subject is, to the reader of the story, entirely secondary in importance. Insanity is a dark sea on whose shore we have not even yet ventured far; and science is a frail boat which may or may not hold the points of compass. Whether demonic possession was the delusion of a blatant superstition, or should ever become material of an exact science, Jesus, if he knew, did not think it necessary to explain. He delivered no homily on evil spirits. He delayed to elucidate no views on the nicer problems of mental disorder. He simply went to work and healed the case.

It was a bad case; one of the worst of the in-

curable, against which the rude medical art of the
times was hopelessly helpless, and about which the
humanity of the times did not feel any responsibility.   Few pitied and most forgot the homicidal, sui-
cidal wretches who had been driven from home and
from all human society.   It needed Jesus to invent
tenderness to the insane.   It swept through his
heart that night in a surging movement of pity and
power.

We have here one of those sombre pictures in
which a great moral emotion has taken the brush
and painted in the only high lights.   The gloom of
the land of caves filled a dismal background.   A
large herd of two thousand swine, disturbed by the
cries of the maniacs and disinclined to sleep, were
stirring uneasily on their pasture at the top of the
steep grade which ended in the water.   The fishermen, uncomfortable and puzzled, were gathered
closely about their Rabbi, — to protect or to be protected, they hardly knew which.   The maniacs were
gibbering and shrieking; he, the worst case, bleeding with self-inflicted wounds where he had cut himself with sharp stones.   In the centre of the group,
tall and quiet, Jesus stood thoughtfully.   The moon
brought out all the nobility of his face and form.
He seemed to absorb light from the sky, and to
radiate it upon the little spot of earth on which he
trod.

The maniac, or the demoniac, — call him as you
please, — had something of the shrewd wit not uncommon to the deranged.   By whatever law illuminated, he recognized the supreme superiority of the

Nazarene more quickly than most sane men. The
friends of Jesus were confounded to see the lunatic
on the ground at the Rabbi's feet in the attitude of
worship, and to hear him crying shrilly:

"Thou son of the Most High God!"

"Thou spirit unclean!" replied Jesus authoritatively, "come out of the man!"

A few moments of great confusion followed this
command. The shrieks of the lunatic, his protests,
the disturbed comments of the fishermen, the re-
newed entreaties of the maniac, were hardly quieted
by the calm replies of Jesus.

Suddenly sharp cries came from another direction. The keepers of the flocks above were calling
for help. The great herd of swine, alarmed by
the unusual scene and by the shouts of the maniacs, thoroughly demoralized, had taken fright, and
were running down the declivity. In the moonlight
they could be plainly seen rushing from shadow to
shadow, from the pasture behind to the lake below.
The keepers ran to and fro helplessly. It was a
perfect stampede; one of the curious animal impulses which no man can ever understand, and few
control. Before it could be stayed, the whole herd,
unable to stop on the steep grade, the foremost
crowded by those in the rear, had pushed to the
edge of the water and were drowned.

Strange things were said about this scene. Jesus
was accused of having ordered a legion — that was
to say, a large and indefinite number — demons
from the man into the animals. His disciples, sure
only of this one thing, that their master was the

kindest, the tenderest of all men living, or who had
ever lived, remembered that he had conversed in-
dulgently with the maniac, suffering but not commanding in the man's disordered mind this view of
the stampede. Peter, John, and James, and the
rest, were simple men. The demonology of their
times was much less mysterious to them than their
Rabbi. Whether the swine went over, or were sent
over, was a matter of little consequence to them.
Whatever Jesus commanded or permitted needed no
explanation. The animals were gone. But the man
was here, sane — a happy, reasonable person, asking
for clothes and food and home; acting like other
people, and pouring passionate gratitude at the feet
of the healer, who stood quietly amid the confusion,
his peaceful face brushed by a wing of sadness.
Was he thinking about the swine in the lake? The
mystery of animal life sacrificed to that of man had
not begun to arouse a question in the ordinary mind
in those times. His extraordinary mind, or extraordinary heart, always moved first in the direction of
pity. It was not one of his easiest tasks in life
that, in the capacity of a dispenser of mercy, he had
sometimes to choose between the lesser pity and the
larger.

At all events the man was saved, the brutes were
lost. The owners of the property were exasperated.
The residents of the region were terrified. They
intimated to the healer that his presence among
them was not desirable. Had he been an ordinary
juggler, they would have ordered him off. But this
was not jugglery. Jesus was no common sorcerer.

The most ignorant man on either side of the lake knew better than that. In truth they were all very much afraid of him. The cured maniac, longing to keep close to the healer who had given him back his reason, but gently forbidden to do so, traveled here and there, joyously relating the story with the authority of a hero in the scene. The whole coast was astir. Every other popular emotion seemed to have melted in terror. Jesus was made so uncomfortable that he took to his boat again, and returned across the lake.

CHAPTER X

FIVE THOUSAND GUESTS

HE was at home once more, but he was not permitted to rest. Crowds larger than he had left received him. He was surrounded and overwhelmed. It seemed as if all invalid Galilee were moaning after him. In the heart of his busiest and weariest hour an urgent demand came up. He was wanted for a life and death case. An officer of the Jewish church, an important person, Jairus by name, had a little daughter, dearly cherished. She was scarcely twelve years old, just at the lovely age, — not yet past her play-days, but already with the dainty airs of a little woman, — a winsome maid, her father's darling. She lay at the point of death, and in hot haste messengers had been sent for the Nazarene. But the distress of the father outran the swiftest feet. He touched the unconscious child with the despair of one whose last kiss cannot be returned by the dearest lips in the world, and went desolately out to try in person to find the healer; at whom the regular physicians had scoffed. But the physicians had given up the case.

At the feet of Jesus, Jairus flung himself down like a slave, and such an agony went up in his face and attitude as a cold man could not easily have

resisted. Jesus, melting with sympathy, tenderly
reassured the father, and started at once in the direction of the ruler's house.

But what a throng! When he tried to pass
through the people, they closed like a round wall
about him. It was, indeed, a wall of human misery,
blank and vast. Jesus felt almost stifled by it, as if
it were crushing him. The unhappy, the evil, the
sick — oh, the uncounted, neglected sick! — uprose
upon him. It was like an insurrection of the woe
of the world, catching sight, for the first time, of the
only alleviation it had ever seen. The healer's face
changed perceptively. He seemed to stagger for the
moment in that riot of misery.

Such a mass of humanity pressed upon him that
it was impossible to move.

At that moment, stealing past the push and rush
of the thoughtless throng, a timid hand touched the
fringe of his talith; and, terrified, withdrew instantly.
But as instantly he felt it, — who knew how?

" Who touched me?" he asked quickly. No person in the crowd replied.

" Strength goes out of me," insisted the healer.
" Who was it?"

.   .   .   .

Jesus and Jairus walked together to the ruler's
house. The father did not speak any longer. He
was afraid of offending the Rabbi. After those first
hot words, the first wild moment, what could he do?
When the servant came, weeping, and told him that
it was too late, — not to trouble the Master, for the
little maid was gone, — his heart had broken in one

mad outcry. This great healer, this mysterious man, so famous for his tenderness, so marvelous for his pity, must needs fail him, — *him*, Jairus, out of all Palestine, and that in the hour of his terrible need! The fact could not be denied that Jesus had stopped on the way to a dying patient to cure an old, chronic case.

The woman could have been healed just as well to-night, to-morrow, next week. But he had lingered. And the child was dead.

What had he, the desperate father, said in his anguish? Had he blamed, had he reproached the Nazarene? But, if he had, Jesus exhibited no offense at the outbreak. His sympathy with the poor father was far too high a thing. He could not stoop to notice how the madness of grief had treated him. A lower nature may do that.

" Do not be afraid," he said tenderly; " only believe!" But his face was very grave. And, by a single motion of his expressive hand, he ordered all his disciples back but three, — Peter, James, and John, his dearest. The group entered the ruler's house.

The house was not silent; Oriental mourners had already taken possession of it. Obtrusive wails and groans, mingled with genuine sobs and tears, filled the place. Jesus seemed surprised at the condition in which he found the family.

" The child is not dead," he said decidedly. Some of the neighbors, who did not altogether believe in the famous healer, began to laugh. It was a derisive laugh, — a cold sound in that house of woe, —

and it did not please him. A keen rebuke shot from his mild eyes at the unseemly scorn.

" Nay," he repeated, " she is not dead. She is asleep."

He spoke in the tone of a man who was not to be gainsaid. He did not try to make the most of the case. He did not say, " Yes, this is death. But I am lord of death." It would have been far easier to do than to cling to his view of the·truth as he did, against the convictions of the family. He went into the sick-room and looked at the child.

" This is sleep," he persisted. . . . The father's sobs had ceased. The mother lifted her face, discolored with tears, worn with watching, and piteously raised her hands. The three friends of the Rabbi stood reverently wondering.

Jesus silently regarded the little maid.

She lay unconscious, and was quite rigid. The rare trances known to medical science show less evidence of death than the child did. She lay on her pallet, cold, with the pathetic, wondering look which death casts upon childhood, as if she said :

" Why, this is what happens to old people ! "

Jesus looked at her with a strange expression. His eyes seemed to say :

"It is between me and thee, little maid. We understand."

He was known to be very fond of children, and they of him; he was sometimes seen with them climbing over his lap and laughing, as they put their arms about his neck with the unerring identification of those whom they can trust, which only children and dogs possess. Mothers brought their babies to him for his blessing, and it is recorded how lovingly he gave it.

Now he looked at the little girl with the tenderness that is only to be expected of those in whom the love of children is profound and genuine.

She seemed to quiver beneath his look, but her color and her attitude did not change. Then he took her by the hand.

Her little, wasted fingers lay for a few moments in his nervous and vital grasp ; then he felt them tremble. . . . Who sees the instant when the lily blossoms ? Who could have detected the moment of time in which the child began to stir ? Was it his hand that moved, or hers that directed his slowly upward till it reached her pillow, and so came upon a level with her face ?

It did not seem sudden or startling, but only the most natural thing in the world, when the little girl laid her cheek upon his palm. . . .

" Give her something to eat," said the healer, quite in his ordinary tones. This sensible and commonplace order restored their senses to the excited household. But Jairus remembered how he had thought of Jesus, — perhaps how he had spoken to him, when the Nazarene stopped to cure the chronic case ; and the father felt ashamed ; but he did not know how to say so. And the little arms about his neck were warm ! How could he think of anything else in the world ? Jesus seemed to take this as a matter of course. That was the wonderful, the beautiful thing.   Jairus felt as if he could worship the Rabbi.

The whole countryside rang with the story.

"Death! A second time! Why, he cheats the grave, as another may cheat in war or a bargain! Who is this man who does the deeds of the living God?"   But Jesus had denied that the child was dead.   He never retracted the denial.

It would have been easy for him to rise just then on a great flight of popularity, had he chosen to make the most of this reanimation.   Instead, he made the least of it.   Content with the doing of the thing, not concerned for the name of it, he went serenely on, as if his own reputation as a worker of wonders were the last thing in the world about which he.had a care.   In point of fact it was.   He had so much loftier aims that he could well afford to let the lesser go.

He had at this time, if no more leisure, at least more solitude than usual, in which to reflect upon his position and his future ; for he had dismissed his chosen friends on an evangelistic tour about the country, dividing them two by two, selecting these couples with great care, that they might supplement one another's temperament.   We wonder to whom he united John the preferred, — gentlest and loveliest of companions !   Whose calmer nature moderated the hot temper of Peter, the spokesman of the group ?   Who had the warm faith to melt the doubts of the skeptical Thomas ?   Whose penetration kept watch upon the moods of Judas the treacherous ?

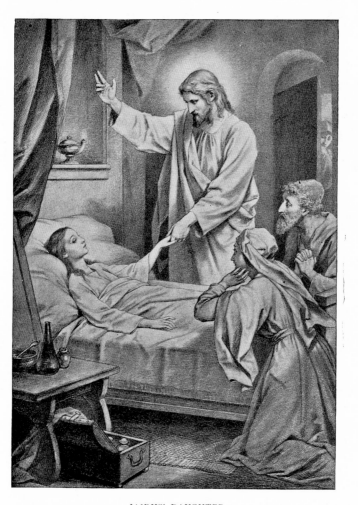

JAIRUS' DAUGHTER

To these men Jesus now solemnly made over a measure of his own gift; as if his power to relieve human misery were a thing communicable at his will to one who loved and trusted him. These men received a certain amount of quality as healers, and of success as missionaries. In his enthusiasm for humanity Jesus did not draw the line at anything, but tried to make his disciples wonder-workers as efficient as himself.

" Raise the dead," he said. It is not recorded of them that they did this. Had he too much faith in them, or they too little in him ?

When the twelve came back to their Rabbi, there had reached him news so black that the experiences of their missionary trip — although they told him all about them volubly enough — were put well into the background. During their absence had occurred the terrible supper at the palace of Herod, when a girl danced away the life of the greatest of prophets and one of the grandest of men.

The execution of John, after all, had been sudden and was unexpected. Jesus was overwhelmed by it.

He received the intelligence in silence, and went away alone as soon as he could. He spent that night by the sea in the solitary prayer which, while it made such havoc of his vitality, seemed strangely to renew the very treasure that it wasted. No man was witness to those hours of grief and of resolve.

In his personal bereavement a consciousness of personal peril now began distinctly to mingle. Jesus was not the man to be deceived by this thrust from the government. If he had ever doubted before, he could doubt no longer that, as a political suspect, he himself was liable to mortal dangers.

A strange story reached his ears about this time, which did not tend to allay his discomfort or the fears of his friends. For, when the rumors about his career went up to the palace, the murderer shook. Herod Antipas, turning pale with the superstition of guilt, uttered a cry whose weakness has gone into history with his unenviable name.

" This," he said, " is John, the man I beheaded. He has risen from the dead to torment me ! "

Jesus, worried by dark facts and darker rumors, was thrown more and more into an inner solitude which no one could approach. His growing conviction that it was impossible to make the people understand the purpose of his life made him, at this time, a very sad man.

An event soon occurred which revealed, past all mistaking, the significant and to him fatal truth. Up to this time he had secretly hoped something from human gratitude and from human intelligence. He was soon to learn that he had nothing to expect from either.

It was at Bethsaida, upon the lake, — a pleasant fishing-town (" House of Fish," as the word goes), full of the cheerful bustle and the charming scenery which lend such vivacity to maritime life. There were two Bethsaidas, not of the same province. The peril of Jesus was now so obvious that he had found it necessary, for the time being, to take himself out of the political jurisdiction of Antipas. From the fortress of Machærus John's meek spirit had bravely gone to God who made and loved it.

John's troubles were over; but Herod's were not; and those of Jesus had just begun. Haunted by remorse for the cowardly slaughter of an innocent prisoner, Herod Antipas was very uncomfortable. But his superstitious uneasiness quickly developed into a more solid and reasonable alarm.

The whole country was ringing with the name and with the achievements of the Nazarene. The missionary trip of the twelve had immediate results which were almost disastrous. They had circulated the doctrines of their Rabbi so widely that it was impossible any longer to restrain these within local limits. Everybody was talking of Jesus, — of his mysterious personality, his incredible deeds, his partly understood claims. That these could be anything but political, it was impossible for the Roman or the Hebrew mind to conceive. The palace now began distinctly to fear an insurrection.

Jesus was no hot-headed enthusiast, narrow of sight, and blundering into avoidable dangers. For a man sacrificing himself utterly and with passionate gladness to a principle, he was remarkably careful in his public movements. He never anticipated his perils unnecessarily. He was perfectly sane, self-possessed, even adroit in his relation to affairs. He never forgot the true mathematics of a great work, which may put the terms of the equation a long way apart. He did not allow, as smaller souls may do, a false ideal of courage to blind him to the true.

The time had not come to hurl his life away; a premature sacrifice was not in his plan. Herod

Antipas could make no immediate trouble for a suspect beyond his own boundaries, and out of sight
might be out of mind. Even for a day or so it
might be worth while to be absent from Herod's
range of vision. Jesus prudently went into Iturea,
the dominion of Philip the Tetrarch.

Upper Bethsaida (known as Bethsaida Julias),
at the northeastern corner of the lake, was only six
miles from Capernaum by water, though much further by land, and by either route the town was easily
accessible.

Jesus took his boat and sailed across the lake.
The wind was light, and the voyage was a slow one.
Seeking seclusion above all things at that time, he
had chosen to land south of Bethsaida, off the plain
of Batihah, in an uninhabited locality.

It was a brilliant day. The sun and the sea were
vivid. The sky was strong. The spring air was not
too hot, but soft and pleasant. It was Nisan, the
Month of Flowers. Vegetation was at its richest
and brightest. Scarlet anemones ran everywhere.
Touches of color, like candles of white and pink, told
where the rock roses burned. The highly cultivated
grass was like plush to the eye and to the hand.

The boat rocked gently upon the water. The
fishermen moored it, and followed their Rabbi,
wondering. For, see! It looked as if all the world
had come to meet him. Plainly, he was to be
overwhelmed again.

This was far larger and other than a local crowd.
It was swelled by pilgrims *en route* to the Passover,
and already it was perceived that the very persons

whom he had left behind, a throng accumulating as it moved, had overtaken Jesus. The people, wondering only why the Nazarene had sailed away, had come around by land from Capernaum ; and were rapidly massing to meet him when he landed, intending to head off his departure if, in fact, he meant to leave them. The consequence was a reception several thousand strong.

The keen eye of Jesus swiftly took in the size of the crowd. He perceived that he was to have no ordinary audience, and that it would require no common handling. He walked thoughtfully on to meet it.

It was a lonely plain where he landed, and, after glancing at the topography of the place and the position of the crowd, he climbed a knoll and began to give himself to their wants. The usual proportion of the diseased were in the throng. Even to-day, the traveler in the East is impressed with the hopeless, superstitious sick, who fill the roadsides wailing for relief which cannot be given to such ignorance. The sight of invalids drinking milk in which a line of the Koran has been washed, or of the disabled, suffering wounds to be stuffed with cayenne pepper, or the acutely ill swallowing prescriptions compounded of scorpions, silkworms, Spanish flies, and centipedes, gives us an idea of the kind of thing with which Jesus was always surrounded.

The demands upon him that day at Batihah were enormous. He healed and preached, and healed again. He denied himself to nobody, and refused no act of mercy. He spoke with unusual fervor and healed with memorable power. The people seemed hardly to know which they wanted more, — health for the soul or health for the body ; and hung upon him heavily, taking either or both, or anything that he might give. Meanwhile their number was growing steadily, and became and remained utterly absorbed in him.

The day began to decline. The hot look passed from the cheek of the lake. The colors of the sky softened. The wind died down. The thick, short grass took on the golden radiance which strikes slantwise from a dipping sun.

The throng numbered now as much as five thousand men, and many women and children who were not counted. These were of various nationalities, — Hebrews, Greeks, Romans, Arabians, Persians, Phœnicians, — and were more or less gorgeously dressed in the gay Oriental taste which the Eastern countries shared in common. It was a motley audience, but it was a very picturesque one.

Jesus had made himself heard quite plainly, though in the open air and by so many ; but as he approached the end of his afternoon discourse, his voice deepened and lowered with feeling, as if he felt that more depended upon the events of this day than he could explain or others understand. The hush in his own heart extended itself to his audience, which was so still and breathless when he ceased to speak that his last words roused an echo, gently answering him.

Then a little bustle set in, and across it he heard the footsteps of two or three of his friends, who had

fallen back to common life again, and had resumed
its cares. One of his disciples was speaking:

" Send the people away, Lord. They have nothing to eat. Look at them ! "

Then the preacher, himself pale and weary, rousing from the abstraction of oratory, saw how faint
they were, — these people who had come so far, and
had been so entranced by his address that they had
forgotten even to notice that they had not eaten, and
that they had no food with them. It was an involuntary tribute to him, which he could but notice.
It gratified him, and gave him some hope that his
hard day's work had not been wasted.

He shook his head when his anxious friends repeated their desire to disperse the crowd, and order
them away. It was some distance to Bethsaida village, and the way was wearisome. The hospitality
of Jesus was warmly aroused. With a hearty impulse to treat his audience as his guests, he made a
few practical inquiries into the condition of the com-
missariat of his own party. Significantly, Andrew
exhibited five loaves and two small lake fish. This
was all which the twelve had up to this moment provided for their own meagre supper, and for his who
had preached and healed all that severe day. The
question of purchasing supplies was now discussed.
But it was calculated that between thirty and forty
dollars would be needed to provide any sort of entertainment, however simple, for so vast a number of
guests. To the poor missionary band any such sum
as this was out of the question, and the twelve were
much disturbed that the Rabbi did not make short

work of the situation and command the crowd to
break up.

It would have gone away at his wish. Just then
it would have done anything for him. Impulsive,
ardent, excitable, the throng was his. The people
— the sick whom he had cured, the troubled whom
he had comforted, the erring whom he had startled,
those longing for better lives whom he had invigorated — at that moment adored him so that they did
not see how they could leave him. This moved
him, and he felt as if he could not send them away.
A happy look swept his face. It was one of the
rare moments when he felt that he was loved by
the humanity he loved, and that what he did and
suffered for it was not all thrown away. It is pleasant to think that he had this hour of comfort, and
that he had it just then and there.

Suddenly came this unexpected order: " Make
the company sit down. Separate them in groups of
fifties on the grass. Then feed them as I shall command you."

The disciples, who had learned by this time to
question no order, however astounding, which their
master might give, obeyed him, perplexed enough.
With precision the immense throng was divided, and
delegates were deputed to attend to the wants of
each division in its turn. This man of peace showed
a military skill in the management of great bodies
of men. The practical good sense, so rare in the
exalted temperament, but so evident in his, marshaled his thousands like an experienced general.
Indeed, we must remember that, in the handling of

masses, Jesus had acquired an extraordinary experience.   Palestine, a small country, about one hundred
and sixty miles long and seventy broad, was more
thickly settled than Massachusetts.   This little land
is thought to have held between four and five millions
of people.   There were two hundred and four town-
ships in Galilee alone; the smallest had a population
of fifteen thousand souls.   Nazareth itself was a city
of four or five thousand at the least, possibly of
many more inhabitants.

Palestine teemed; and there was great compact-
ness in the apportionment of life.   No recluse in the
wilderness, but a man always in contact with men,
Jesus had exceptional opportunities to develop those
elements of power which only masses of humanity
can call forth.   Of these opportunities he made,
from first to last, an exceptional use.

On this day in the Month of Flowers — a day
which proved to be one of the conclusive crises of
his life — he indulged his wish to entertain his
immense audience.   He did not often indulge himself in anything.   He who had no home of his own,
no chance to enjoy the happiness of being host; he
who would have made so gracious and so great a
host, so generous, so thoughtful, so full of fine care-
fulness for the comfort of his guests, felt a touching pleasure on this evening.   Excepting one other
instance, somewhat like it, the occasion stands alone.
This social entertainment personally given by Jesus
was a beautiful scene.

The people in their brilliant, many colored costumes reclining on the vivid grass looked like flowers.

One of the recorders of the incidents, with more imagination than might have been expected of the plain and severe historians to whom we owe all that we know of Jesus, spoke of the brilliant ranks as garden beds, or *parterres*.

Jesus in his blue talith, on the height above them, looked down ; slightly flushed with happiness, and smiling.   His white linen head-dress gave a certain pallor to his complexion, which was more delicate than that of most of his countrymen ; as his features were more regular : these had something of the Greek symmetry modeled by the Hebrew force. His countenance was both winning and commanding. In hours of exaltation, it drew the heart up to it by a kind of glory that awed, while it attracted.

His appearance at that moment was one of great beauty.   His expression was that of more than usual peace.   It was one of the last times when those who loved him saw him ; saw him free from anxiety or pain ; and they remembered it as long as they lived.

His men had brought him their scanty provision for supper, and he had taken it into his outstretched hands.   His eyes were fixed upon the sky.   His smile settled into gravity ; this slowly assumed the look of prayer.   Soon it was perceived that the Rabbi was asking the blessing of God upon the evening meal, and the twelve bowed their heads with the impulse of worship.   Many in the throng did the same.   Jesus used the Hebrew form of grace proper to be spoken over a meal of bread.   He said : " Blessed art Thou, Jehovah our God, King of the world, who causes to come forth bread from the earth." Somewhat suddenly, he gave the order to offer the food which he had blessed.

His friends, half in consternation, much embarrassed, but trusting that it would all come out well, somehow, began to distribute five loaves of bread and two fish, among five thousand people.

This obedience and confidence seemed ridiculous, but proved sublime.

What was to be said ? What was to be thought ? For five thousand ate, and were satisfied ; and ate and could eat no more. And they left upon the grass so much food, beyond the power of so many hungry people to make way with, that the astounded committee of the twelve went about, and picked up many basketfuls of scraps and untouched provisions. These were cheap wicker baskets, such as careful people carried on journeys, and used wherefrom to feed beggars.

The wonder soon became understood among the throng. It raised a tempest of enthusiasm. The people were about dispersing, but now nothing could move them. Who could leave a man who could do a deed like that? They rushed towards him. They clambered up to get nearer to him. Huzzas arose ; cries of admiration rent the still air. It was beginning to darken ; but no one thought of home or shelter. No one thought of anything but the tall, serene form, the gleaming face, just beginning to grow indistinct in the dusk; those outstretched hands, that presence of serenity and of strength ; the loving heart, the mysterious gift, the mighty tenderness, with the power to use it, and the will to use it,

as no other man had done. Everybody tried to get
nearer to him. Broken shouts arose, defining into
words:

"This is He!"

"The Messiah! The Wonderful! The Anointed!"

"Here He is! Here is He we have sought so
long! No one else could do such things! Our
own eyes have seen! It is the King!"

Then from the valley, as the shadow darkened
and the outlines of the crowd became clouded to his
eye, Jesus heard the shout taken up and carried on:

"The King! Let us to him! Our King! Our
King!"

The groves echoed the cry, and it reverberated
with a curious sadness from rock to rock. The
lake seemed to receive it wistfully, and to repeat it
under breath of her lightest waves, as if she felt
afraid to say it aloud for his sake, because she loved
him.

Jesus stood looking down; — now a dim form, a
dimming face, high above the clamor of the people.
He seemed at one instant, in the oncoming night, to
blur and blend into it, like a mystery which might
melt into it and vanish forever; at the next, to stand
there like some grand, eternal fact, carved out of
the solid rock, and never to be shaken. He did not
speak.

For his penetration was not deceived. He knew
that in this happy evening hour, while the sun
dipped and the wave whispered, and the light on the
grass went out; while the people shouted, understanding nothing, and loved him without consider-

ing him, — he knew that the turning of his fate was decreed.

It has been said of him that he never trusted a mob. The wisest of men have been deluded by the adulation of an audience. He was not, even by this one, his kindest, his most pleasing. He knew that he could not depend upon these people to spare him or to save him; that they would huzza to-day, and forget to-morrow. Did he understand that, having helped him to his doom, they would leave him to it? We like to think that he did not, alto-gether, — not quite yet. Even a few hours' respite was something to the tired man. But, while he stood, drowned in his own deep thoughts, the enthu-siasm of the people had made headway against a silence which they took to be that of irresolution or assent.

The shout arose again; this time with hot deter-mination:

"Jesus, our King! We will *make* him King!"

His quick divination perceived now the position in which he stood. Five thousand men were solidly moving from the plain, up the knoll, massing upon him from all points, with the intention of trying force upon him, if flattery and entreaty failed. By a bold *coup* his audience, his patients, his guests, — all these people who were in debt to his sympathy and kindness, — meant to capture him bodily, and drag him to the front of a great political rebellion. What should begin as a riot would end in a revolu-tion. An outburst of hero-worship would grow into an uncontrollable tragedy.

CHAPTER XI

A DECISIVE CRISIS

SOME hours had passed. The "first evening," the "evening between the evenings," and the "second evening" were gone. It was midnight; and he was at last alone.

It had been a hard contest; but he had conquered the people. This was a much more difficult thing to do — as his throbbing heart and exhausted nerve told him — than it had been for him to feed five thousand men on five loaves of bread. In the estimate of his strange power one must rank very high among mystical gifts the art, the force, the wit, the will which peaceably dispersed the mob that night.

The personal friends of Jesus, swept into the general excitement, were almost carried off their feet. They would have liked nothing better than to see their Rabbi with a crown on his dear head. They considered no throne too good for him. They would have headed the rioters with equal zeal and indiscretion; and might have been in a Roman dungeon before another sunset. Jesus found it as important to control them as to dismiss the multitude of men who had gone into such a frenzy over the events of this exciting day.

To the dismay of the twelve they were ordered to take to their boat at once and sail away, and that without his company. This was confounding. What a disappointment! Not to stay and see what was going to happen? To leave the Rabbi alone with the mob? To have no share in this tremendous thing? To be sent home like children who could not be trusted in great public affairs? It was hard. But they obeyed him, for the command was given in a certain tone of his, not too often used, but as irresistible as whirlwind, torrent, conflagration, or any force of nature when it came. When Jesus spoke in this way, it no more occurred to his friends to withstand him than to defy Jehovah. They went. Uncomfortable and unhappy, they set sail without him, and headed for the western shore of the lake.

Jesus was now left quite alone upon the plain of Batihah. He climbed to its highest hillock and sank, for he was worn out, upon the ground.

He recognized perfectly that the crisis of his life had come. It was all in his own hands now, — rather it was all in his own heart. It was his to choose between glory and shame, between success and failure. Strictly speaking, it was not a choice between life and death. In either event, he stood but scant chance of life. An ordinary man would have been blinded by his position. A demagogue would have suffered himself to be carried on the shoulders of the people into the maddest and greatest of Hebrew insurrections. The duller zealot, meaning generously, but thinking imperfectly, would have rushed headlong and tried to retreat too late.

The trap would shut down on leader and on people alike; and it would snap with a Roman lock.

Jesus recognized the fact that he lived in a time of anarchy and under an iron autocracy. From five million Jews Herod the Great had exacted three millions of dollars a year, — a heavy tax for the average income. Desperate poverty filled the land which it stirred to perpetual revolt. The people were so poor that to be on the edge of starvation was a very common thing. Among the crowd that evening, no one knew how many there were who had no food with them simply because they could not afford it. The sympathy of Jesus with this kind of suffering was swift and steady. The first personal petition in what was known to literature and to worship as the Lord's Prayer was: Give us our daily bread. The Jews had not the resources in themselves or in their conditions for a successful revolution against the proudest power of the world.

The political astuteness of the Rabbi from Nazareth has never received anything like its appreciation.

Jesus had extraordinary comprehension of affairs. In the lonely watch upon the shore of Gennesaret that night, he measured the forces of nations and grasped the situation of the civilized world. His own exalted enthusiasm, his personal success, his passion for humanity, did not confuse him for a moment as to the practical facts. He was familiar with the history of his people, — of their riots, their famous insurrections, and the fates of their unsuccessful leaders.

He perceived distinctly that in any revolution, for any cause, under any leadership, subject Jerusalem would stand no chance against omnipotent Rome. There would be an hour of fire of glory, of romance, of splendid patriotism, of brilliant resistance, and then the worst must be expected. Many a man has gladly given his life to be the chief figure of such an hour, and to go into history as a patriot defeated but magnificent.

It is easy to die a hero. How hard to die a victim! Jesus had to choose between the two. Lead his people on a hopeless national revolt he would not. Yet their political expectations were the sole basis on which they were likely to meet him. Their only intelligent idea of their Messiah was that of a powerful and obliging being who would free them from Rome and make a nation of them. He, Jesus their Christ, just for this hour their idol, he must disappoint them. But, if he did it, he must meet the consequences. There lay his terrible dilemma.

True, there was another way. Yes . . . there was the other way. There had always been this other method of dealing with the great problem of his life. He had not used it, — never once to his own advantage. It had been to him a holy treasure held in trust; called upon only under what he believed to be the orders of God. Suppose he fell back upon it now?

There in the midnight and the moonlight, with the lake at his feet, in silence, in exhaustion, in the utter solitude of a man who knows that even if his dearest friends were with him they could not understand him, and so feels less alone to be without them, he thought the question through.

There was this other way. Powers which other souls knew not were his. He had not tested this beautiful and dangerous difference from his kind all this while to no avail. He had not cultivated his mystical force for over two years without a faith in it, and a comprehension of it, that had grown with the force itself. Between his first timid exercise of functions occult and sacred and the great deeds which he had done in the last six months there was a long march. He had learned much from the education of his own power. But it is not to be forgotten that he learned everything from its restraint. How much more than he had wrought had he left undone! How much more than he had given had he held back! How much more than the wildest enthusiasm of his maddest mob believed him capable of might he have achieved! How much more might he yet achieve? . . . Ah, how much!

His thoughts moved back to the first conflict in the desert near Jericho. Severe and decisive as that had been, it was the trial of the theory, not of the facts of life. It is one thing to forecast experience and adjust it to principle in imagination. It is quite another to face the actual crisis which experience has slowly and painfully brought. Sore with suffering yet throbbing with achievement, the mind comes up with a shock in the clutch of the situation which it has so long contemplated at a distance with all the ease of remoteness and much of the sense of unreality. The visions of the desert were now the

struggles of the hour. Jesus was not free from the
strange law by which a soul is often subjected to the
same kinds of trial all through life. This terrible
monotony in suffering he knew to the piteous end.
He had now to front his old questions, and meet
again the ghosts of the spiritual foes that he had
laid at the outset of his career.

Should he take that other, that omitted way ?
Should he pursue his Father's plan, dim, inscrutable, so far above his age and his people that it had
no more coherence to them than a delusion of the
demonized whom he healed ? Or should he do the
thing, the only thing, from his position comprehensible to his race and his times ? Should he levy his
mystical powers ? Should he summon invisible cohorts to his aid ? Should he carry out the national
aspirations, not as a man among men, but as a God,
scorning men and their methods, — flinging aside
human restrictions and assuming divine prerogatives?
Should he confuse, baffle, smite, slay, triumph, by
inexplicable means ? Should he work out the mission of his life under human laws or above them?

The Jews had the primitive idea of royalty, of its
purpose and its prerogatives. Jesus had quite another. The words " king," " kingdom," " throne,"
meant one thing to them, quite a different one to
him. In his brief, intense public life, wherein the
energies and fervors of a very long career had been
crowded into a little over three years, he had never
been untrue to the dreams of his first youth. His
exaltation did not desert him in the stress of his
tremendous experience. He had kept his great

ideal. He had never deviated from his unapproachable consecration. His belief remained unshaken that he knew the purposes of God in his life's history, and that these were not the expectations of men. He had been selected for a fate as solitary as it was sublime.

His was the kingdom of the soul. He was the King of the spirit. His was the realm in which the little life of nations, their wars, their revolutions, their political schemes, their paltry clangor, could not enter. The ambitions of Augustus Imperator were petty beside the aspirations of Jesus. Nothing less than the permanent control of the world would ever realize these. But this force must come from within, not from without.

His legions were the elements of human character; his court was in the human heart; his throne was humanity itself. Of its obligations and of its possibilities he had a perfectly new conception to enforce.

This he had tried to make his practical, commercial people understand. He had preached, but they were puzzled; he had lived, but they were perplexed. He had suffered, but they did not comprehend why or to what end. He had hoped against evidence and struggled against fate. They did not, could not, would not understand.

Now! To sweep over everything like flood or simoom; to start and surge on like any common revolutionist, — this they could comprehend. The patient, humble Rabbi, curing the sick, comforting the unhappy, helping the poor, was a mystery. What should be done with him? With it? A leader of revolts was altogether a simple problem. Add the mystical element, to which the Hebrew mind was quite accustomed. That was not half as perplexing as a modest man of power honoring the claims of duty in a plain way, using great gifts for no clearer end than to make people well, pure, and happy.

Suppose he took off the check imposed by his subtle sense of spiritual honor? Suppose he gave his mysterious nature the rein? Suppose he brought to the situation but a little portion of the forces, of the resources, which were his, and which he now knew were his? If he had chosen precisely here to add the extra-natural touch to the natural powers? . . . What a dazzling vision! What success! What glory! How much more than the prospects of a politician! It was the future of a spiritual statesman. Jesus Christ was the only man of his age who could have hurled Rome from the throne of the world. But he could not have done it under common laws, and that he was meant to do it under the superhuman he did not believe. He would not touch it on that basis. What then?

. . . .

The crisis was so profound, he had been so absorbed, the night was passing in such emotion and exhaustion, that the solitary thinker had not noticed the change of weather. Suddenly a breeze fanned him in the face from the southerly, and he perceived that it had veered and was rising steadily. With his quick consciousness of the situation of others, — always putting it before his own, — he perceived in-

stantly that his friends were sailing against a head
wind, and remembered that it was by his particular
command that they were not ashore.

He rose at once, and stood looking off over the
lake, shading his eyes with his hand from the brilliant Oriental moonlight. He could see from the
point where he stood that the little boat was having
a hard or even a dangerous time with what was now
a severe squall, if not a gale.

The claims of his solemn night's vigil yielded instantly to the interruption which mercy made upon
them. He hurried down to the shore of the lake.
His own trouble could wait. That of his disciples
could not and should not.

Six miles by water, but much more than that by
land, the distance to the western shore spread before
him. He had no boat. On that coast, now deserted,
none was accessible. It was far on in the night, and
no help was likely to reach the party; they might
drown before anything could be done for them.

Overcome with anxiety for his chosen friends, Jesus performed one of the few really impulsive acts
of his life. He stepped directly into the water. It
was soon deep, and grew rapidly deeper. The space
between him and the struggling boat was far too
large for the strongest swimmer. The wind had
now become a tempest. The waves ran high, and
both wind and waves were against him. But he did
not stop to think of that. Exalted, insistent, he
trusted himself upon the little sea. His heart was
so full of distress for those he loved that he could
not think of himself. His soul was so full of trust

in God — his high mood vibrated so in harmony with
the being of his invisible Father — that the laws of
nature seemed to him at that moment like his serfs.
. . . Through them or against them, reach the
boat! Defy the waves! Trample the water! . . .
Who can tell? Had he ever done the deed before?
In those long and lonely nights by the lake, un-
watched, unseen, had he ever experimented with his
mysterious faculties, trusting himself by these alone
upon the waters? Could he have explained in this
way any of his singular appearances or disappear-
ances which his friends were not always altogether
able to follow? Had he ever freed himself from
the thrall of the land, from the bondage of the keel,
in some weary and restless mood which only the
freedom of the water could calm? Was the event
of this night the movement of an educated or an
untried faculty? Or was it rather the overflow
force of that hour of exaltation when five thousand
men had been nourished by his human vitality and
his mystical power? Was his soul still so vibrant
with the vigor of a greater than human life that the
extra-natural was the most natural thing for him at
at that moment? However that may be, the moment bore him on. Ecstatic, he trod the water as
men do in dreams, while living, or fancy that they
may do waking, after death. All lovers of the sea
will understand something of this instinct, which
lies like a sleeping faculty within them. Moving
swiftly, moving joyously, tall in the moonlight, pale
and solemn, he had the look, he seemed to have the
qualities, of an apparition.

Such the occupants of the little boat took him to be when he glided into their range of vision. He approached them rapidly. His hands were outstretched as if to gather them. His face melted with shining pity. The boat lay over upon her side; she was capsizing fast. But the fishermen cried out in superstitious terror. With the impulse of their class, in all ages and all lands the same, they were more afraid of the supernatural than they were of drowning.

"A spirit! See! That is a spirit!" Then they saw the apparition smiling, just as the Rabbi smiled any day on land, — the sweet, familiar smile which had become the sun of their days and the moon of their nights, the romance of their prosaic lives.

"Have courage. Do not be afraid," he said, "it is I."

But the fishermen huddled together upon the windward rail of the sinking boat. Thomas shook his head skeptically. James and Andrew whispered together. John held out his hands towards the vision of his Master longingly. But John was gentle, and waited for others to act.

The group clung to each other like frightened animals. Jesus stood quite still. The water was pouring and dashing about the unseaworthy boat.

Then up spoke he who was always the first to gather courage, and the surest to express it for the rest of the twelve. Peter — never timid, seldom silent — flung out these impulsive words: "Lord, if it *be* thou, order me, too, to walk upon the water! I would come to thee!"

This challenge was quite satisfactory to the fish-ermen. It was their form of psychical research. It was a perfectly reasonable test, to their minds, of the nature of the phenomenon. An apparition might walk on Gennesaret for aught that one knew to the contrary; but plainly, to enable a fisherman to do so was out of the province of spirits. But if it were their Rabbi, their own Rabbi!—

Smiling, half amused, half tender, the figure beck-oned. At the gesture Peter sprang promptly into the foam. . . . Why, he could tread the sea,—he, too! Greatly excited, he took a few steps. The surface of the water bore, or seemed to upbear, him. Then the brave man suddenly lost his head.

The waves were running furiously. The Rabbi looked a long way off. It proved to be no easier to walk on the lake than it had always been. Peter became so confused that he began to go under. At the chill of the water and its rush into ears and throat, his jet of courage and trust went out like a candle dipped in a wave. From sheer nervous collapse, the sturdy man of the oar and the sail was about to drown in earnest.

Then he felt his hand grasped. What a vital, powerful touch! No other hand on earth could hold the sinking so.

"My Rabbi!" cried the panic-smitten man,— "my Lord!"

As if she, too, recognized her master, the boat began to right herself.

Jesus stepped aboard in perfect silence. The fringe and hem of his talith and tunic were wet; but his garments were otherwise dry, or only dampened by spray. He looked mildly at Peter, who fell dripping and gasping at his feet.

Awestruck, the fishermen dropped upon their knees, their faces, beside their bolder mate. Whispers, inarticulate at first, then growing stronger and quite distinct, passed from lip to lip.

" Thou *art* the Son of God ! "

Jesus smiled remotely, solemnly. He did not reply. He sat down among the demoralized sailors, and by a mute gesture ordered the boat to put about for the shore.

The events of this evening had been so disturbing, or so unexpected, that Jesus, in face of them, found his plans more or less disarranged. Besides, the Sabbath, on which no Jew could travel, was close at hand. It was now, we may think, the night of Thursday to Friday. The boat made a difficult landing, not precisely in Bethsaida, — which was then the fishing-port or Fisherton of Capernaum, but to the north of the Plain of Gennesaret, — and in the light of a Friday morning, calm enough after the storm, the little party landed near home in considerable perplexity.

The keel had scarcely grated on the sand before it was perceived that a large concourse was collecting to meet the tired Rabbi, who, wherever he went and whatever he did, could not escape his inevitable crowd.

The throng on the northeastern shore of the lake, the evening before, had dispersed in utter perplexity and some resentment.   Thousands of men, who were

ready to drag him into the front of a revolution, had
scattered, *en route* for the Passover, disappointed
and bitter. They wanted no more of a Messiah who
refused his proper position at the head of the Jewish
nation. The popular idol must realize the popular
dreams. When the Anointed came, ease and idleness
would come with him. Fruit would ripen every week.
Grain would harvest once a fortnight. The neces-
sities of life would fall into a man's hands without
working for them. Comfort and luxury would run
attendance on every whim. Miracles would multiply
for the asking. Every day some wonderful thing
would happen to amuse one. Life would become
a brilliant play, in which the spectator sat to be
entertained. First and finally, Israel would be a
nation again, and Rome would fall before her. Who
knew but the Hebrew Messiah might sit on the throne
of Augustus?

With this Rabbi, who would not be what was
expected of him, the majority of the mob had done.
They scattered about their own affairs in a very ill-
humor. But the Rabbi had his friends left, and
some of them followed him to Capernaum as fast as
possible. The severe gale of the night, however, had
blown a certain portion of the Gennesaret fishing
fleet over towards Bethsaida Julias. When morning
came, where was the Nazarene? He was known not
to have sailed in his own boat, which was seen to set
off without him. It was sure that he had not gone
by land, for he would have been met or overtaken.

A story, vague, amazing, began to take form.
In what manner had Jesus traveled from Batihah

to Capernaum ?   People whispered and wondered ;
curiosity grew.   The most incredulous or the most
credulous, those most eager to see him for his own
sake or for theirs, took passage on the storm-driven
fishing-boats, whose presence in the vicinity was a
convenient accident, and came across the lake in
search of him.   Take it altogether, he was received
by a large and excited multitude of people.   He
began immediately, in his characteristically quiet
manner, to attend to the sick, as was always his first
impulse.   He went about his usual work precisely as
if nothing out of the common course had happened,
healing, teaching, and preaching, as he saw the
opportunity.   He had a wonderful respect for *daily*
duty, for the ordinary demands of life ; with which
he never suffered the extraordinary event to interfere.
But the movement of the extraordinary had now set
in upon his history.   He was not to be able much
longer to ignore it.

It began that Friday by an ecclesiastical persecu-
tion, of small proportions, but of wily and ominous
intent.   A certain delegation of Pharisees and of
Scribes, who had come up from the capital with the
purpose of entrapping the great nonconformer,
attacked him almost as soon as he appeared in the
vicinity of his home, by an accusation of heresy.   It
took a form grave to the creed of these pompous
sectarians, but nothing less than ridiculous to a
modern mind.

The Nazarene had allowed his followers to eat
without previously washing the hands, according to
the full Pharisaic ceremonial.   Terrible omission !

Fatal fault! Fists were clenched. Phylacteries and
fringes shook in the bitter anger of religious intol-
erance. Rumors of the strange scene on the plain
at Batihah had spread like fire among dry leaves.
Jesus had fed five thousand homeless, hungry people
crowding a desolate place, without keeping them
waiting while he insisted on the petty lavations of a
sect. He had put hospitality, humanity, and good
sense before dogmatism and formalism. The delegation arraigned him openly for impiety.

The Nazarene stood silent for some moments after
this public onslaught. He was weary from the events
of the day before. He was spent from the sleepless
night, from the solitary struggle upon the hills, and
from the deed that he had done in the tempest.
Who measured the strain upon the mortal frame
given by his powerful conquest of the forces of nature,
by that act of mercy and of mystery? His dearest
friend did not know that Jesus had come to the crisis
of his mature life, and that he knew he had come to
it. A man conscious that the grandest success in
the history of human power was in his grasp, but
deliberately electing the cruelest of defeats; a man
aware of near martyrdom, but, for the sake of a
principle too noble to be understood by other men,
refusing to evade danger by a footstep; a man
passionately craving love, sympathy, and loyalty, but
conscious that he was about to estrange them all; a
man not baffled, but still master of the situation, —
he challenged his church and his state.

His delicate lip curled slightly with a scorn so
obvious that his silence seemed surcharged with it.

Then, unexpectedly, he roused himself and faced the heresy-hunters.

Without a thought of himself, he turned arraigner. Without a care for the consequences, he hurled at the delegation from Jerusalem a series of the great rebukes for which this gentle, this compassionate man has become famous.

"You teach the commandments of men, not the commandments of God! You wash cups and pots and tables. . . . Yet you dishonor father and mother. . . . You are hypocrites!"

.   .   .   .

"Rabbi, knewest thou how much the Pharisees were offended?" The most timid of the disciples came trembling to him afterwards and anxiously put the question.

"They are blind leaders of blind men," replied the Nazarene calmly. "Both shall fall into the ditch."

But his thoughts were not as calm as his voice or countenance. He preached in the Capernaum synagogue on the Sabbath; a powerful discourse, absolutely without evidence of fear or faltering. He preached upon the topic which was in everybody's mouth, the supper of the five thousand. He avoided no question and parried no complaint of that great event. He was as straightforward as if he had been the safest priest or courtier, protected by the favor of the authorities of the land, instead of the suspect, homeless and hunted, that he was. He shot out the truth, and disdained the results. He startled his audience. He made astounding assertions:

"This is the work of God," he said. "I am the bread of life. . . . He that cometh to me shall never be hungry. I came from Heaven, not to do mine own will. I came to do the will of Him who sent me. . . . He that believeth on me hath everlasting life. . . . The living Father sent me. . . . The words that I speak are spirit and are life."

So he spoke, commandingly and courageously. But his heart was heavy; so many abandoned him suddenly that he felt like a man shunned. Perhaps he had not expected this trouble to come so quickly, so sorely. He was so loving a man, he depended so much on human tenderness, as all highly organized souls do, that coldness and desertion almost broke his heart.

One day he turned pitifully to his chosen, the twelve, who clung to him while others left him.

"Will *ye* also go away?" he asked with pathetic wistfulness. Tears started to his sad eyes. His delicate face pleaded with the fishermen, his rough friends, as if he cried out to them for something that he *must* have. To their dying hour these men remembered that moment, and the time came when they thanked God that Peter had answered for them all:

"Master, to whom shall we go? The words of eternal life *thou* hast."

But the public agitation was now so great that Jesus found it necessary to escape it for a time. He resumed at once his interrupted plans of travel, aud went with the twelve towards Tyre and Sidon; a calmer region, where temporary safety allowed him to continue the work which was more important to him than his own fate.

But there were indications of a certain change in him which his followers observed. He had lost something of his cheerfulness and ease of manner. He grew more grave, more sad. He was much alone. He was often absorbed. He sat sunken in thought. He knew many sleepless nights. He spent his vigils in prayer. He seemed somehow removed from his friends by a consciousness of trouble untold. At times he looked at them longingly, lovingly, as if he would have said something which yet he never said. He turned away in silence which they did not dare to break. His lips parted, trembled, and closed. What sorrowful secret did he withhold from them?

CHAPTER XII

THE MOUNTAIN: AND THE TOMB

THE time came soon enough when he told them;
concealing nothing, revealing all that they could
understand and more. But he bore his dark secret
for a while yet, in the loneliness which he had endured so long that every nerve now began to writhe
away from it, and his heart to cry for a little human
comprehension. No man is so sensitive to sympathy as he who has lived the longest and the most
strongly without it. The time comes when he must
have it, or sink; the very force of character which
has enabled him to dispense with it turns again and
rends an exquisite organization by force of tenderness. The very depth of nature, which has been
lord of the emergency, now becomes its subject.
Jesus was approaching such a mental crisis.

He was now an unpopular wanderer, homeless,
and in peril. The malice of the church which had
already excommunicated him was backed by the
power of the state which hated and feared him. As
long as the mass of the people supported him, neither palace nor Sanhedrin dared resort to extreme
measures. But the people had begun to desert him.
He had known their delusive attachment. He was
to know their caprice and their cruelty.

The last six months of his life in Galilee he spent as a hunted man, practically an outlaw from the more dangerous centres of population; pursuing his missionary labors as well as he could against odds in remote places. Some of the most interesting work of his life was done in this despairing time. He treated the deaf, the dumb, the blind, the leper, the maniac, — Jews or Gentiles, it mattered nothing to him, — every anguish that needed him fed upon him. Dramatic cures and eloquent discourses, bountiful mercy and beautiful thought, crowded his days. He seemed to press them with kindness, with pity to all the world. He gave himself passionately, utterly, to suffering soul or suffering body. He lived as great spirits do who know that their time is short. But the greatest goes dumb before this record of spiritual royalty.

Yet was he so watched and suspected that he was obliged to conceal even his kindnesses, if he could. He made many unsuccessful attempts to keep his greatest cures as secrets, but the nervous excitement of his healed patients prevented this.

It was one of the special hardships of his life that its noblest objects created its gravest dangers. The necessity to be silent, to repress, was always upon him. It took difficult forms. A man living to a certain great end, yet was he forced continually to withhold its furtherance. About to die for a supreme truth, yet he was often obliged to check its expression.

One day at Cæsarea Philippi, a significant conversation took place between himself and his twelve friends.

"Whom," he asked suddenly, "do men say that I am?"

"John the Baptist, or Elijah — Jeremiah, or some other prophet," was the prompt reply.

"But whom do *ye* say?" persisted the Nazarene.

Then Peter uttered these memorable words: "Thou art the Christ, the Son of the living God."

"Blessed art thou!" murmured the Rabbi, much moved. "Thou art a rock. I build my church upon thee!"

His face blazed with a beautiful happiness, which those who loved him saw but seldom now. But this momentary glow died quickly down into the dull remembrance of his true position.

"See to it," he said sadly. "Tell no man that I am Jesus the Christ."

Up to this time there had been but few occasions in his life on which he definitely admitted his own celestial claims. After this time he did not attempt to evade them. They had now grown quite clear to his mind. It cannot be said that they never clouded over. It cannot be said that he had passed all question, all doubt, all the subtle suffering which the mere consciousness of his own mission and nature brought upon him. But he had met the sun. Behind the darkest hour he knew that he *had* seen it shine. He lived a life of intense determination to believe in the Fatherhood of God at all odds, at any cost. His trust in his mysterious relationship to the Deity was racked to the limits of human endurance.

.   .   .   .

One day the dispirited twelve, themselves tired of trouble and danger, were gathered round him like homesick children. Something in their affectionate trustfulness touched him to the quick. They, too, like the rest of their race, had expected a political Messiah; they had hoped to see their Rabbi King of the World. His failure to become what he might, and now his evidently growing unpopularity, troubled them. His declining fortunes sorely tried their faith. Nothing tried their love. Yet they were in a hard position. He felt it for them.

He had sat in profound silence for some time, entombed in thought. Unexpectedly raising his sad eyes, he looked at his followers so appealingly that he who was dearest of them all crept near to the Rabbi, and softly laid a hand upon his arm. The eyes of John and the voice of Peter asked:

" What wouldst thou, Lord ? "

But Jesus answered nothing at all. He continued to gaze at them so steadfastly that even Peter could not talk. The little group held their breath. A sudden terror, nameless, formless, began to clutch their hearts. The look by which a great love answers foreboding that it cannot relieve crept solemnly upon his expression. They read in his broken face the spelling of one awful word. His lips could not, would not frame it till his pitying eyes had said it.

Death ! . . . Their Rabbi, their lord, their dream of life, their vision of human power and splendor, of divine vitality — *die?* The thing seemed so incredible that its full shock could not reach their senses. But they looked back into his quivering face again, and they saw that terrible truth was on it.

. . . .

As soon as he could speak, or they could listen, he told them what he knew. Did he tell them all he knew? It was impossible to say this, or indeed to say where his prevision of his fate began or ended. The tragic movement of events taught these plain men many dreadful lessons. At that moment they were rent between the feeling that he could not be doubted in anything that he said, and the passionate protest of belief against accepting enormity like this. They repeated the words slowly, in broken sentences, with stiffening lips.

"Jerusalem . . . Condemned . . . of the Priests . . . To be killed . . . three days . . . Rise again " . . .

Their thoughts grew rigid like their muscles about these impossible ideas.

Impulsive Peter broke into a passion of reproaches, finding fault, as hot-headed persons do, with the being one loves most, because affliction has smitten him. Peter acted as if the Rabbi had become morbid, and needed a healthy mind to check him.

But John, whom Jesus loved, crept closer, and buried his face from sight of all the rest upon the shoulder of his Master. When the dearest disciple heard this presentiment or prescience of doom confided to his friends by Jesus, John put up his hand entreatingly, and laid his finger on the white lips which articulated the horrible words.

Did John understand more than the others, or better? For the disciples were not fine of perception about what Jesus had said. They found it almost impossible, when they came to think it over, to interpret him literally. He must mean this or that; must refer to some unknown decline or increase of fortune. He was indulging in parable. Or, perhaps, he thought of the general resurrection of the dead, whatever that should signify.

One day Jesus found these good men wrangling as to which of them should hold the highest political office when he came to the throne of the Hebrew nation. He turned away, astonished and mute. After all, had their minds gone no farther than *this?* If they, with their opportunities, *could* not understand, what should he expect of the rest of the world?

The Nazarene was now living intense days. They passed in spiritual fervors which encroached upon a wasting, but always revitalized strength. His preaching indicated the exaltation under which he moved. When was he more eloquent? His language could not be more terse. His thought, fed by his heightened feeling, was seldom, if ever, more valuable. Immortal quotations from his addresses date from this time: "Let a man deny himself . . . to follow me. Whosoever will save his life shall lose it. . . . Whosoever will lose it for my sake shall find it." What profit to a man if he gain the world and lose his own soul? . . . What shall he give in exchange for a soul?"

A week had gone. Dedication had done its work

upon his sensitive organization. He had grown pale,
thin, shining. His eyes were larger than usual, and
their hollows had darkened. His veined hands had
shrunken a little, as the human hand does with certain temperaments, giving the first signal of bodily
change under suffering or sickness. What illumined
his patient smile? A sacred fire was in his eye.
His disciples watched him in dull wonder.

There came a night when he bade the three on
whom he most depended to climb the hills with him,
and gave no reason beyond the familiar one, that
he would ascend to pray. Peter, James, and John
were tired with the day's traveling, but no one of
them objected. The Rabbi's manner was something
not to be argued with.

They were at the foot of beautiful Lebanon, highest and whitest of mountains. It was an Alpine
ascent, involving a night spent in air too rarefied
for comfortable breathing, if one made the snow-
touched summit. The little party did not, but
mounted to a nearer foothill, and wondered why
this toil was added to a hot day's march. Jesus
climbed in advance, apart. His stout staff fell
firmly on the rocks. He showed less than usual
signs of weariness. Yet his friends knew how worn
he was.

The great mountain divided Jewish from Gentile
territory. It was an imposing height, and the view
therefrom was significant and inspiring.

The sun had set. Cool was coming. The road
started among cultivated slopes, and wound upwards
through orchards, vines, and grain fields. Figs and

apricots, mulberry, corn, and melon interchanged outlines and colors of leaf or blossom or forming fruit. The air was sweet. The world was ripening. Clumps of oak succeeded to this richer level; dwarf shrubs and rock ravines thickened as the climb grew steeper. Turf, gravel, stunted cedars, gorges and crevices, began to take the place of warmer scenery. Warm became cool, delightful to the sun-smitten travelers; and now from above them the scent of snow! The group drew it in to thirsty senses and to weary frames. Strength came, as it always comes with snow. They felt invigorated and excited. The hot, dusty world lay below them, as life lies below death, — a trouble escaped. Their spirits rose, and so their souls.

To the dull watchers down in the plain and valley, stately Lebanon gave no sign that mystery swept over his head that night. Life went on as usual to common minds and in common circumstances. Who guessed that a wonder thrilled the mountain? The lowland and the heights are far apart. Lebanon was always a beautiful summit, and the eyes of the sad or the sick turned to it on this as on many other evenings.

Sunset on this peak has been captured by the vivid pen of one who knew it well.

"Close upon the rose color deepening into red" came "a death-like pallor, and darkness relieved by snow." . . . "A deep ruby flush was slowly followed by warm purple shadows." The Sea of Galilee, "between its dim walls of hill," was lighted with "a delicate, greenish-yellow hue. The flush

died out . . . and a pale, steel-colored shade succeeded. . . . A long, pyramidal shadow slid down
. . . and crept across the plain. Damascus was
swallowed up by it . . . the pointed end of the
shadow stood out distinctly against the sky — a
dusky cone of dull color against the flush of the
afterglow. It was the shadow of the mountain itself, stretching away for seventy miles across the
plain — the most marvelous shadow, perhaps, to be
seen anywhere. . . . The sun at length slid into the
sea, and went out like a blue spark."

In the color, in the glory, remote from men, apart
from the fret of life, a group of four passed from
twilight to dark, in the attitude and in the absorption of worship. Jesus had prayed aloud with his
three friends, calling upon them — did they ever
reveal what endearing blessings? He had now
moved somewhat apart from them that he might
have the privacy of personal and silent prayer.
They watched him reverently. But they were very
tired. The Master prayed a long time to-night.
And if one should fall asleep, and offer him that
disrespect?

The three, struggling against the drowsiness which
began to overcome them, suddenly stirred and
started. They sprang to their feet. Every man of
them forgot that he was sleepy, thought and cared
no longer for himself or for his feelings or concerns.

For, what had happened? Or was happening?
Was the mountain on fire?

Who was that? *What* was that? Where was
their Rabbi, — the plain man whom they were used

to seeing every day, the unpopular, hunted preacher, with his blue talith stained by the climb up the mountain, and his dear face furrowed with care? He had vanished as the shadow of Lebanon had vanished on the landscape when night melted the hard outlines of day away.

He was gone, that hunted missionary, bowed with responsibilities and dangers, comrade of grief. In his stead, what a vision! Behold beauty, splendor, joyousness, a kingly form; light on his hair, on his features, on his arms and hands. His dark linen talith had taken on the texture of clouds, and the color of white fire. His feet, an hour ago travel-worn and dusty, now glittering, refused to touch the earth. He trod on the mountain air. He floated lightly, — as fair, as refreshing, as refreshed as the snow beyond. His countenance was as if it had been a medallion, carved out of living light.

A mist of gold broken into rainbow, brushed into pearl, surrounded him. From it looked dim outlines, half foreign, half familiar, with the Hebrew lineaments; faces of ancient saints and sages cherished by the Hebrew imagination and faith.

The three simple-hearted men, to whom the sight of these bright phantasms was given, fell flat with terror, which arose quickly into ecstasy. Half intoxicated with the presence of the transcendent, never before granted to their experience, they began to babble like children in happy delirium, not knowing what they said.

But what should be said of *him*, the portrait in that frame of glory? Where was the worn face?

Where the wasted hands, the troubled figure? Like the dust of travel, escaped in a bath of fire.

Pain and wanness vanished from him like the staff which had helped him up the mountain, and now lay forgotten. Humanity, transfigured, had mounted into — what? This was no more the man they knew, who shone ineffable before them. Then who?

The fishermen were nervously anxious to tell everybody what had happened. This wonderful thing must bring all Palestine to the Rabbi's feet. Were they not its elect witnesses, good men and true, whose testimony could not be scorned?

To their dismay, they were authoritatively ordered not to say anything about it. Nay, even the remaining nine of the twelve were to be told nothing at all. Peter, John, and James were astounded to find that this splendid secret was theirs, and theirs alone. They did not know whether to be more honored or more troubled by the confidence.

They descended the mountain silently. They looked askance at Jesus, wondering that he appeared just as usual. They were afraid to address him. They whispered among themselves and glanced over their shoulders now and then, like people who had seen sorcery. They were not imaginative men, but they were loving ones, and they found it natural to connect the great scene on the heights with the strange mood which now consumed the Rabbi.

What store of strength did he need for the next act in the tragic drama whose scenery had now begun to shift with darkening swiftness?

Had his unseen Father, in whom he believed so profoundly, taken this desolate son to his heart in the splendors of a mystical hour? Did it need the night on Lebanon to fortify Jesus for the days which were to come?

He told no person. But he came down the mountain a changed and determined man. No more uncertainty, whether apparent or real, troubled his purpose or controlled his movements. From that hour, he turned without one hesitating motion to meet his doom. It has been said of him in a few strong words which discourage a weaker version of the crisis: "From that time he set his face steadfastly towards Jerusalem."

The history of martyrdom has its grandeurs, its follies, and its delusions, like that of all other human enthusiasms; and, in its awful processes, minor men have exhibited great qualities. Thousands of them have studied, in passionate desire to repeat it, the bearing of Jesus of Nazareth. But when has it been reduplicated? Who has trodden such a road as he with such a step? It was so human, so sensitive; it winced so from anguish; it indicated at every blood-drop suffering so acute that ordinary sympathy has not the nerve to follow it; it was the footfall of flesh on fire; yet it trod like metal on stone.

Bravely to accept the inevitable calls forth a kind of self-respect which often honors human character, and takes the form of fortitude or courage. Jesus elected the avoidable; forced it, hastened it, and faced it as if he had been king, not captive of his

fate. He moulded his own sufferings with the serenity of a sculptor modeling the statue of a god.

The Nazarene now set forth upon the itinerary of his last journey through Palestine, moving from province to province as occasion dictated, facing or fleeing immediate danger, as the large plan of his sacrifice seemed to him to require. His dearest friend never saw him falter. Relentless, determined, — seeing it all the while, — he trod into the trap which church and state had laid for him in the capital.

Who, in the preconsciousness of a terrible fate, lives as if it were not to be? Which of us, knowing that he is to die, can act as if he were to live? Jesus went straight on with common life. Daily duty presented to him, as it always had, the foremost claims. He preached, he taught, he prayed; he healed, he rebuked, he forgave, he comforted. He gave his last six months of life to everything but his own interests, to every being except himself. His patients thronged his path early and late, as they had always done. Sickness and sorrow accumulated in his way, leaning upon him more heavily than ever. The woe of the world clung to him more helplessly, more persistently, as if it were a sentient thing, and had a dim foreknowledge that its opportunity was short.

His own spiritual force responded visibly to the calls upon it in these intense months. He preached with an ecstatic absorption. His mental powers grew at once more profound and more simple. His discourses at this period were many, and remain matchless. When has the *intellect* of Jesus Christ received anything like its recognition? We have

been accustomed to think of him so exclusively as a great religious influence that the supreme quality of his mind has escaped us.

Very many of his immortal thoughts, dating from this crisis, were apparently and deliberately thrown away in private instruction. His acquired lack of confidence in mobs gave him reserved opinions about the uses of public address. He began to question its permanent value. He became deeply conscious that he must now seek permanence rather than immediate effect for the truth which was about to cost him his life. He began to trust his thought more and more to his personal friends.

Type and the press did not exist. He had none of the conditions of the modern reformer.

Yet the Nazarene forecast the methods of influence which would be in power centuries afterwards. The most eminent orator of history, he preferred the medium of a few intelligent and controlling minds. He confided his system of faith to twelve unlettered men. Did he know that these would become the editors and authors of the greatest publication in the world?

There was a suburb of Jerusalem which he came to love and to seek, a convenient and pleasant retreat (scarcely two miles away) for a traveler wearied of the town, or for personal reasons unsafe within it. In the course of a few brief visits to the capital, — troubled, hurried stays that sent him forth from the city sadder than he came, — the heretic preacher, in these last dark months, had opportunities to cultivate his warm friendship for one family resident in

Bethany. This was the preferred household of three which came nearest of any that he had known since boyhood to giving him a sense of home.

No closer ties than those between brother and sister deviated the attachment of Lazarus and Mary, who were unwedded, and of Martha, a widow, from their gentle guest. The four made a circle of those solitaries whose shared, yet separate lives, form the best material for friendship. A beautiful devotion, deferent from the hosts, faithful on the part of the guest, grew into delicate intimacy.

Martha, proprietor of the home, a wealthy house-holder, a little fussy and arbitrary, as good house-keepers are; Mary, the devotee, a little neglectful and absent-minded, as dreamers are ; and Lazarus, the younger brother of the family, made an interest-ing group. Their affection became peculiarly dear to Jesus. His wasting heart threw tendrils around them. Their open home was precious to the lonely man.

It is pleasant to think that, at this troubled time of his life, he knew something of a home of real ease. He had been so poor, so hunted ; he had so much of privation, and so little of comfort! The hospitality of the poor and of the middle classes, spasmodically offered, gratefully accepted, had been his usual lot. He had met it cheerfully ; but his sense of homeless-ness was pitifully acute.

He once wistfully compared his condition to that of the wild creatures of the forests and the skies. The foxes and the birds had their holes and their nests. The Son of Man, he said, had not where to

lay his head. These plaintive words constitute one
of the rare complaints of his hard life.

His experience since the evening on the mountain
had been more than at some other times a desolate
one. At the very outset of his first journey to Jerusalem (traveling by way of Samaria), he had been
refused outright admission to a village where, being
tired out, he had arranged to spend the night. This
breach of the commonest laws of Oriental hospitality
was so incredible that the indignation of the twelve
knew no restraint. They demanded, in a rage, that
the Rabbi should smite the offending town with the
wrath of heaven, clearly believing that he could do
it if he would. Gently rebuking them, the wearied
man patiently took his march again and humbly
walked on to another village. He showed no resentment.

Worse than this had happened in Judea. To one
of his public addresses at Jerusalem befell an ominous interruption. Something, hurled by an unseen
hand, struck him violently. It proved to be a stone.
Smarting with the pain of a severe blow, quivering
with the nervous shock, the preacher paused and
steadfastly regarded the crowd. He perceived clear
signs of an intention to mob him by stoning him to
death.

He changed color. His fine lips parted. What
just denunciation would they roll forth? What awful retort? Earthquake, fire, flood, sunstroke, the
blows of the winds, or the resources of sudden death
which lurk in the human body — were these at his
disposal? Which would he select from the invisi-

ble ranks of his mystical guardsmen to protect himself? to punish his assailant?

He chose the sting of a gentle word. " Many
kindnesses have I done you. . . . For which of them
do ye stone me ? "

Heartsick and hopesick, he had been lovingly received into Martha's luxurious home. He had sat
with Mary under the tents of green branches erected
in the court, or near the house, on Festival Week,
and rested in the flickering of cool shadows, talking
quietly of the great thoughts with which his mind was
throbbing, while the mistress of the house bustled
to and fro ordering his upper room, or preparing
for many guests. Of these he was the most distinguished. He was treated accordingly. The social
position of Lazarus and the ladies of the family was
so prominent that their unconcealed devotion to the
Nazarene made them no special trouble in ecclesiastical quarters; they were, for whatever reason,
let alone in their heresy. At all events, they never
wavered from it. They became and remained his
fast and affectionate friends. Every comfort that
wealth and love could command their hospitality
crowded upon him. The worn-out man, accustomed
to a rude and simple lot, gratefully drew one long,
sighing breath in the soft air of gentle surroundings.
His exquisite delicacy of nature rested in it, like a
bruised nerve, long lacerated and neglected. Far
beyond common woe or want as his personal emergency had gone, all human distinctions looked
smaller than ever to him; and he had never rated

them as of much consequence. But the educated *sympathy* of refinement he did not, for he could not, undervalue. He needed it too much just then. It came at the right time. Friendship, at its best and sanest, he tasted with a touching gratitude; the ripe and beautiful fruit he laid gently down when the hour came; no one heard him complain because he must relinquish it.

.   .   .   .

It was in Perea, and the travelers were moving with caution. He had found himself in such imminent peril in Judea that he had kept out of the province for a time, teaching, healing, and preaching as usual wherever he went. He was about a day's journey from Bethany. A sudden message reached him from his friends there:

"He whom thou lovest is sick. Lord, hasten to him!"

But Jesus did not hasten to Lazarus. The inexplicable mood which he had more than once shown in emergencies took possession of him. With apparent disregard of the appeal, he went on about his work where and as he was. Two days passed. Strange silence came upon him. He would not talk about the thing.

Two days! A man might die and be buried in the East in that time. And this his chosen friend, of whose lavish hospitality he had freely partaken; this the household where, above all others in Judea, he loved and was loved! It began to be rumored that the healer was afraid to go to Bethany; that he would let his friend die, — like any timid, com-

mon man, — rather than risk his life so near Jerusalem. His disciples interrogated him persistently.
But the most that they gained was this enigmatic
explanation of his conduct: " It is that you might
believe."

The sick man was asleep, he said. " When I go,
I will awaken him." Then the twelve remembered
the little maid, the child of Jairus, and how the
Rabbi spoke about her, affirming that she was not
dead. " If he sleep, he shall do well," they answered
cheerfully, for they were much relieved, being anxious about their master's reputation in this matter.
But Jesus turned upon them one of his long and
silent looks."

" I tell you plainly," he said with decision, " Lazarus is dead."

Suddenly, at the end of two days, he gave the
order to start for Bethany. And now the fishermen
took fright themselves. They begged him for his
life's sake and for theirs to keep away from the region of the capital. They reminded him of the stone
which struck him on that startling day. They reminded him that if Lazarus were dead there was
nothing to be done.

But he looked at them and strode on. His staff
scattered the dust far ahead of his party. It was
almost impossible now to keep up with him. His
unaccountable indifference and delay had warmed
into what seemed an unreasonable anxiety and hurry.
The talith that he wore that day was white, and
his tall figure looked like a pillar of light, as he
moved rapidly forward, in advance of his disciples,

who plodded after, rough and faithful, obedient and
perplexed, — perplexed as they always were. They
spent their lives in an intellectual strain. A man's
faith is worth something when it burns through such
mental conditions as theirs.

They overtook him before they came to their
journey's end; and the group entered Bethany together.

The first news which reached them was as bad as
it could be. It was, indeed, as the Rabbi had said.
Lazarus was dead. More than that, he was dead
and buried.

. . . .

Lazarus was the most prominent citizen in Bethany, and the circumstances of his death were on
everybody's tongue. The village was astir with
mourners. Neighbors gossiped about the dead man's
tarrying friend, — not kindly. Muttered reproaches,
displeased and distressed faces, met the healer everywhere. Before he had set foot within the borders
of the village, he felt himself to be the most unpopular man in it. He looked a little surprised at this.
He had grown more and more restless during the lat-
ter part of the journey; he had eaten little and with
difficulty; he would take no rest at noon, but hurried along; his nervous system seemed to be on an
unusual tension; his expression was less serene,
more intent, and now it began to indicate sudden
pain. He panted slightly, as if he had received an
unexpected blow upon the face which affected his
breathing. He had stopped — so strong was the
popular feeling — with his group of friends about

him, and made no movement to advance into the village.

A grumbling by-stander viciously observed that the Nazarene was not in a hurry to enter the house where he had been so well treated, and whose bereavement he could have prevented if he had taken the trouble; for there seemed to be no doubt but that he was a very distinguished healer.

Jesus entered into conversation with no one, but stood silently, looked so troubled that his disciples felt discouraged. What did it all mean? How would he defend himself when people called him a craven or a faithless friend? Why had he let it happen as he had? Why? Why? Why?

The old, unanswered question faltered to their lips, and worried their hearts. Their minds found no reply to it.

At last one of them plucked his robe, and whispered to him that Martha was coming. Jesus raised his eyes, it seemed reluctantly, to meet hers. He was prepared for any reproaches.

But, upon the first glance at her, his whole expression changed. Hers was subdued, affectionate. The voluble housewife, touched by grief, had acquired a dignity and a gentleness which made another woman of her. Her demeanor was self-possessed. Her voice was controlled. Her eye met his frankly. No veiled reproof was in it; scarcely a question troubled it. It trusted him.

"Lord," she said affectionately, "if thou hadst been here" — She choked and stopped, but collected herself bravely. "My brother would not

have died," she added. "But I know that even
now, whatsoever *thou* shalt ask of God " —

"He shall rise again," replied Jesus quickly. He
was plainly more moved by the confidence of the
family than he could have been if he had been
covered with the hottest reproaches of grief and of
disappointed friendship. He seemed anxious now to
meet Martha on her own ground, and to interpret
the inexplicable position in which he had placed
himself.

"Yes, Lord, I know. At the last day," said
Martha drearily.

Jesus lifted his face, his clasped hands parted and
outstretched above the weeping woman's head. The
by-standers had ceased to whisper. Evening was
coming on. The light was low. The air was quiet.
Clearly through the stillness arose the voice of the
Nazarene, uttering for the first time the great words
that have thrilled the mourners of the world for
two thousand years, from the wail of that anguish
to the cry of our own, and which will be uttered in
triumph till the burial hour of death itself shall
strike : "*I am the Resurrection and the Life.* He
that believeth on me, though he were dead . . . shall
live." . . .

Mary was not like Martha. She could not go
hurrying out among all the neighbors. Her heart
was breaking. She could not speak. She would
answer no questions. She was crushed by the astonished despair which begins when the first excitement
of the burial is past. She was lying tearless, deso-

late, comfortless, when Martha came back for her. The superior will of the elder sister could not do much with the grief of Mary. The gentle mourner had developed the unexpected decision which suffering gives sometimes to the docile. Mary shook her head when Martha, in considerable excitement, took her by the hand, indicating that they were to go forth together, and at once.

"But the Rabbi calls for you," urged Martha, with some of the impatience which the stronger feels for the weaker sufferer.

Mary arose without a word, veiled herself, and went out.

Now Jesus dreaded this meeting with Mary; she would make it harder than the elder sister had. She was so sensitive, so dependent; her nature was all love; Lazarus had been her idol. They had been nearer of an age than he and Martha; they were playmates in their little years and confidants in their larger ones. Mary was very dear to Jesus. Her high-minded nature, her thoughtfulness, her delicacy, her essential womanliness appealed to him. And Mary had trusted him; he remembered how much!

Bereaved of her brother, bereaved of her friendship, shaken of her belief in everything that had made the Rabbi precious and grand to her, *could* she trust him still? She had not the force of will for it. But she had the force of love for it. One look into her delicate, haggard face told him that. In spite of everything that had happened, she trusted him utterly. This was the kind of trust for which he sought all his life. Where had he found it before?

" If *thou* hadst been here," she began, in Martha's very words, " he had not died, — he had not died ! "

But there she faltered and broke quite down ; and the poor girl sobbed so piteously that the coldest eye in the crowd softened, and many a neighbor turned his face away. Mary had thrown herself upon the ground at the healer's feet ; her lips and her tears touched them. His face worked ; he was greatly moved ; it seemed as if he could not bear to look at her.

Suddenly the by-standers heard a heart-breaking sound. It was the groan of a strong and sensitive man, who has repressed the expression of grief till it has revolted against him, and will obey him no longer.

The Nazarene was weeping.

.   .   .   .

Lazarus had lain in his elaborate tomb three days ; being four days dead. It was the fancy of his people to believe that the spirit clung to the flesh until such time, when it parted therefrom forever ; and the laws that govern the insensate body when deprived of its lord, the soul, should, as a consequence, begin to act without hindrance.

The tomb of Lazarus was by the wayside, carved into the limestone of the hill on which the village was built. It was, in fact, a spacious cave running deep into the rock ; one descended into it by many steps ; it was protected by a heavy, movable slab. The silver foliage of olive-trees softened the scenery above it ; flowering vines hung over the façade of the vault, and everything that wealth and family deference knew how to do had signalized it; but there was nothing cheerful about it. The Hebrew grave knew not the hopes of a happier faith, and little of the delicacies of modern feeling. Lazarus was dead. He was buried. There was no more to be said. He was locked back into the cells of the earth's ancient prison, and despair, the jailer, held the keys.

"Where have you laid him?" the healer had asked, in a voice almost inaudible from grief.

Some one had silently pointed in the direction of the family burial place.

Some one else had said:

"See! How much he loved him!"

Whispering and muttering, the collection of people, which was now large for a village crowd, had followed the Rabbi, his disciples, and the bereaved family. The outside mourners hastened to swell the number. As they approached the tomb, they began to wail aloud officiously. This seemed to trouble the Nazarene; and one of the twelve tried to hush the dreary sounds.

The sun was now declining fast. The evening was cool. The sky was a deep, palpitating blue, brushed with rose, that had taken on the form of a great wing, extending almost from west to east. This was an unusual effect, and attracted attention. Shadows were already beginning to dream among the olive-trees. The air was remarkably still. Not a leaf stirred. There was no more breath in the wind than there was life behind the stone that locked the cavern. The living themselves felt suffocated. Respiration seemed to be ceasing in the world.

Jesus stood alone, apart from his friends. He and the tomb faced each other. He regarded it steadily. The sepulchre seemed to frown. The wing of rose-color in the skies deepened slightly. The tint was reflected upon the white robe of Jesus. His hands were clasped so tightly that they seemed welded together; and his fingers darkened towards their tips, where the circulation was checked. The features of his face were rigid. He observed no one. No man dared address him.

What thoughts, incommunicable, incomprehensible, traversed the solitary corridors of his mind? The supreme deed of his life lay before him. What if he failed in it? What had he staked on it? His reputation for common, human gratitude and loyalty to friendship was precious to him. His fame as a compassionate healer had its noble value. If these went, what should he leave? The memory of a man who had preached great truths and neglected practical virtues, — a prospect peculiarly abhorrent to him. But if these went, what else would go with them? What grander name, what more transcendent claim? If the events of the next half hour did not verify the most solemn, the most mysterious assumptions of his history, what would be lost? The hopes, the ideals, the future of one heart-broken man? Nay; the hopes, the ideals, the future of a world. For thus he did believe. "I am the Resurrection," he had said; "I am the Life."

The moment was so critical that he covered his face with his hands, that no man might see its exigency. But all men felt that he was praying.

When Jesus lifted his face, the people fell back. The stillness without was as deep as that within the tomb. He pointed to the stone.

" Roll it away ! " he commanded.

Recoiling hands obeyed him. Ghastly fear had settled upon the spectators. Many of them would have escaped the scene if they had found themselves able to stir.

Jesus advanced slowly. He had grown very pale. Otherwise he showed no agitation. He treated the tomb authoritatively. He had the aspect of a king about to overthrow a great foe.

" *Lazarus ?* "

Something in the accent laid upon this single word shook the souls of those who heard it. Could a dead man hear ? Should the buried answer ? Jesus bent as if he would have entered the place of burial.

" *Lazarus !* Come forth ! "

The shuddering breaths of the people could be distinctly heard. For a moment there was no other answer to this awful summons. Then the sepulchre replied. She yielded hard. Centuries crowded those moments. Dusk was deepening. Within the house of death it was quite dark. . . .

Are we sane men or delirious ? We are too many to be mad ! Cling together ! Close up, shoulder to shoulder. Take courage and reason from one another's eyes. For what, in God's name, do we see ? . . .

Stooping to pass through the low door of the tomb, the outlines of a fearful figure stirred.

Lazarus, four days a dead man, hindered by his grave-clothes, moved with difficulty. He slowly raised himself upright, walked out a few steps, stood bewildered among all the people, and solemnly regarded the Nazarene.

CHAPTER XIII

INTO JERUSALEM

WHAT was to be said? Jerusalem and her suburbs trembled with wonder and dismay. The astounding story admitted of no qualifying interpretation. It must be accepted or rejected altogether.
It soon became evident that rejection was impossible.
Lazarus had been a live man a week ago. Dead,
and four days buried yesterday, he was alive to-day.
It was only necessary to visit Bethany and see for
one's self. Hundreds hurried, gaping, to the spot.
Curiosity inundated the village. His house was besieged. It was only a matter of hours before the
incredible facts were dashed into the face of the
church. The governing authorities took fright.
The Sanhedrin was hastily convened. The case of
the Jewish nation against Jesus of Nazareth was
formally opened that very Friday, within twenty-
four hours after Lazarus had emerged from his
tomb, and stood staring amid the flowers, in the
approach of night, among the appalled and silent
witnesses of the inconceivable truth.

Strictly speaking, the preliminaries to the arrest
of the great heretic were all illegal. The Sanhedrin
had no civil or criminal jurisdiction, except by the
mercy of Rome, and the hastiness of their procedure

was in itself irregular. But all formalities, ecclesiastical, civic, or humane, were distorted by one mad thrust. Lazarus had come out of his grave, — how, who could pretend to explain? But he was out, and the Nazarene had done the deed. The people were frenzied with the thrill of it. They were massing from all quarters to rally about Jesus. The cry, "Messiah! the Messiah!" rang through capital and countryside.

Pharisees and Sadducees, priests and scribes, stood quaking. The greatest insurrection of Hebrew record seemed to be upon them. It would be no insignificant riot if this terrible Rabbi should lift a finger to enforce his royal claims. Then Rome would stir. Her legions would awake. Her awful force would roll upon the rebels. The Temple, the nation, would be ground to dust that a wind might blow away. And whose fault that? His, — all his; this rustic pretender's, this indomitable preacher's, this scandalous heretic's! The venom against Jesus, always sullenly lurking among the religious classes, now developed into sudden rabies. One of those passionate ecclesiastical hatreds which challenge all other forms of rage swept through the Sanhedrin.

In the uproar of indecision, — all united only in fearing and abhorring the Nazarene, no two agreed as to what should be done to him, — the cold voice of the chief ecclesiastical officer was heard.

Joseph Caiaphas, being High-priest of the Jewish nation, and forever to be known by this deed that he did, arose and adroitly put the case. In a few cynical words, sedulously adapted to inflame the

animosity and alarm of the Sanhedrin, he brought
it to his will.   The sinister suggestion, that here was
one man's life against the life of a nation, was
enough.   A glow of what was called patriotism suffused the convention.   Jesus of Nazareth was hotly
indicted as a criminal subject to the death penalty.

In Jerusalem what restlessness, what malice!   In
Bethany what happiness, what peace!

Jesus had done one of the bravest deeds of his
life.   He had gone straight from the opened sepulchre to the house of his friends.   In the blazing
state of public feeling, this was a dangerous step.
The rumor of the resurrection had fired all his
friends and foes, and, in the region of the capital,
his foes held the balance of power.   Why did he
not immediately and quietly slip away, as he had
often done before when the wonder-working force in
him had gone too far for his own personal safety?
But his heart and purpose took him, and he went
home with Lazarus.

Curtained by the soft, warm night, the family
group trod in a celestial hush.   For very awe the
neighbors and spectators held aloof, following at the
distance of their fear.

Four silent figures moved on together up the village street.   No man dared approach them.   Mary
and Martha fell behind; Martha was sobbing with
joy, but Mary was as still as a marble saint.   Before
them, separate from tears or smiles, from common
human laws or expression, two leaned together and
apart from all the world.   Dim in the darkness, Laza-

rus clung to the strong arm whose support he sought.
He seemed to be listening yet for the voice that had
summoned him from the fastnesses of death. But
Jesus did not speak. Moving like spirits, the twain
passed on. And so Lazarus came to his house. The
mourners had left it but an hour ago. The over-
turned tables and couches — the customary signals
of affliction — were not yet replaced. The disorder
of death and burial still pervaded the expectant
court and the beautiful rooms. All were empty.
The family were alone. No profane eye witnessed
that solemn coming home. At the threshold Jesus
paused, and extended his arms in benediction and
in welcome. Lazarus fell, like a shadow, at his feet.
The women dropped upon their faces. No one
spoke. The faint light from one hanging lamp left
by the mourners revealed the majestic form but not
the inscrutable face of the Nazarene.

. . . In this shelter of awe, of joy, of remoteness
from all usual pains and pleasures, he remained for
the respite and the risk of several days and nights.
Jerusalem began to mutter for his life, but he stayed
on. He was visible to no man. Shut in with the
solemn experience of that one family selected to
know the ecstasy of heaven while enduring the anguish of earth, he veiled himself.

Who shall say what interchange of feeling or of
thought in that quiet space passed between himself
and the living man who had been dead? Who
knows if Lazarus needed yet the glorious vitality,
the supernal power, which had dragged him from
dissolution? Is it to be thought that Jesus, careful

for the permanence of the mighty thing that had
been done, chose to watch for a little over the man
on whose body he had wrought the deed of a divinity? He had done it under the limitations of a
man. What if Lazarus showed signs of weakness,
of relapse into the disease which had slain him? If
he should sink suddenly? If the astonished vital
force, wrenched back into the mortal frame by the
law above laws which it had obeyed, should hesitate
anywhere? Dead Lazarus lived. Who could say
that he would continue to live?

Sensitiveness to possible failure, and anxiety for
results, exist in proportion to refinement of power.
In those days smitten with awe and ecstasy, whose
scroll no one unrolled with the shielded family at
Bethany, did the heart of their great friend quiver
with an anxiety over the condition of Lazarus which
even they could not divine or share?

These were the last days of happiness or calm
which Jesus of Nazareth was to know in the land
that he had tried to bless with his mysterious personality, and which now resounded with curses upon
his gentle head.

This last little cup of peace was tinged — as everything in his life was discolored with suffering — by
the solitary and tremendous responsibilities attach-
ing to him who could give a dead man life.

The future of the Christian faith rested at the
crisis, to an extent impossible to measure, upon the
necessity that Lazarus should remain a live man for
a sufficient time. It has been said [1] that he lived
on for thirty years.

[1] Tradition.

Bearing within himself the experience of corruption, what vigor did he need to reconquer the sources
of life! How did he get it? Holding the awful secrets of death, at whose door humanity has knocked
in vain for knowledge from the break of time till
now, did he ever reveal them by a word, a sign?
Did curious Martha or reverent Mary ever share
with him one lesson of his terrible and blessed education? Rather to his last hour did there rest upon
Lazarus something of the dignity of death. His lips
were closed. No person pried upon their reticence.
His lips were closed like those of the sepulchre from
which he had been summoned, and to whose dark
hospitality he must — who can guess with what
untold reluctance? who can say with what inexpressible hope and courage? — on some day return.

Be these things as they may, the dead man was
alive. By hundreds, by thousands, the witnesses of
the fact poured into Bethany. So intense was the
public excitement that the Sanhedrin were at their
wits' end. It is a matter of history that, before the
month was out within whose dark span the greatest
of dramas was to thrill the world, the authorities of
the Jewish Church seriously contemplated an attempt to put Lazarus to death again.

The Nazarene was now in imminent peril. Threats
of excommunication against any person who acknowledged his Messianic claims vied with popular in-
ducements to effect his arrest. It was determined
at all hazards to put a stop to his career. The danger became so acute that Jesus reluctantly left
Bethany.

The strange impressions under which his movements were ordered produced a plan of action which
gave for the moment to the most courageous of men
the appearance of retreat from his fate.

" My time is not yet come," was a favorite phrase
with him. Suddenly he disappeared. Jerusalem
and Bethany sought without success for him. The
detectives of the Sanhedrin tracked him in vain.

At a sufficient distance from their malice; in a
little town known as Ephraim, always remembered
lovingly for the shelter that it gave to the hunted
man at the cruelest crisis of his lot; on the borders
of the wilderness, he crept into a temporary safety.
But he dared not, or he did not, long remain in any
one retreat. He was soon heard of in Perea, and
even in certain districts of Galilee. The itinerant
habits of his public life were still strong upon him.
He could not keep still. He could not stop work.
With intensified energy he pursued the service to
humanity which he so passionately loved. To lighten
suffering! To ease sickness! To help poverty!
To shame guilt! To confirm purity! To heal, to
comfort, to teach, to warn! With exclamatory force
these motives propelled him. Those last few weeks
brimmed with marvels wrought out of a dedication
which would have burned him to ashes but for his
illustrious sanity. He kept his perfect self-possession. He never lost his eminent calm. He worked
as if he were to work on forever.

Lepers crawling to him ran from him: they came
corrupt; they went clean. The born blind groped
to him, and left him, lingering reluctantly for the

last sight of his face, — the first human countenance that they had ever seen, the one to be retained by the newly responsive, sensitive retina as the tenderest it should ever see. His heart, his mind, were full. It seemed as if he gave himself no time to consider his own fate. He ignored his own perils. He worked as if he had been the most popular Rabbi in Palestine.

The condemned heretic never wore the aspect of an offender.

He did not even have the comfort which comes from the grandeur of suffering greatly endured and let alone. He was haunted and taunted by the pettiest things.

In the territory of Herod deliberate traps were laid for the views of Jesus about divorce, it being the purpose publicly to draw from him expressions of opinion which would expose him to the vengeance of the monarch, whose family history made him irritable on this delicate point.

John the prophet had perished for such cause. Why not this other? Jesus parried the diabolic casuistry with adroitness which astounded and silenced the wiliest polemicists in the province. They could not even involve him in a rabbinical controversy, that might have opened a fresh charge of heresy against him then and there.

He was pursued by paltry annoyances even among his own friends. Those nearest to him fretted him with incredible obtuseness. His very dearest cut him with the slenderest blades.

His favorite disciples wrangled even then about

their official positions at right and left of him when he should come to the throne. He found it impossible to make them understand the very essence of his claims, the very basis of his doctrines. Feminine ambition laid a little finger on his great troubles, and the mother of James and John preferred a formal petition for the advancement of her sons when he should come into political power. He knew to the full the incoherence of human fate which does not relieve great souls moving on grand errands of small worries, or free the noble from paltry cares.

His chosen twelve gave themselves over to jealousies almost too petty to credit or to record, while this sad and solitary man, going patiently to defeat, was making ready for death.

There now began the most extraordinary episode in the annals of missionary travel, — the last journey of the Nazarene to Jerusalem. While yet in a safe position, he abruptly elected to thrust himself into danger. Sheltered, he tore himself out of his refuge. It was the bud of the year. Passover time was coming on. It was not necessary for him to attend the great festival, — he, an excommunicated church-member, whose deference to ecclesiastical customs could do nothing but irritate. But, as if he were yet one of the most honored of her rabbis, he chose to respect the religious observances of his church. Quite as if nothing had happened, exactly as if nothing were at stake, he started with his twelve and some other friends, forming one of the little festive bands with which Palestine was now stirring joyously.

He was under no delusion. No false hope played with his unerring intelligence. He knew perfectly what that journey meant. Deliberately he chose to put himself into the very throat of danger. Steadily, sturdily, without one backward step, without one hesitating movement, he marched to his doom.

Its very details were made, at that early day, quite evident to him. How, no one asked. Upon his exquisite sensitiveness the whole horrible minutiæ were stamped. All through those tired days and waking nights he lived his fate through before its time. The delicacy of imagination, which is the essence of power and pleasure in the highest organization, is always the fatal source of its pain. He knew to the uttermost the relentlessness of this law. Add to this his mystical enlightenment as to facts unknown to other men. Here was illumination whose working is no easier for us to explain to-day than it was for his fishermen friends to comprehend as they turned their faces towards Jerusalem with him in the laughing spring weather. They alone among all the happy pilgrims were going upon an awful errand which they did not, would not, could not understand.

He tried to explain it to them as they traveled. He told them dreadful things. He used unsparing language. What he should undergo, and when and where, he related with distinctness. He spoke with calmness of unendurable torment.

Where were the senses of his friends? Dulled by trouble, or blunted by love? Dazed, perhaps, by the sheer force of events which hurried them along a course inconceivable to their prepossessions. They acted like people stupefied by the conviction that they knew better than their Rabbi what should happen to him. Aching for sympathy, he found himself denied it because his dearest friends did not credit his preconsciousness of his fate. They treated him as too sanguine persons treat those more sensitive, and hence more anxious than themselves, dismissing the matter as the nightmare of an unhealthy temperament. Yet it were unphilosophical to blame them. He never did. It was a severe education that their affection for their Lord brought upon these simple-natured men. They loved him according to their capacity. At least it was the best kind of love that he had. He clung to it more and more wistfully as the end drew on.

Burning Jericho swam in a crater of heat. The travelers would have known where they were by the temperature, if not by the map. They must pass through a scorched and treeless region to reach the place, and they arrived exhausted. This was the town where the inhabitants could wear nothing warmer than linen in winter. And spring was bursting into summer now. The heat was oppressive to strangers, and more than hard enough to those who had traveled on foot, and who reached the city at the end of a long day's march. The sky was like a metal cover shutting one down into a brazier set upon coals. The air was a furnace.

Jesus felt his strength attacked by the climate of this place. It was a little misery, but it made his greater sufferings more difficult to bear. The scented gusts of fire beat without mercy upon his burning face and brow. The too-sweet odors of Jericho the Perfumed aroused distaste in fine senses. He lifted his eyes wearily to the balsam-plantations, whose rich gums devoured the freshness of the air. These were the famous plantations once given by Anthony to Cleopatra, and sold by her to Herod. Here was a bustling town. The streets were full and noisy. Trade chattered everywhere, — the great balsam traffic of Palestine, which made this spot the centre of schemes and frauds, and the meeting-place of commercial natures. Rome took heavy revenues there, and made much account of her tax-collectors, whose duties were not light in such a place, and whose persons were bitterly unpopular with her subjects. The Hebrews shunned these men with a distrust as scorching as the atmosphere.

The chief collector, wishing to see the great Rabbi as he entered the perfumed city at the head of his band of pilgrims, climbed into a thick tree by the roadside to escape the crush of the crowd, for he was an under-sized man, and also to escape its enmity, for he was not an obtuse person. There he quietly took the measure of the famous preacher.

He saw a tall, finely modeled man, browned by the excess of the sun, but singularly without redness or rudeness of complexion. Jesus was walking slowly. His staff looked ready to drop from his tired hand; it had a white tint at the tip, like a sceptre of silver blazing in the hot air. His face

bore signs of weariness both of the spirit and of the
flesh, but none of weakness.

A puzzling strength seemed to fortify this exhausted pilgrim. The collector examined him with
a discernment in which reverence began to get the
better of curiosity. He did not speak to the distinguished Rabbi. He would have liked to do so; his
heart went out in such a wave of longing as this
man of public experience had never felt to any private citizen. Official life had done its cold work
upon him; sly opportunities had not passed him by;
the consciousness of always being unpopular had
told upon him; he was accumulating peccadillos;
ideas of honor to which he had sworn allegiance at
the outset of his career were somehow slipping into
phantasmagoria. The man of the world who had
sunk a little lower than he was meant to go, or than
he had ever thought to be, regarded the Nazarene
with a strange pang, half shame, half moral resolve.
Then he saw that Jesus had stopped, and was looking him full in the face.

"Come down, Zacchæus," said the Rabbi; "I
sup at your house."

It had not been a cautious thing to do, but Jesus
had done it with his usual independence. The Jews
hated the collector, but Jesus became the guest of
Zacchæus at Jericho without asking his countrymen's permission. The moral crisis in the life of
an unpopular and tempted man appealed to him so
powerfully that he put aside every other consideration to reach it. This one soul above all others in
Jericho needed him. Here was one of the opportu-

nities to help an individual which he never disregarded.

The collector entertained the Rabbi deferentially; he poured out the hospitality of an opulent home with the generous gratitude of a man who has been forced back to his true self by the power of a higher nature. But the people muttered.

At this stage of his royal career, what kind of a king was that? Zacchæus was not recognized in respectable Hebrew society. Should the Messiah of the nation fellowship with an outcast? Jesus ignored these complaints. But they stirred sound-waves in the hot balsamic air, and echoes of them came into the capital. Every Passover pilgrim carried his own tale. The conduct of the distinguished heretic was the subject of discussion in every tent, in every shop and house; there was not a political or ecclesiastical caucus in Jerusalem which did not hiss with his name.

Jesus found his acquaintance with this man of affairs at Jericho a comforting episode to himself. This successful effort to uplift the moral tone of another was a temporary diversion from the acute consciousness of his own lot. The two parted with a mutual regret. The man of the world looked reverently at the Nazarene: he felt that the man of another world existed; he had never believed it before; he tried to express his thoughts, — he who was adept in the diplomacy of Roman official life, — but he could not, and he turned away to hide his emotion.

Jesus moved on at the head of his pilgrim band. The bright morning blazed like a huge camp-fire.

The party walked on among the plantations. Jericho on her oasis added the breath of leaf-honey
to the perfumes of the balsams. In the sickening
scents, the path swam before the eyes of Jesus. His
thoughts swam, too. That brief distraction vanished
out of them. Jericho, its welcome, its hospitality,
the collector and his moral emergency, began to dim.
Images of unspeakable things which had beset the
imagination before returned. Outlines of terrible
scenes began to fill in. Jesus walked giddily, and
was seen once or twice to stagger. . . . The sun
smote his head and made a rim around it. . . .
What was that? *Thorns?* He passed his hand
over his brow and then examined the palm carefully.
What color did he see? One of the twelve spoke
to him. He found it impossible to answer. He
walked on silently. His head sank upon his breast.
. . . What sights! What sensations! Surely they
would pass soon. He quickened his steps. But it
all kept pace with him. . . .

So he came into the great gorge through which
the road from Jericho wound harshly towards Jerusalem. It was a steep, rocky cut, rough to pass and
haunted by robbers. Six hours' travel on foot took
the ascent from six hundred feet below to nearly
three thousand above the level of the Mediterranean.
It was an exhausting climb.

Jesus walked at the head of his Passover band.
Shadows and lights from the broken features of the
rocks that lined the way alternately illuminated and
veiled his ascending figure. The gorge grew ruder.
Its dreariness deepened. He looked down into its

grim depths with a sick repulsion; they seemed to be waiting below for him.

" Though I walk through the valley of death " — Old words from the Scriptures of his people came to him. He reinforced his strength for the ascent, which he made powerfully and silently. Once or twice he slipped unaccountably, and seemed to weaken; but when asked what had befallen him, he made no reply.

At moments he moved like a man who carried some strange, intolerable burden.

. . . What was that upon his shoulders, bearing heavily upon them, crushing him to the ground? Had the light spring air acquired weight? He put up his hand and brushed off something unseen. It seemed to him to have a frightful shape, significant of disgrace, portending agony.

" Through the valley of the shadow . . . *Thou* shalt be with me."

.   .   .   .

And now the festal bands began to gather themselves in preparation for the journey's end. Jerusalem lay yonder; the city of God and of his people. Soon the marble and gold of the Temple would cut the glittering air. Soon the ancient Songs of Ascent would swell from ten thousand throats as the pilgrims climbed the last slopes to the sacred city. Soon the joyful solemnity of the Passover supper would blot the hardship of the pilgrimage from a weary memory. The lambs, already bound and bleating, with gentle, patient faces waited for the sacrifice.

JERUSALEM FROM MOUNT OF OLIVES

It was Bethany, the peaceful hamlet carried on the shoulder of the Mount of Olives. Jesus and his party had lingered here. It lacked now six days of the Passover. He longed for a temporary rest, for the touch of tried friendship. His emergency was so great that he felt a pathetic need of a little comfort.

The usual Passover crowd was increased to an extraordinary size. From all corners of Palestine and all quarters of the East, sightseers had added themselves to the customary pilgrims. Cold curiosity, political and ecclesiastical malice, blotted the religious anniversary.

The name of Jesus of Nazareth was on every lip. Rumor had run far and wide with the recent events of his career. It was said that he was coming into Jerusalem at the head of phalanxes; that he was prepared to take the city by some adroit feint or solid blow; that he was ready to defy Rome, to head a successful insurrection, and to capture the throne. It was no longer a secret that the Sanhedrin had indicted him, and that this condemned heretic would not fly. On the contrary, he had faced his fate deliberately, and had been seen within two miles of the capital. Crisis was in the air. All the world hurried to be present at the climax. Crowds poured out into Bethany to obtain a sight of the great offender.

But in Bethany he was loved and trusted, and Bethany met the general agitation by a feast whereat he was the guest of honor. It was a Sabbath feast, for he had arrived on Friday evening. Although

the supper was held in a private house, it partook of
a public character.

His personal friends, the most distinguished citizens in the village, were prominent in the entertainment.   Living Lazarus himself, the startling object
of every gaze, was present.

Martha's housewifely genius was lavished upon
the occasion.   She meant to make this a splendid
affair.   True, Lazarus was alive and the Rabbi had
come, but supper must be properly served nevertheless.   Martha was very busy.

But Mary had slipped away out of sight, no one
knew why ; and it was a general surprise when she
was discovered in the attitude of worship at the
Rabbi's feet.   A precious perfume swiftly filled
the dining-hall, and it was seen that Mary had
broken a box of spikenard and was anointing Jesus
with the costly tribute.

The treasurer of the twelve — he whose name has
become the synonym of infamy — spoke up curtly
with caustic reproach :

" This spikenard was worth nearly fifty dollars.
Why was it not sold and the proceeds given to
charity ? "

Strictly, there was not much force in this charge
of extravagance, for fifty dollars would have been
a small price at Rome for an alabastron of Indian
nard.   But Judas had the adroitness of an undetected peculator.   He set up pseudo-philanthropic
standards, and recalled the general poverty.   It was
well known that two hundred dinars (about thirty
dollars) could be made to provide bread for five

thousand families, and that one dinar made the wages of a day-laborer.

" This vast sum should have been given to the poor," urged the treasurer severely.

The eyes of Jesus softly sought those of Mary. He smiled gravely.

Mary glanced from him to her brother, then looked back at the Rabbi. Her heart was so full of adoration that she could not have spoken a word. Lazarus watched the two in the sacred silence which now so often enveloped him. He made no effort to enter into the scene.

Slowly raising one white, tremulous finger, Mary pointed at her brother solemnly, and sank upon her knees at the feet of Jesus. There she veiled her face. The eyes of the guests filled.

A fragment of the broken alabastron rolled in the direction of Judas, who observed it uncomfortably.

Jesus turned his head. The brilliant dining-hall floated before his eyes. His breath halted for an instant. He glanced at his feet, from which Mary was tenderly wiping the scented ointment. Almost imperceptibly he started, as one does who sees something painful which is unnoticed by others. . . . Was that blood ? What stabbed — what hurt him so ?

A burning tear, a single one, had fallen upon his foot from Mary's lowered lashes.

" Let her alone," said Jesus, not with unsteady lip ; " she has done this for my burial."

Now he regarded his treasurer with a firm eye ; it gave out no irritation, no resentment. Jesus spoke gently.

In a few poignant words he suggested that charity was never without its opportunities and its objects.

" But me ye will not have always." Then his wistful voice rose into the ring of prophecy :

" I tell you wherever this Gospel shall be preached, this thing that she has done for me shall be spoken. It shall be a memorial of her throughout the world."

It had gone abroad that the Nazarene had now in deed and truth come to the front of his revolution, and that he was about to make his entrance into Jerusalem in the triumph and splendor which the people love to see wasted about their heroes, when, springing from the humblest to the highest rank, the strong will and the superior soul accept the station that they have created for themselves.

The man and the moment had met. It was said that Jesus had at last cast away his unaccountable reluctance to filling his true position. It was said that he was done with all those qualms and peculiarities which had prevented him from taking the natural advantage of his popularity. It was known that the indictment against his life, the enmity of the church and the state, had produced no effect upon him. Nothing checked his purpose. Nothing modified his courage or his independence. He had boldly left his shelter at Bethany. He was coming down the Mount of Olives. He was advancing towards Jerusalem. Intense excitement pervaded the capital. Roman officer and Hebrew ecclesiastic were nigh to love each other for the first time in their common hatred of the Nazarene. The Sanhedrin were stupefied. The government, though scornful of the rustics, was perplexed.

It seemed the easiest thing in the world to capture this agitator now.

But in fact it had never been more inexpedient to do so. Whence had his friends sprung? The earth, the very air, seemed to have created them. Who would have believed that this hunted heretic had such a following? *Unpopular?* Why, it was as if the whole world had wings and flew to him. It was too true that Jerusalem hated him with deadly persistence. But Jerusalem was under the restraints which control a host. Her streets overflowed with pilgrims from all parts of Palestine, and with visitors from the East. This multitude of strangers, familiar only with the main facts in the life of the Nazarene, and unembarrassed by local dissensions, were quivering with cordial interest in him. His direst foe dared not strike out till it was to be seen which way the currents would set.

From her Temple to her gates, Jerusalem watched for him.

Who knew what secret service had been planning the *coup* of this brilliant day? What unknown resources had the carpenter commanded? What unestimated forces could thrust over the talith of the Rabbi the purple of the King? What legions were at his back? What splendors glittered before him? What mounted guardsmen, what shining mail, what serried edges of spears, blazed around him? On a caparisoned charger he was mounted proudly. His war-horse already scented blood. Magnificent in attire, imperious in carriage, he was coming on to capture the city. His long reserve, his

false humility, had tossed off its mask. The true
force of this remarkable man had now expressed
itself. To make himself Dictator, to become King
of the nation, was clearly his intention. The people seemed to be at his feet. What would be the
consequence?

The unrest deepened in the capital. The officers
of Rome could not deny that they shared it, though
treating the matter with well-bred indifference. The
Jewish Church sent her delegates into the crowd
with orders to report what was to be seen. Hurried
councils and secret threats and plots muttered in
Temple and palace.

The mob rushed on. The jam thickened. The
uproar increased. The Nazarene was said to have
descended the mountain, to be crossing the valley, to
be climbing the sacred hills of Zion. In an hour —
in minutes — he would be in sight. He and his
retinue were coming up rapidly, splendidly. In a
moment — Ah, there!

The cries of the multitude rose to the heavens.
For a space, one could neither hear nor see. A craze
to witness the gorgeous spectacle seized the quietest
man in the crowd. A kind of glorious madness set
in. Who would have believed that this country
Rabbi could have commanded such a demonstration?

Ah, behold! at last! That is he. Here is the
heretic. See the madman. Look at the Sabbath-
breaker, the blasphemer, the excommunicated Rabbi.
There is the revolutionist, the pretender. . . . Rub
the eyes well. Look again. Doubt your senses, but
look once more.

The day was quiet and warm. Spring sang outside of the city. The sky was a pallid, pure color.
All the people were in their Passover clothes. Festal
bands were coming up everywhere, and these from
without and those others, the throng from within the
capital, met in a mass.

In the centre of it was a plain man. He rode a
young animal whose neck had never before known
the bridle, — the colt of an ass, which, it was said,
had been mysteriously found, or strangely offered
to his service. No trappings, no tricks of effect,
deviated from the simplicity of his mount. No steed
of war bore him on his errand of peace. He had no
arms and no armor. There was no retinue. Not a
guardsman lifted a spear-tip to protect this defenseless
man. His courtiers were a motley group, fishermen
and common folk: they walked behind him sturdily;
they had strong, serious faces, like those of men
whose characters had been tried and were capable of
further test; their garments were poor; a few women
were among the lot, modest and with thoughtful expressions. When one came to examine the Nazarene
himself — oh, amazement! He was but the simplest,
the gentlest of men. *Pretender?* Nay, the most
unpretending hero who ever showed himself at the
front of a national crisis. He was clad in his ordinary dress, the hyacinth-colored talith of the Rabbi.
The blue of his robe and the tint of the sky were
felt to harmonize without the reflection that they
did so. His head was bare. It wore no crown but
the touch of the Passover sunlight.

His nervous hand held no sceptre. Some one came

up as he passed through the suburban gardens, and reverently offered him a spray of a palm-branch; he took it appreciatively.

Palms were everywhere. The trees were stripped of their branches. Men and women tore them and flung them. A green carpet fell at the feet of Jesus, and he rode over it. Hosannas rose higher. The people went mad with the welcome of him. They cast off their cloaks and spread them in his way. He rode on as if he had been riding over velvet and treading upon pearls.

Now came a fresh outburst of voices and of warm-hearted words:

" Blessed be our King!"

" Peace in Heaven!"

" Glory in the Highest! Praise God for His mighty works! Blessed be Jesus our King!"

It was afterwards said that the most loving of these outcries came from the long-sick whom the healer had cured; and some of them from the sick of sin to whom he had given the health of purity; and some from the bereaved to whom he had restored the dying or the dead; that especially the very poor, and the altogether neglected, and the heart-broken whom he only had ever tried to comfort, and persons of no consequence whom only he had ever remembered, were in his retinue that day. These mingled their hosannas with the plaudits of the stranger pilgrims who had come out of the city. It was said, indeed, that Jesus was borne into the capital on the love of those who knew him best, and the trust of those who knew him least.

But as he rode along, it was noticed that his eyes were fixed upon Jerusalem. The stately city, hindered by Olivet, visible only at two or three points of the journey, now rose haughtily before him, terrace upon terrace, straight from the Valley of Kedron, as if from an abyss. From the Palace of the Maccabees and that of the High-priest to the towers and gardens of Herod, Jerusalem shot up glittering. Her architecture had a cold look. Something about it seemed to smile cruelly.

The countenance of Jesus melted and broke. Those nearest him heard murmured words, — one involuntary cry :

"Ah, Jerusalem! If thou hadst known" — Then he commanded himself and rode on. His face was wet. Something inexpressible on it wrung the heart to see. But his demeanor was high, and so quiet that those whose hosannas had rung the loudest began to fall silent, one by one. A sudden hush smote the vociferating throng.

In a silence which no man could understand, either in himself or in another, Jesus, the prophet of Nazareth in Galilee, passed through the Gate Shusan and entered the royal city.

Thus the great democrat, traveling like a peasant, assuming and asserting nothing, avoiding lawlessness, spurning display, humble and gentle, followed and blessed by the poor, and loved by the unhappy, treated the practical chance of political power.

Thus he put aside the opportunity of his life and of his age.

CHAPTER XIV

IN THE TEMPLE

WITHOUT a symptom of fear the indicted man went straight into the Temple and remained there for a while. His manner was perfectly self-possessed, and he preserved a noticeable silence, making no public address that day to the turbulent people. Sheer amazement at his courage held the hands of the law back from him. Unmolested as he came, he returned that night to Bethany and to his friends.

There they gave him such solace as they could. It was little enough. His demeanor forbade intrusion. The very air that he breathed seemed surcharged with unknown tragedy. He was still cheerful, but the lines on his face grew tense. To the loyalty of the twelve the three at Bethany added an eager devotion, and two of these a subtler comprehension. The solemn reticence of Lazarus, the watchful tenderness of Mary, protected Jesus from idle talk. His puzzled disciples would imitate this reserve, this calm.

Here for a space he felt that he was so loved that it mattered less whether he were understood or not. He tried for the moment to throw off his intolerable burden. Love and life seemed to be of necessity one force united to demolish the fact of death.

Quiet affection, home, peace, temporary respite from trouble, wrought upon him something of the incredulousness of pain and mortality which it is their nature to arouse in us all. The images of his torment retreated. That night the overstrained man knew the bliss of a little sleep. He needed to, for it was one of the last when rest was possible, either by the friction of events, or from the condition of his own brain and nerves. He awaked to thank God that any had been permitted him.

But in the morning the consciousness of everything returned. His true position was not to be ignored. He faced it at once, and went directly into the capital. He acted like one who was more fearful of seeming to fly from danger than of danger itself. He was as a man moving upon a terrible errand whose object might be defeated if he deviated by a thought's breadth from a certain course.

Those most in his confidence could not tell how definite his impressions were becoming of the manner or the moment of his fate. Did he go into Jerusalem each day knowing or unknowing whether it would be his last? Could he or could he not yet perceive precisely whence the blow would fall, or who would strike it?

The group at Bethany held the breath, and choked the sobs, and adored him the more because they could not help knowing that but for them he might not have been in the strait that he was.

For this thing was true, and time has confirmed the fact. But for Lazarus, the story of Jesus of Nazareth might have been a different one to tell.

Loyalty to friendship, sympathy with sorrow, — the tenderest, the greatest deed of his life, directly placed it in the final peril.

The popular feeling aroused by the wonder wrought at Bethany did not decline. The Sanhedrin became very much afraid of it. "The world has gone after him," said Pharisee to Pharisee.

Unconsciously (for it would have broken her heart to know it), Mary, the gentlest, the most loving of women, had herself added a mesh to the net which Bethany was destined to weave around him. The Indian nard lavished upon his feet served to mark the steps by which he was to be tracked and trapped. For this little incident had an unusual effect upon a low mind. It took disproportionate hold of the thoughts of Judas. The petty peculator had missed the opportunity to defraud on a large scale. He resented the loss of wealth which had never been, but might so easily have been, his. Then he was irritated by the social embarrassment of the Sabbath supper at Bethany. The gentle reproof of Jesus had rankled.

Out of any twelve picked men chosen for an important purpose, there is more than apt to be at least one failure. The treasurer of the society of Jesus had become that one. Judas had started in honestly enough. To begin with, he thought he loved his Rabbi, but the mercenary acid was in his nature. Dishonor had eaten its way by unnoticed degrees. He had deteriorated under the commission and concealment of small pecuniary irregularities.

Judas, the only Judean of the twelve, had been

an ambitious man as well. He counted upon political preferment when the Nazarene should come to
the throne ; he had relied more upon this than had
one or two others of the group who had said more
about it. He hid his expectations, but fondled them
accordingly. His present position gave him treacherous hopes. He looked to nothing less than to be
Treasurer of State at Jerusalem, perhaps even at
Rome. He was bitterly disappointed at the turn
which the affairs of Jesus were taking. Instead
of capturing a throne, the misguided revolutionist
seemed to be walking straight into a Roman dungeon. Judas was displeased with the whole situation. It began to occur to him that the disciples
had a case against their Rabbi. It struck him that
he had not been personally well treated.

Judas was not a brave man. He had the timidity
produced by undetected dishonor. He now began
to dwell upon the risks of his position. What
would become of the followers of the Nazarene in
the event of his downfall? He remembered the fiat
of excommunication — most dreadful of all things
to a Jewish mind — already extended to include all
persons who admitted the claims of this Messiah.
There had been other messiahs. There might be
others still. Was it possible, after all, that his Lord
was a pretender? How madly had he thrown away
his chances! This descendant of David, this heir
to the Theocracy, had entered Jerusalem without
a claim.

The thoughts of Judas began to coarsen fast.
Shapes of monstrous ideas groveling, crawled around

him. He tried to escape them at first. He called upon his early ideals, his young trust and affection. But his lost integrity did not respond. His sense of honor protested feebly for a little, but it had hardly life enough left in it to articulate. One day he put out his hesitating hand and choked it.

He had gone away from the others to think this thing out by himself. In a moment it was suddenly plain to him. Now he knew what he should do. He did actually stretch his grasping hand into the hot air, and bring the fingers together as if he were strangling some small, living creature. His face had grown old when he rose and came back to the side of his Rabbi. It was withered; it looked like the face of a corpse. For the highest in us is the vitality of us, and, in order to kill his honor, a man must kill himself. From that moment Judas moved about the living world like a dead man. He was done with it, and it with him. He made a few attempts, in which there was something to pity, to contend with his own condition. But the laws of moral corruption are as inexorable as those of physical decay. There is such a thing on this warm earth as a dead soul.

On Monday morning Jesus seemed restless, but his wan face was set with resolve. He was walking rapidly into the city, when he suddenly turned very faint. His broken night, part of it passed in the woods on the Mount of Olives, had poorly prepared him for the day's strain. He tried to find some fruit by the wayside, selecting a fig-tree, on which it seemed that some of last season's fruit might yet be hanging unobserved. But none was to be found, and with a momentary assumption of the royal manner which he sometimes wore, rebuking the tree (as he might have rebuked the faithless, fruitless city before him for its disregard of his nature and his needs), he went on.

The twelve wondered at this incident. The Rabbi was never impatient with little annoyances; he never scolded; this must have been a parable; but what? The fishermen walked behind him into Jerusalem puzzled, always puzzled. That Passover week was a dense and terrible darkness through which they beat about blindly, like birds caught in the clouds of a tempest. All they understood was that they loved their Lord, — their sad Lord, who was not going to be King, after all. The whole world was turning against him: he needed them; he had never needed them so much. They clung to him lovingly, but in their hearts these simple men were terrified at the position in which they found themselves.

Jesus arrived in the Temple at an early hour. Here he found the very same abuses which he had tried in vain to reform at the outset of his ministry. In the Court of the Gentiles the shops were full. Wine, oil, fruit, doves, were selling rapidly. Here were the brokers vociferating, precisely as they did three years ago, when he had lashed them out. The old wrongs were going on in the same old way. He felt the disappointment which any public teacher feels, in returning to the scene of a former effort, to find that everything that he has done to destroy an error is apparently thrown away. He looked about him for a while in bitter silence. Almost forgetting for the moment that he was approaching the end, and was not still at the beginning of his career, he began enthusiastically to repeat his wasted experiment to purify the holy place.

No whip was needed this time to scatter the offenders. The authoritative force and influence of Jesus had greatly increased. His voice was a lash. It struck and stung. The porters carrying unlawful loads by a short cut across the Temple to save steps, the brokers, the merchants, all the unwholesome pack ran scattering before the command which sprang from his lips.

Among the bedlam of noises, the bleating of lambs, the flutterings of frightened doves, the curses of the brokers, he stood, mournfully smiling. This excommunicated man ended his public career as he had begun it, by an act of passionate devotion to the honor and the purity of his church. Not to conform to the false because it was the ecclesiastical, but to protect the true because it was sacred, was his last as it had been his first devout and fearless care.

Attracted by the commotion of the scene, and trusting to the reputation for human mercy which always followed the Nazarene as if it had been white fire raying about his head, the beggars and decrepit folk from without the gates of the Temple began to clamor for him. As if to show what the religious idea really meant to him, Jesus turned quickly from the desecrated Temple courts to these miserable people.

Now, indeed, the mournfulness went out of his look, and for the moment his own high joyousness flashed back to it. His instinctive happiness in relieving suffering could not be repressed. They crawled to him, — the crippled, the neglected sick, the loathsome, and the blind ; and for one hour of eager gladness he gave himself to them. He healed with a dazzling swiftness never seen in his touch before; he comforted with a tenderness which might have melted the very stones in the Temple pavement beneath his unsandaled feet. — What a smile! It was soft fire from heaven itself. The artist who could have painted him as he looked then would have scorned the aureola. Jesus needed none but the light of his lips and eyes.

Now he had never cured any of his patients in the Temple before, and the scene aroused an awed attention. Many crowded in to hear and to see, and the physical discomfort of the press was as great as the moral irritation produced by the healer's success. The priests looked on darkly. Pharisees and Sadducees and Herodians whispered with sullen displeasure.

Nothing which this patient, gentle man could do was right, — his noblest acts most wrong of all. The ecclesiastical officers were the more angered because he gave them so little ground of legal offense, and they watched him narrowly with a helpless rage. The spectators looked at the priests, and many, who had begun to shout for Jesus affectionately, were alarmed and grew cowardly quiet.

But it happened that the chorister boys in the

Temple, the sons of the Levite priests, had come out
to see the sight, and were not as quick as their elders
to catch the idea that the tide, on whose brilliant
flow the Nazarene had entered the city yesterday,
had already begun to ebb.

These boys came out, in their little consecrated
robes, and clustered around the Rabbi. Some put
up their hands and played with his talith. One or
two leaned against him with a graceful attitude, half
nestling, half aloof, prettily independent of too much
show of emotion, as a growing boy is. He who
loved children so heartily stopped to chat with the
boys, and to welcome them ; for he was gratified by
their affectionate attention. Then the boys, remembering how all the world had cried after him the
day before, took up the words that they recalled most
easily, and began to shout in chorus, as they were
trained to sing, rhythmically :

> " Hosanna ! Hosanna !
> To the Son of David
> Hosanna ! Hosanna ! "

The chorister boys wondered why no one took up
their tribute to the great Rabbi, but only a few
voices joined in the children's hosannas ; these came
from some of the poor folk, the cured patients of
the healer, who were sobbing and laughing for joy
in the Temple court. The mass of the crowd was
ominously silent. The chorister boys, puzzled, put
the hem of the Rabbi's robe to their lips, and stoutly
gathered closer to him, with the battle instinct of
boys coming up in them, and so repeated their
chant :

"Hosanna!
See the Son of David!
Hosanna!"

Over this beautiful bulwark of youth, of trust, and
of song the eyes of the heretic healer sought those
of the officers of his church. For a moment there
shot from his a blazing question, to which their falling lids had no reply. Then the priests called the
chorister boys and ordered them away.

But the Rabbi, quoting softly from the Scriptures
of the people, was heard to say:

"Out of the mouths of babes . . . is perfected
praise."

The chorister boys went away unwillingly, looking back with manful reluctance at the Nazarene,
who watched them affectionately till the enfolding
architecture of the Temple shut them from his sight.
He was so grateful for the trust of these children
that it makes the heart ache to think how small a
measure of human love did comfort him in the
dark week when he needed all that Palestine could
hold.

He left the Temple at once, and went back to
Bethany. A sudden reserve had wrapped him.
He did not talk. Once he raised his hands to his
ears with an involuntary motion, as if he would smite
them deaf from something that he only heard. . . .

The clear, young voices of the boys rang on for a
little in his brain. He heard the ideal youth of the
world's future crying to him. It might have loved
and honored, it might yet honor and love him, — how
much, who could tell? Oh, to live and know! . . .

Where were the hosannas? They had changed to imprecations. One terrible word crashed in upon the silenced choral.

" *Crucify!* " Who said that?

No one; nothing but the inner voices of his own fine organism, throbbing under laws which the coarser being could not formulate and never knew.

Jesus collected himself and walked on to Bethany. He spent a part of the night in the house of his friends, wishing to give them the happiness of thinking that he rested; but midnight found him in the groves of the mountain. The olive-trees "were kind to him." Pacing among their silver arches, kneeling at their roots, his figure, solitary and solemn, moved from restlessness to exhaustion all night long. Prayer with him had never been an easy reverie; rather, the truest application of mind and heart. It had always been energy. Now it was growing agony. Dawn touched the brow of the mountain. The sharp, slender outline of the highest leaf on the tallest tree received the glitter, like a spear. He did not sleep. He had slept for the last time.

On Tuesday he went back persistently to the city. His friends at Bethany, in anxiety all the more acute because it was so ignorant, perceived that no human love could any longer influence him to save himself. It was hoped that the arrival of his mother for the festival of the Passover might have moved him to take some precautions. But nothing made the difference. He was determined to dare the worst.

Walking with the twelve, he passed the fig-tree

which had refused him fruit yesterday when he was faint. The quickest eye among the disciples observed instantly that the tree was withering, and exclamations of surprise arose from the group. Jesus took advantage of this episode to utter some of the most remarkable sayings ever propounded by any teacher of mankind. He laid down, in a few trenchant words, his theory of prayer; burning it in upon the confused minds of his friends, as if through them he would have branded it upon the intelligence of the world. He seemed as if he were pleading with all time to understand him.

"Oh," he cried, "have faith in God! . . . Ye yourselves could do more than this. . . . Whosoever shall not doubt in his heart, but shall believe that those things which he saith shall come to pass, . . . shall have whatsoever he saith : . . . when ye pray . . . believe that ye shall receive . . . and ye shall have."

"But," he added, qualifying this astounding assertion with the gravest warning, "when ye stand praying, if ye have anything against any one, forgive! forgive!" . . .

He went into the Temple without an obvious tremor. The crowd was larger than yesterday's. The delegates of an enraged church were on hand to receive him. The day began by an absorbing scene. Before he was allowed to open his lips, the priests and other important ecclesiastical representatives officially questioned his ordination as a Rabbi, and hence his right to preach to the Hebrew people.

The sleepless man, his brain on fire for rest, turned

upon the polemicists instantly. His mind showed no signs of weariness. It worked with unerring obedience to a celerity and adroitness of thought which was confounding. He parried the onset of his antagonists by a keen rejoinder. Religious and legal casuistry show nothing finer of its kind.

"Assuredly, I will give you my authority. But pray answer me one question first. Whence did the baptism of John come? Of Heaven or of men? Answer me!" he commanded.

The priests fell back and consulted. Here was a dilemma! To say from Heaven was of course to be asked, "Why, then, did you not treat John's system of faith as if it were sent from Heaven?" To reply, "He taught nothing superior; he was a very ordinary person," was sure to enrage the people, who stolidly held to it yet that the murdered .teacher was a prophet.

"Answer me!" repeated Jesus.

An aged priest was pushed forward as spokesman. Candidly he said:

"Indeed we cannot tell."

"Then," replied the Rabbi, smiling quietly, "neither do I tell you by what authority I do these things."

The officers of the church looked at each other uncomfortably, and openly gave up the battle for the time. Who would have believed this rustic from Nazareth capable of such astuteness? The country Rabbi had an intellect with which it proved dangerous to cope. It seemed one must study the man and his methods before venturing too far with him in public debate. The experienced controversialists wavered. The priests ranged themselves in his audience from very confusion, not liking to seem to run from him; and now, having an open field, Jesus cast every personal consideration behind him and began to speak.

He preached as if he had never preached before, and never should again; as indeed he never did. He spoke most of the day, and taught much by the parable. He was interrupted by several important episodes, but preached steadily on between them. Each sect had its turn at him, in a common endeavor to entangle the Rabbi to his own destruction.

The Sadducees worried him for his views on the marriage relation, as it was connected with a belief in personal immortality. The Pharisees maliciously waylaid him on the subject of Roman taxation, — as for instance: If he were in fact the King of the Theocracy, could he be subject to Cæsar? This was a skillful and dangerous trap. Jesus did not fall into it. This friend of the people upheld the law of the land. He would have nothing to do with socialistic mania. He has proved himself to be the greatest revolutionist of all time, but he was the revolutionist of character. He did not concern himself with codes. These, he assumed, would take care of themselves. He seemed perfectly indifferent to them. He had the burning conviction that, if his moral creed were accepted, the abuses and oppressions under which the mass of the world suffered would right themselves. He held fast to principles, and did not waste himself in ways and means of application. The simplicity and grandeur of his position in this respect were never so brilliantly apparent as on his last appearance as a public teacher in the Temple of his nation. His wiliest adversary was silenced for the moment by very admiration of him.

But theological controversy had not done with him. All day the leading schools of the church contended over the calm and gentle preacher, who exhibited such unexpected intellectual supremacy that it put their best men on their mettle to contest with him. An influential lawyer, who tried to entangle him into some dangerous public expression about the Hebrew statutes, received an astonishing reply. It has since become the basis of theoretical sociology, and of the practical civilization of the world. It was the superlative of the day's effort, and had such an effect upon the trained debaters who heard it that it was naïvely said :

" After that, no man durst ask him any questions."

Now he himself turned questioner : " What think ye of the Christ ? " he suddenly asked. But the confused controversialists looked feebly at the commanding face and figure of the preacher. No satisfactory reply was forthcoming. Jesus took the occasion subtly to intimate his celestial claims, but he did not dwell on them, and turned to another subject.

The plain people, who heard him with touching attention, were gathered about him. They lifted to him faces whose perplexity seemed to approach him

with a force that he found it impossible to resist.
They looked so poor, so meagre, so nearly starved,
and so wholly miserable! Oppression sat heavily
on their ignorance and helplessness. He turned
to their ecclesiastical officers and influential citizens,
— pompous, sleek, comfortable men, living on easy
incomes, enjoying social distinction, scorning people
of the lower classes, and scarcely aware that these
had any rights. Jesus seemed overwhelmed with
the contrast, and with the thoughts which it started
in him. It was as if he took up into his heart in
that one moment all the blind struggles of the down-
trodden and ranged himself beside them.

With church and state on his track, with death at
his throat, Jesus flung his last challenge down. The
most terrible arraignments of his ministry now fell
from his merciful lips. Without a care for himself,
he scathed the very men who had it in their power
to slay or to spare him, in language which the
worms of the earth would have resented.

"Woe unto you, Scribes, Pharisees, hypocrites, —
woe unto you! You make long prayers and devour
the homes of widows. . . . Lawyers! you bind heavy
burdens on poor men's shoulders, and will not lift
them by a finger. . . . Pietists! you pay tithes, but
have neither judgment nor mercy! Blind guides!
Full of iniquity! Serpents! Generation of vipers!
Woe unto you!"

It was his last outcry for the "common people,"
whom he had always loved, whom he represented,
and for whom he was willing to die. It was his last
plea for the purification of his church, and for the

integrity of the national religious character. If he
had a chance left, this arraignment of ecclesiastical hypocrisy and of social oppression would have
hurled it away. The courage which it must have
cost was something so evident and so sublime that
his listeners were stunned. The attack was received
in stony silence, ominous to the last degree.

Jesus paid no attention to the effect of his denunciation, unless it could be said that he clinched it by
turning his attention to a very poor woman who just
then had offered to the Temple treasury the smallest
sum allowed by law. He openly selected her contri-
bution as the most important of the day, and passed
at once quietly to the next incident.

This proved to be one which was profoundly interesting to him. A delegation of Greeks who were
visitors at the national festival proffered a special
request for an interview with the distinguished
Galilean. Jesus was in the Court of the Women at
that moment, a part of the Temple wherein no foreigner was allowed; and he went out of it to receive
the strangers. A brief but impressive conversation
ensued. Something about these visitors appealed
to him strongly. He was sensitive to their breadth
of thought and finish of manner. Greek culture
presented peculiar attractiveness to an independent
Hebrew mind. These foreigners had such sincerity,
such ardor in the pursuit of truth, they were so
unhampered by tradition, they were so natural, they
were such winning men, that his heart went out to
them. He would have liked to fling himself into
one mighty effort to illumine the undeveloped spirit-

uality in this beauty-loving people. He thought of the opportunities of a journey through Greece — perhaps to Rome itself — or into the farther East. It came upon him with a crushing force that the world lay yet beyond his short, sad ministry.

Galilee and Judea had refused him. Jerusalem was even now crouching for his life. But Palestine was not all. Three years were not a lifetime. The end? Nay, he was but at the beginning. Effort, sacrifice, achievement, — these might all go on in breath and joy. — Death was not the only way. . . . Such a vision whirled before him of the possibilities of living that he felt for the moment swept away by it. He saw himself carrying the truth for which he was martyr to the end of the known earth; to peoples kinder to him than his own; to strangers who would listen and love him and believe.

But this was to-day. There would be to-morrow; then Thursday — Friday —

His expression changed visibly. He parted from the Greek strangers with emotion. He could have wished that he had not seen them. . . .

Who spoke? No, it was thunder. Yes, again, who spoke? The voice came from above the meek, bowed head of the Nazarene. Some said that the air of the April day had uttered itself, but that no man could translate the language, for it was an unknown tongue. But there were by-standers having fine ears who prostrated themselves upon the pavement of the Temple; for they said that they heard words which no one could forget, and that these gave awful credentials to the mysterious teacher.

When these reverent persons raised themselves from the marble court, they saw the Nazarene standing rapt and listening. All the trouble had gone out of his face. He looked as if he had received a reinvigoration of life. He was reinspired of hope, of peace. At that moment no man dared address him.

Jesus had appeared in the Temple of his people for the last time. Whether accidentally or intentionally, his closing public address fell into a thrilling picture of the final judgment of the human soul before the bar of God.

In this discourse he assumed distinctly for himself both royal and divine claims. In it he gave some startling definitions of character. What was done to the obscurest of miserable men was done to him, he boldly said: " *I* am hungry — sick — in prison. You feed and visit *me*."

Words like these overthrew every conception of religious duty known to his church. They were received in gloomy and pondering silence. He had left the Temple and the capital without much public demonstration : few voices huzzaed ; none hosannaed. He began to feel his growing unpopularity as he walked meekly away.

But his friends, never any too sensitive to his moods, were blunt to his condition now. The twelve began to indulge a little national vanity at that untimely moment, and to chat about the grandeur of the Temple. They pointed out to him the huge, white blocks, some of them twenty-four feet long, which proudly supported the walls ; and they dwelt upon the glory and indestructibility of the building.

"The time is coming," observed the Rabbi quietly, "when there shall not be left one of these stones upon another."

Forty years after, when the capital of the disgraced nation went down in dust and flame, men remembered the words spoken by this patriot, and how — forgetting his own fate, and thinking only of hers — he had foretold in tears the doom of the city that he loved. On his way back to Bethany he rested with his party on the brow of the Mount of Olives. There, Jerusalem could be seen with a certain beautiful insolence of bearing; pallor of marble and glitter of gold ornamented her as if she had been a bride or a queen. She seemed to return the gaze of the martyr whom she was hounding down, with a chill intelligence.

The twelve, now sobered and puzzled, crept close to him in this quiet spot, and began in earnest to ask him for explanations. What fate was indeed before the royal city? What awaited himself? Or them? What was a fisherman to do with the situation into which his devotion to the fallen fortunes of a defeated Lord had brought him? What was to happen if they lost him? What did all the parables and mysteries mean?

Then he broke his reserve, and told them that at which their hearts stood still. They were brave and hardy men. But they began at last to understand that this prophet whom they had served so long was the King of sorrows and of failures, not of joys and of success; and that his officers were the picked men of suffering, not of pleasure. It was not power which awaited them. It was ignominy.

The treasurer of the association listened, with the rest, to these disturbing revelations. He heard them with a sour dismay. He thought it indiscreet in his Lord to speak so frankly at such a time, being, as he was, a practically defeated man. But Judas found these intimations personally useful. He made no remark upon them. His dark soul brooded upon what he had heard in sinister silence.

The party went on thoughtfully to Bethany. In the twilight one furtive figure set forth from the villages unnoticed, and fled along the road back to Jerusalem. Dark was down when this man re-entered the capital. With a kind of frenzied hurry, as if he feared that he might wish to recall what he was doing, if he gave himself time to think, he dashed up the marble steps of the palace of Caiaphas. At the door he stood, in the hot evening, with cold drops running down his cowering body. Half minded to fly, he went in. At a whisper the servants admitted him, and the silken curtains of the reception hall dropped behind his shaking figure. Eavesdroppers were scattered. The High-priest of the Hebrew Church and the trusted officer of Jesus of Nazareth were together.

Jesus came to his friends at Bethany looking so exhausted that they thought their hearts would break. They begged him to rest in his own room that night, for they reminded him that he had

preached all day without sleep. But he refused them gently. And while they were yet pleading with him, he departed from their tender urgency, and went out into the groves.

There, with the scalding brain and the deathly faintness of vigil, all night he waked and prayed. The mountain worshiped. But the palace blushed. The polished slabs in her walls would have cried out for horror if a single movement in the will-power of the mystical solitary on Olivet had given them tongues wherewith to save him. But they were as mute as the laws of nature made them.

Undetected, undeterred, Caiaphas and his council closed one of the compacts which history is ashamed to record, but which the moral instinct of the race never suffers her to forget.

Plainly, the crisis of the revolution has arrived. It must be met by any means, fair or foul. Never mind the method. Rid the nation of the Nazarene!

Who will put this pretender into our hands when he is not protected by the presence of the people, — the deluded people, whose confidence we have been unable to wrench from him?

Who will give him over to us in dark, in stealth, and in dishonor blacker than any with which we have a mind to stain our pious reputations?

Yonder stands our opportunity. Fortune flings at our feet one of his own men, — a trusted confidant. Incredible! But this brilliant luck is ours. Beckon the cringing figure. See to it that he makes his own proposition. Close with it on any terms! Close with it without an hour to consider or to re-

call! This is of the deeds which are best done with the least reflection.

The High-priest, cultivated to the point where one represses rather than expresses scorn, made some effort not to draw back his robes from contact with the low fellow who offered the person of his Lord and friend for betrayal to the law. Haggling with the ignorant man, the great Priest beat him down, as if they had been petty tradesmen bargaining for the sale of a Passover lamb in the streets.

Jesus of Nazareth was sold to the National Church — and the price was paid in silver from her treasury — for three pounds and fifteen shillings; the ransom of the lowest slave.

On Wednesday he did not go into the capital. He passed the day in Bethany, shielded for a last respite from the worst, cherished among his friends, loved, and a little understood. The eyes of Lazarus, the tenderness of Mary, the longing of John the dear disciple, clung to him throughout the day. On his mother's beautiful face age grew rapidly. He did not look at her often, — he could not bear it. It came to be so that he could no longer bear the presence of any who loved him, for the more they loved, the harder it was; and it was at a very early hour that he left them all and went away alone.

The group of his friends stood in the court of the house of Martha and watched him as he walked in the direction of the olive woods. On his white face dwelt the distance from human sympathy which is peculiar to the appearance of the sleepless.

THE CENACULUM

SAID TO BE THE HOUSE OF THE LAST SUPPER

ful preparations for the great religious banquet of
the year. Since for every reasonable and sincere
observance of his church Jesus had always shown respect, it was like him to give the due to this occasion.
On this last evening he performed, as he had always
done, the simple duty of the hour, precisely as if he
had expected to live for double thirty years. Ecclesiastical legend has dotted the land of Palestine with so
many traces of the great Rabbi's movements in which
history can put no faith, that a profound interest
attaches to the few localities which there is any reason to suppose may have been really identified with
his experience. The house in which he was entertained for the last supper of his life is thought to be
one of these few. It is still to be seen, a stone house,
outside the walls of the existing city, and in its time
stood so far south of the heart of the capital that it
escaped the general ruin.

It was a comfortable, in some sense a stately house,
of a degree befitting the position that Jesus had now
assumed as the foremost figure of the nation. It had
a large, upper room suitable for banqueting, and
giving through sufficient windows a wide outlook.
Couches surrounded the low, curved table on which
the red wine and water, the bitter herbs, the lamb
slain and blessed at the Temple and roasted entire,
were set forth in paschal order. There was no servant in attendance, nor did the owner of the house
present himself among the group to whom he had
rented his room of state. The Nazarene and his
twelve were alone and unobserved.

It was early evening when Jesus appeared walking slowly from Olivet, looking upwards at the Temple, whose splendid outline and colorings smoked with the burning of slain sacrifice. The smoke coiled lightly against the unclouded sky, and vanished in vague forms on the upper air, like the passing of a spirit. He watched it without remark.

Ten of the twelve were with him ; they, too, walked quietly. They were met by their paschal committee, Peter and John, who had been appointed to make arrangements for the supper. The group assembled in the spacious upper room of the stone house, and closed the doors.

Jesus took his place at the head of the table. He had never before held the position of host at the solemn festival of his church, and had not personally offered sacrifice. He thought of this in almost the same words that had come to him when he partook of his first Passover, he then a boy, blinded by his consciousness of mystery and by a passing preconsciousness of suffering : " I shall be the sacrifice."

That was at the beginning. This — this was the end. He sank down upon the cushions of the couch. An attitude " of rest, of happiness, and of liberty " was necessary to the paschal feast; the tense muscles of his troubled figure battled with the appearance of ease. He glanced at the slain sacrifice, — poor, dumb symbol of suffering no less mute than his own ! How power and helplessness met in pain and death ! The evening light struck straight upon his face. He looked out through the window with eyes that were not limited by its proportions.

The stone walls of the house widened and wavered to his gaze. No point of compass seemed to restrain his vision. It was as if he looked fairly on Olivet; a shadow was sombrely moving up the mountain. Yonder was unseen Bethany. Invisible Galilee sat hidden somewhere in the darkening map. There lay Nazareth, Capernaum, the Lake, home, youth, freedom, — the eager scenes of three dedicated years, crowded with passionate hope and toil, with unswerving belief that he was walking God's way, that he was forcing everything to the wishes of his Father, — of his Father unseen, unproved, but trusted in spite of that. And now? What was the outcome of it all?

The color of the evening entered the room solemnly. He felt the peculiar grip at the heart that comes to a man who knows that he is looking for the last time at the setting of the sun.

He was so absorbed that he had not noticed at first that there was a disturbance among the twelve. Even on that night, at that hour, they were quarreling pettily over the order of their precedence in taking positions at the supper table. Judas had somehow managed to get himself into the seat of honor, at the left of the Rabbi. Peter, seeing this, had gone over to the lowest seat on the opposite side. The others were noisily arranging themselves on the divans as they pleased. John was standing irresolute. Jesus beckoned him to the couch at his own right hand. The meal opened in discomfort.

Could they not have spared him, even then, this last reminder how weak they were, how full of undisciplined nature, how deaf to the real message

of his life with them? In three years how little
they had learned! He looked at them with infinite
sadness. They seemed to him like children. He
spoke to them patiently. The meal proceeded with
decorum.

But what was the Rabbi doing? He had risen
from his couch and laid aside his talith. Girded
with a towel, as a servant is who waits on his supe-
riors, he was moving about meekly with a basin and
ewer of water in his hand; and, before a man of them
could stay him, they perceived that he was bathing
their feet, — a menial act, the humblest which he
could have performed. Shocked beyond power to
refuse, most of the twelve submitted to this strange
ceremony. But Peter protested hotly: " No, — no !
You shall *never* wash my feet ! "

" Then," observed Jesus, smiling gently, " you
have no part with me."

" Lord," cried the impulsive disciple, " wash my
hands and my head also ! "

The room grew as still as the inner chambers of
the heart. Peter's heavy breathing could be heard
distinctly; the tears stormed down his cheeks as
the Rabbi wiped his rough, large feet with the servant's towel. But John, when in turn his Master
stooped to serve him, hid his face in the pillows of
the couch for delicacy.

In order Jesus passed to Judas. There for a
moment he paused. It was thought by those who,
being nearest, most plainly read the expression of
his face, that he would have omitted the treasurer
from the perplexing ceremony. But he did not.

Drawing himself to his height, he seemed for the instant to rise above the traitor like a flame that might fall and annihilate him. Then the Rabbi's kingly figure bowed itself, and his fine hands offered to the basest soul in Palestine the same humble service that he expended on better men. Judas endured the act without speaking, but he writhed under it.

Jesus resumed his talith silently. His appearance seemed to have gained, not lost, in dignity by this singular digression from the usual relation between chief and subordinate. With more than royal demeanor he returned to his couch, and authoritatively began to explain his reason for what he had done.

" Ye call me your Master, as indeed I am. Yet I, your Lord and Master, have washed your feet. Wash ye one another's feet! Is the servant greater than his lord ? "

Such a lesson in personal humility did he now set forth as a man could not have forgotten till his last breath had gone out in the struggle between the nobler and the smaller in him ; nor until he had learned where lies the difficult border-line between the force of individuality necessary to achievement, and that force of vanity which usurps the energy and the fair fame of the other.

The twelve thought how they had wrangled about a seat at a supper, and they hung their heads.

To themselves they said, — and some whispered the words to their neighbors, — " We will never do a petty thing like this again. Next time we will be larger-minded ; we will please him better."

This was one of the resolutions wrung from shame when opportunity is past. There was to be no next time. For two thousand years that meal in the stone house has been known to men as the Last Supper. Yet the minds of those who partook of it did not seem to grasp the fact that it was not to be one of many more when they should be the guests of their dear Lord; he quiet, pale, tender, and looking, please God, something happier than he did to-night. Love deluded them, as it always does the loving. They could not understand.

The time had come to undeceive them thoroughly, and Jesus could put it off no longer.

The sun had long since set. The room was lighted only by its festal lamps. A patch of starlight and darkness lay out beyond the windows, and seemed to draw towards them like a curtain. Now through the quietness strange words were heard; they came indistinctly from his lips, as if he found it almost impossible to utter them. His familiar face, broken with grief, turned from one of his friends to another. He seemed to be appealing to them to give denial to that which he was forced, by a power beyond himself or them, to assert.

" For one of *you* — shall betray me."

Anguished cries interrupted him. " Nay, nay ! The thing is too dreadful to think of. . . . Lord, not one of *us*, — not one of thy very own ! For three years we have followed and trusted thee, — loved thee. Lord, thou wrongest us ! (Has suffering, think you, touched his brain ?)

" He will not answer. What a look he wears !

The Passover lamp flares on his quivering face. Who dares address him? Not I — nor I. Where is Peter, the spokesman? Put the question, Peter! Ask!"

But the power of speech for once had died out of Peter's throat and lips. His rugged face worked with disturbance.

Across the table sensitive John, overcome with the painfulness of the scene, had hidden his face upon the breast of his Lord. He raised it once, trying to calm himself by a glance upwards at Jesus, and at that instant Peter caught his eye. A swift signal mutely conveyed the entreaty :

" Ask! He loves you best."

But John could not command himself to speak just then, and while he hesitated, low murmurs were heard creeping from trembling lip to lip around the paschal table.

" Lord, is it I? Or I?"

Some sobbed the words out, covering their faces for shame that they could so much as bring themselves to utter them ; and some shot them out sternly, like men pushed by a mad fate, who would know the worst at once. So much had been inexplicable all this while! Could a man be forced to infamy against his will? Who knew but this was another mystery, another trouble?

At that moment their love for Jesus seemed to them the greatest fact in the world: they felt as if heaven and earth were armed against it; they felt as if there had never been men so wronged as they.

" Lord," whispered John when the tension of the

scene was at its height, "who is it? who shall it
be? Tell me!"

Jesus whispered to him a few words in reply. At
this moment the treasurer on the other side, growing
too uncomfortable to keep still, leaned forward and
helped himself out of the dish that stood before the
Rabbi. Jesus dipped a bit of bread in the paschal
gravy, and without a smile handed it to Judas. The
treasurer accepted the courtesy, turned scarlet to the
brows, and sharply rose from the table.

"Do it quickly, Judas," said the Rabbi in a stern,
loud voice.

When the group collected themselves, they were,
besides their Master, but eleven. Judas had skulked
away, having been sent, it was supposed, to provide
supplies for the Rabbi's comfort to-morrow.

When he had gone, there seemed to be fresh air
in the room. Each man took a long breath, and
noticed that his neighbor did the same. There set
in at once one of those subtle changes in the moral
atmosphere which every one feels, though no one
explains. Jesus himself visibly responded to some
powerful emotion.

He now began to talk to his friends freely. He
told them heart-breaking things. Were theirs all
sanguine temperaments, untaught by nature to prepare for trouble? For even then, at the last
moment, they found it almost impossible to believe
in the tragedy that was upon them. He tried to
blunt the edge of the blade for them before it
struck. His whole heart seemed to go out in thinking of *them*, — how they would bear this, how they

CHRIST AT THE LAST SUPPER

could endure that, how they should act under such circumstances. He who needed comfort as man never needed it before, as no man has dared say that he has needed it since, only had a care to give it to those who loved him, and whom he loved best. He called them by affectionate terms, — "Little children."

"I am with you for a little while longer," he added plaintively, when he saw how startled they were. "Love one another! Remember how I have loved you."

He spoke so touchingly that a man must have a soul of frost who can recall his words without emotion.

The disciple whose independence of thought no emergency could altogether fetter spoke out brusquely :

"Whither goest thou, Rabbi?"

"I go where ye cannot follow now," said Jesus firmly.

"Why not?" persisted Peter. "I will lay down my life for thee!"

Jesus smiled, — a smile which no man could read.

"Thou shalt deny me, Peter, before the cock crows."

Inarticulate sounds of horror ran round the group. Every man looked at Peter with indignation. He had flung himself upon the floor; his only reply was to put up his hands and stroke his Lord's feet. No one could see his face. Voluble Peter was past answering. He was saying to himself, "I will show them! He will see!" His rough hands, gnarled

by the sheets that hauled the sails of Gennesaret,
continued to stroke his Rabbi's unsandaled feet.
The eyes of Jesus filled.

The evening was passing; all too rapidly, all too
heavily. Across the countenance of Jesus advanced
an immeasurable shadow. He took up the Passover
loaf and broke it, with a solemnity so significant that
every eye in the room now fastened itself upon him.
His low voice faltered a little in the Passover blessing, and when he said :

" This is my body, — broken, and for you. Eat."

He poured the wine into the paschal cups. It ran
a deep red in the light of the festal lamps.

" This is my blood," he added ; "drink."

In a silence like that of the after world, the group
obeyed him.

With bowed heads, with streaming cheeks, with
shrinking lips, they ate, they drank ; wondering, but
asking him no question now.

The cup trembled a little in his hands as he
pressed it to the lips of John. In his eyes rested
the solitary look of far prevision which his friends
had learned to know.

What did he see? Cruciform oak, nails, the
point of a spear, then the gush which comes from
the heart?

But what did he see ? Far down the years quiet
groups in holy houses, sitting with bowed heads. The
dull white of broken bread, the gleam of red wine,
the pure tint of silver, show and shift across the scene.
The afternoon wanes to dusk. Prayer and sacred
song are softly audible. This is one of the hours

whose memory flits far across a driven life. Doubt remembers it, and moral peril, and sorrow leans on it. It comes to mean a power in the world of men, gentle as that of motherhood, strong as that of worship. With wet eyes, with hushed hearts, those who celebrate this solemnity do think of *him :* they murmur a name, — it is *his ;* they melt with tenderness for suffering, — it is *his.*

The feeling that his own race, his own day denied him, the future gives him. Millions offer what the few refused. The true heart of the world will not foreclose its sympathy from this man acquainted with grief.

With wide, grand eyes gazing out through the windows of the upper chamber of the stone house, he saw these things and spoke not of them. Sacrament was in his silence.

He broke it by some of the most beautiful words that ever came from his lips. He began, in a voice scarcely above a whisper, to offer to his friends his last directions, to extend his parting benedictions.

The Passover lights burned low, and seemed almost afraid to reveal his face, which melted into dimness, which struggled into form, and wore a wonderful expression. Sobbing was heard about the paschal table. Some hid their faces in their hands, but John wept upon the arm of his Lord. Peter had not moved from the floor where he lay at Jesus' feet.

"Let not your hearts be troubled. Ye believe in God. . . . Believe in me. . . . I am the way, I am the truth, I am the life. . . . I will not leave you comfortless! I will come to you! . . . Now I go my way. I go to Him that sent me. In the world ye shall have trouble. Have good cheer. I overcome the world. . . . How many things have I to say to you! But you cannot bear them, — you cannot bear them now. . . . Peace I leave with you. I give you my peace."

He did not speak for a space following these compassionate words; and when he found utterance again, the eleven perceived that he was praying. The voice for whose tenderness they should go starving all the remainder of their lives began to plead with Heaven. They had never heard — who had ever heard? — a paschal prayer of consecration like this one. It signified that the sacred services of the evening were at an end.

"Father, the hour is come. Glorify thy Son. . . . Thou hast given him power . . . that he should give eternal life to as many as Thou hast given him. . . . This is life eternal, . . . to know Thee, the only true God, and Jesus the Christ whom Thou hast sent. . . . I have finished the work which Thou gavest me. . . . Behold the men which Thou gavest me. I pray for them."

Then followed for their sakes such loving entreaties, such thoughtfulness for them at the very ear of God, as it wrung the souls of his friends to hear; and they wept so that they feared lest they lose the entirety of the prayer, whose solemn meaning came to them but slowly in broken phrases: "Let them be one, as we are one; I in them, and they in me.

. . . The world does not know Thee. But I have known Thee, . . . O righteous Father!"

The accents of prayer had but died on the lips of Jesus when they opened again in song. Quite firmly he led the strains of a Passover hymn, as the ritual of his church prescribed. The ascriptions of an ancient psalm dear to the Hebrew faith echoed to the ceiling of the upper room, and floated strongly from the open windows upon the evening air. All the world could have heard the singing. It did not occur to the hated and hunted man to say: "Hush! Speak low, pray softly, but do not sing. Let us not expose ourselves to danger unnecessarily."

In the certain ears of peril, in the grip of inevitable death, triumphantly and joyously, the sweet, deep, voice of Jesus rang out:

> "O, give thanks unto the Lord!
> For He is good!"

The shapes of shame and torture flitted into the stone room. Images which froze the blood at his heart huddled between him and the Passover lamps. But he sang on strongly:

> "Oh, give thanks unto the Lord God of Heaven,
> For His mercy endureth forever!"

The singing penetrated into the open air; the notes of his pathetic voice dropped into the street. Few men had heard Jesus sing, and the beauty of his tone attracted attention. Twos and threes stopped to listen. Many foreigners, not occupied with the paschal ceremony, were strolling about the city. Groups collected at no great distance from the stone house.

A skulking figure, stealing down the street, waved a Roman guardsman back, and listened with the others. Judas Iscariot drew himself into the shadow of an alley and watched. It was but a few moments after this that the paschal party left the upper chamber and came out into the street.

When the singing had ceased, the groups of listeners scattered. Jesus and the eleven passed apparently unnoticed, and set their faces eastward. Having avoided the Temple area, the party turned northward up the valley of the Kedron.

"Lord, I am ready to go with thee to prison and to death!"

"Simon, Simon! I tell thee, before the cock shall crow this day, thou shalt three times deny me!"

"Lord, though I should die with thee, yet would I not deny thee!"

"Nor I, — nor I!"

"Rabbi, whosoever faileth thee, thou canst count on *me!*"

"And me, — dear Lord, on me!"

The speakers in this moving dialogue stared at one another's whitening faces through the sickly color of the late evening. It was not quite dark in Gethsemane, for a full moon, contesting with a stormy cloud, peered through. The garden rested upon the arm of Olivet; it was as if the mountain tried to enfold it, and to conceal it from sight. For the shadow of the cultivated olive grove, always thick, seemed that evening dense. It was a still, cool spot, secure from disturbance; a favorite with Jesus. He

had spent many solitary nights there. Vigil and
prayer whose sacred story no man knew, had dedicated it, — how often! how desolately! The place
was dear to him; his feet turned to it instinctively.
The eleven had followed him, disturbed and subdued.
Now the group stood close together, all pressing
about him.

They fell back when he signified, by a gesture,
his wish for the society of the three whom he preferred. The rest remained, shut out from their Lord's
confidence, but they did not trouble him to ask him
why.

The three walked apart with Jesus into the most
secluded portion of the olive garden. It was darker
here, and strangely still. Jesus stretched out his
arms with a groan. He who had suffered so much
and so long, and who never complained of the worst
that happened, nor ever wore on the feelings of his
friends, suddenly appealed to them by the most
piteous words:

"My soul is exceeding sorrowful, . . . even to
death. Tarry, and watch with me!" he entreated.
Before any one of the three could reply, he had
disappeared in the heart of the grove.

Under the olives it was black about the roots.
Far overhead, the struggling moon brought out
the silver look of the trees; they blended from black
to light, as if blurred with a slow, soft brush. The
sharper outlines of the slim leaves were etched distinctly. There was scarcely any wind; but sometimes a breath sighed, and the moon glanced below.

Around the foliage of one thick tree its neighbors gathered closely, as if they guarded it. The shadow beneath was as dark as death. The light above did not penetrate it.

At the foot of the thick tree, with knotted hands, with face upon the ground, a solitary figure sank.

Human endurance has gone to the limits of pain, shame, and death for all the causes that can torment the souls and bodies of men. Fate and force have met and fought in the name of every conviction that feeds on the will of an unconquerable being, and the war has gone mightily in many a strong heart. But here was a man who carried a burden so isolate that the imagination almost refuses to hold it.

It has been asked, Why did not Jesus Christ become a maniac?

There have been moral alienists who would, if they could, have detected symptoms of mental disease in this dauntless life. But the calm eye of his personal sanity has replied to the interrogations of twenty centuries. He had not even the usual proportion of morbidness or eccentricity which falls to the lot of great minds. Here was a sane man, who believed that the salvation of the human race rested upon himself. . . .

In success, in activity, in religious oratory, in the energies of mercy, this belief had passed for the most part undistressed, if not undisturbed. Gethsemane challenged it. Defeat, disgrace, and approaching death shook conviction to the foundation. At the roots of the olives the smitten man, with up-

CHRIST IN GETHSEMANE

reaching hands, groped like the blind. Above the treetop was the sky; he felt upwards for it, as if it had been a thing that he could grasp and hold. The upper branches stirred ; the brightening moonlight, like some forced and frightened witness, glanced at the upturned face it saw, and fled. The thick foliage closed in again. He had seen the heavens impearled, hollowed like a chalice.

It seemed to him to be held to his recoiling lips, a draught of agony which he must drink. He cried out against it:

" Father! Father! "

He was still so young, so vigorous ! The blood beat strongly in his being. He loved life, as all well souls and bodies do, and his were so sound! Health throbbed in every artery, in every cell. Sickness had never weakened him. No taint had ever marred him. His system had never become the slave of his overstrained nerves. Even the torment of prolonged vigil had not conquered him. He was alive to the last red drop in his fair, pure body ; he was alive to the last energy of his unshaken brain. And his heart? — why, the life of his heart seemed something great enough to supply the forces and the fountains of the world !

Death! — at the top of vigor, at the brim of existence ! Slow torture, and shameful, — and tomorrow ! *Unnecessary* death! . . .

The stillness startled him. Smitten with a sudden sense of his loneliness, he staggered up and gazed about him, looking for his friends. He had spent himself in prayer, had shut himself in to the

society of God.   Yet such a yearning for human
sympathy rushed upon him that it seemed as if he
would drown in it.   He pushed the olive branches
apart, and called the names dearest to him, — Peter,
and James, and "John, John, *John!*" he cried be-
seechingly, like a man who pleads for his life.

But the tired men, sore with trouble, were all
asleep.   They turned stupidly at the sound of his
voice.   Peter sprang.   The lip of Jesus quivered.

"Could you not watch *one* hour with me?" he
gently said.

He went back to the thick olive-tree; there on the
ground he fell again.

The drama of his life returned before him, swiftly
as scenery shot in flame and smoke.   The devout
docility of his childhood, the pure dreams of his boyhood, repassed; and the first surprise of his extra-
consciousness.   He heard the voice on Jordan when
his kinsman, the prophet, baptized among the reeds.
He listened to the message of the clouds when he
floated on the head of Lebanon.   In the Temple,
when the Greeks came, mystery had uttered the
same words:

"*My belovèd Son!*"   What had they meant?
What did they mean now?   As slowly, as naturally,
as the blossoming of character, his explanation of
his own being had presented itself to him.   It had
developed as life develops, with no more haste, with
no more strenuousness; with something of the same
uncertainty and bewilderment; with passages of
glorious confidence; with intervals of humble fear,
but steadily growing and gaining on doubt.   He had

known all the noble self-distrust that only the finest
nature is capable of feeling; and he had known all
the strong trust in another which only the highest
can know.

He had staked everything, he had suffered everything, on the conviction that he was in some supreme
sense different from that which governed the personality of any other man, the Son of his God;
chosen for a transcendent mission; destined to lift a
world of men out of the doom of life.

By the solitary pressure of his own personal character and history, he believed that he was required
to wrest the solid mass of human evil and misery
over into the direction of purity and peace.

If this was not the most tremendous delusion
which ever visited a human brain, then was it the
grandest affirmation. For such was not the task
of a man. It was the privilege of a Divinity.

Nor was this all.

With leisurely power there had forced themselves
upon this solitary being beliefs that set him more
and more apart from his kind. He had begun life
by wondering why he was not like other men; he
ended it by understanding.

As naturally as manhood develops from infancy,
so Christhood had developed from manhood. Gradually, quietly, he had come to perceive that it was
his to live the divine life at the human odds.

But this was not all. It was the conviction of
Jesus that it depended upon himself whether men
should possess the privilege of personal immortality.

He believed that he held in his own hands the

gift of eternal life to the human soul.   He believed
that upon the facts of his life, and upon the facts
of his death, this solitary responsibility rested.   All
through his later life, in these three years of patient
struggle to obey what he believed to be the will of
Heaven for him, he had felt the weight of this
inconceivable burden unevenly; now more heavily,
now more lightly, — not all at once, or he must have
died of it.   In Gethsemane the whole load rolled
upon his shaken frame.

It would have been something, it seemed, if he
had not altogether failed! It would have been much,
if he could have supposed that he had taught his
own age or his own race what God meant him to
teach them.

Torment and death would have been easy to bear,
could he have felt that they were worth while.
But no one understood.   Few cared.   Most forgot.
In Gethsemane it seemed to Jesus of Nazareth that
he had achieved nothing.   He was a defeated man.
He had missed his Father's errand.   Through the
blind gates of death, in a few hours, he must be
pushed, to hold up his trembling, empty hands and
say :

"Father, I trusted Thee, — but I have failed!"

There in the olive-garden lay his poor friends,
asleep again.   Even they could not understand
enough to give him the little common, human sympathy that love saves for the emergency of the
belovèd.   He stole out and watched them, and returned with his head sunken on his breast. . . . He
had bared it to the night air for very anguish, and

he perceived now that heavy drops were falling from his face and body and streamed upon his heart. He looked at them. In the faint light it could be seen that they were red. . . .

By the subtle law which may convert the most sacred private experiences into world-wide value, and which governed every event in the life of Jesus, there have been given to us certain records of an hour known only to himself and to God. The uttermost of prayer, the outermost of sacrifice were in the words upon which the sorrow of the race will stay itself until men shall cease to suffer, and shall no longer need to cling for courage to the heroes of pain. Of these, the consent of the world has placed him first who bore the worst the most nobly, with the least care for himself, and with the most touching trust in God.

" Father, not as I wish ! — as Thou wilt ! "

As his white lips framed these words, the olive-branches stirred above his head, and there, as in the Jordan desert when his troubled life was at its morning, the mystical did visit him. Men called that presence an angel's, not understanding what an angel is. Gethsemane knew the secret of that comforting ; but she holds it.

. . . .

Beyond the grove, in an open space, the now brilliant moonlight caught, stealthily ascending the declivity, the glint of a spear. The sound of approaching feet furtively intruded upon the silence of the garden.

CHAPTER XVI

ON TRIAL

As he stepped out from the shadow into the lighter spaces of the garden, his foot was firm. The signs of acute anguish were gone from his expression and his manner. He had the appearance of one who has absorbed vigor, which makes him unconscious, for the time, of the unendurable. He had received some celestial anæsthetic.

His friends were still sleeping. He called them softly. They sprang to their feet, bewailing and apologizing. They saw him standing straight and still.

"Take your rest now," he said with his own gentleness; "he who betrays me is here."

Before the words had left his lips, confusion seized the olive garden. Tramping steps grew heavier on the pathway. Lights began to burn through the trees. Armor flashed, and military commands became audible. A delegation of Jewish priests and elders, formally accompanied by a detachment summoned from the fortress of Antonia, or by a portion of the large guard posted at the Temple during Passover week, advanced upon Gethsemane.

Judas Iscariot preceded them alone, saluted the

THE BETRAYAL

eight who were left to guard the entrance of the garden, and pushed on. In Gethsemane the twelve were reunited for one tragic moment. Iscariot hurried into the heart of the garden. Peter, John, and James, now thoroughly awake, sprang at the footfall, but the familiar face of one of their own party quieted their fears for a time. Judas, whose brain was confused with the imbecility of crime, made one childish effort to free himself from the suspicion of the deed that he had perpetrated. With a feeble, foolish smile, he stepped forward, put his arms around his Rabbi, and effusively kissed him. A hoarse " Hail, Master ! " passed the preconcerted signal of identification to the arresting officers.

The lip of Jesus curled. Every fibre in his body recoiled. But he submitted to the embrace of Judas, as a god might submit to the touch of a befouled spirit, in the process of some plan of events too grand to be disturbed by a personal repulsion.

He allowed himself ten words in reply. Scorn has never scalded deeper.

" Judas ! Betrayest thou the Son of Man ? with a *kiss ?* "

But the band had now come up. Judas fled to it for protection. The Hebrew ecclesiastics shrank behind the Roman soldiers, who pushed on with the pomp of a detachment commissioned to cut off a fleeing phalanx. Armed shadows swept under the olive-trees, and quickly formed a cordon ; the gentle, unresisting man stood caught within it.

The guardsmen carried torches, and lamps burn-

ing upon long poles. These flared high above the
heads of the group, and dashed the scene on in
strong effects, — lights, shadows, colors, outlines,
coming out emphatically. Dark, Hebrew profiles,
handsome Roman faces, flashed forth; the gleam
of mail, the lustre of swords, the threatening shapes
of heavy cudgels. There were weapons enough in
the party to have quelled a riot.

The moon had now become invisible; a thick
cloud shielded it. The garden would have been
dark but for the torches, cutting reddish-yellow
swathes among the olive foliage, and trembling as
they revealed the quiet figure which now stepped
out to meet the arresting band.

This movement on the part of the captive was
unexpected, and caused a momentary perplexity.
Jesus stood forth alone, in the blazon of the light.
Some surprise was felt to see that he was smiling.

"Whom seek ye?" he asked in a natural tone,
not without a certain lordliness, like that of a
host disturbed by intruders on his own ground.

"We seek Jesus of Nazareth," returned the captain of the troop, in some embarrassment.

"I am he," replied the Nazarene. He spoke
quietly, but there was that in his accent which
caused every man to look quickly upon him; and
when they had looked, there was that in his appearance which caused every glance to drop before
him.

What was it? — the lines of his lip? the attitude of his figure? the ray of his eye? There
shot from him a sudden force that no one could ex-

plain. Whether it smote the body, or the spirit, could not be said. Was it some secret of nature, unknown to common men, like the action of fire, light, or storm? Was it the reply of wronged innocence, or of startled will? Or was it something greater and stranger than these?

In the person of the entrapped Rabbi stood majesty incarnate. Indeed, a stronger term than this passed through the minds of some who were present at that scene, and who carried through life its matchless impression.

The arresting officers fell back. Some of them dropped to their faces on the ground. Judas fled to the rear of the band. He dashed his hands across his eyes, groveling on the ground. But no one thought of Judas. Around the Nazarene was drawn an invisible barrier that could not be crossed. With a smile of deep significance Jesus repeated his question: "Whom do ye seek?" And with hesitating tone the Roman officer, standing at a trembling distance, replied as before, that he sought Jesus of Nazareth.

"But I tell you that I am he," reiterated Jesus. With these words the resisting influence between captors and captive broke. The band rushed forward. The captain laid a hand upon the shoulder of his prisoner. In a moment, Gethsemane had become a battle-ground. The disciples of the Nazarene now came to their senses, and surrounded him. Swords flashed and clubs swung. Shouts and cries clashed through the olive garden, and torches fell hissing to the sod. Peter drew one swift, hot-headed blow, and disabled his man (who chanced to be a servant of the High-priest), not mortally wounding, but deftly mutilating him. But the voice of Jesus was now heard, bespeaking protection for his party, and preventing a massacre.

"Put up your swords," he commanded, "my Father has given me a cup. Shall I not drink it?"

"See!" he added kindly. The impulse and habit of the healer came uppermost even at that wild moment, and he put out his thin, fine hand and reached the wounded man, whose hurt ceased at the touch. The Hebrew ecclesiastics looked uncomfortable. The Roman officers stared. When in the history of war or riot, — where in the battles of Asia or of Gaul, had they met an incident like this? Blood, and slaughter, and revenge, and bitterness, they knew; but a compassion so instinctive that it made a man forget to defend himself, who could understand?

The hand of the captain relaxed on the prisoner's shoulder. For a moment, a distressed uncertainty wavered over the military band. In that space, Jesus shook himself free of the Roman grip. He stood at his kingly height. His eye swept the soldiers and the Hebrews until it seemed as if it would have mown them down, man by man. Crisis was in his demeanor, and opportunity in the bewilderment of the arresting party. It seemed, for an instant, as if by sheer spiritual superiority he might disband them, and escape. . . . But he did not. He turned to his friends, scanning their familiar faces tenderly, as if he would take a last look at what was dearest to him.

"Could I not pray my Father?" he said quietly. "More than twelve legions of angels would He give me if I asked them of Him."

To these startling words, no man replied. He who had spoken them lifted his face to the sky. His hands raised themselves to his breast, and there knotted together. He had the aspect of one who is restraining an unfathomable power by an immeasurable will.

Stars burst through the breaking clouds; his eye traversed the spaces of the heavens from spark to spark. He had a certain military bearing, like that of a commander reckoning his forces. The trained soldiery recognized something of this, by instinct, and it was noticed that many of them saluted, as if in the presence of a great general, whose tactics they could not understand, but whose superiority was not a thing to question.

Twelve legions? How fight phalanxes of spirits? How conquer battalions of invisibles? What could one make of such an army?

These impressions were but the material of a moment. Then the eye of Jesus turned from heaven to earth. By a grand gesture he signified his readiness to surrender, and the hand of the captain fell again upon his shoulder.

They led him, quite unresisting. He felt, before he saw, that he was to be bound. He spoke to them only once, — the tenderest reproach ever offered by captive to his captors:

" Why do you come to me as if I were a thief, with swords, with weapons ? . . . I was with you every day.   I taught in your Temple.   And ye took me not." . . .

As they forced him out of Gethsemane, he looked back for his friends, whom he had loved, and who had loved him, and shared his lot so long.   Their names quivered on his lips.   In the shadow of the olives — was that courageous Peter ?   John — *John* must be here, though all the world besides had failed.

It occurred to him to call them.   But he did not. He perceived with a sinking of the heart, such as he had never felt in all his troubled life, that they had run ; they had deserted him, every man.

His head sank upon his breast as the Roman captain thrust him down the slope of Olivet.

The action of the great tragedy now began to move with such appalling swiftness that the eye is half blinded in the effort to follow it.

Jesus had lived, though not a life of leisure, a leisurely life.   Up to this point there had been time enough for everything.   The childhood of the Nazarene had passed with the orderliness which best educates.   His public career, short and intense as it was, had taken its time.   He had thought and studied, preached and worked, planned and executed, without haste, without rest ; in calm, in thoroughness, and in symmetry.

The end came upon him like a cataclysm of nature.   It was a tempest out of season, hurling him

down in a moment. When one would have turned
to see whither he was borne, he was gone. He had
carried himself before the people of his nation, a
law-abiding man, for thirty-three pure and blameless
years. How did the law treat him? A sham trial,
an illegal sentence, hurried him to a barbarous
death. Between the moment of his arrest and that
of his execution there dashed by, at the most, fifteen
hours.

It was something after midnight when he was led
out of Gethsemane. The April night was not warm,
and it grew chilly as it advanced. Reacting from the
extreme nervous strain of the last hour, Jesus felt
himself grow cold. Instinctively he tried to wrap
his body, damp with the exudations wrung from the
pores and blood-vessels by agony, and suddenly
exposed to the night air. Then the ropes on his
wrist began to cut. He who had been one of the
freest men in Palestine experienced the first sensa-
tion of lost liberty.

Down through the Kedron Valley, up through the
Golden Gate, the military band swept silently into
the sleeping city. No one spoke above a whisper.
The ripple of the brook was the loudest sound. The
moon was now clear again, and the movements of
the party could be distinctly followed by the glimmer
of its spears. The prisoner was calm. He wasted
no strength in futile struggles; indeed, he seemed to
have none to waste. It was observed by some one
that the bound man missed his walking-stick that
had been left in Gethsemane. The Roman officers

were surprised at the evident fatigue of the captive.
At the bridge [1] across the brook, he stumbled from
very weariness, and fell.　A mailed hand dragged
him up, and he struggled on.　No one had ever
thought of the Nazarene except as a man of good
physical strength; but vigil and Gethsemane had
overthrown it.　He was now very weak.

The agents of the Hebrew nation and the officers
of the Roman government entered the city like con-
spirators, trying to cover their victim from chance
observation.　The capital, crowded with strangers
and foreigners, who had come up to town full of
interest in the Nazarene, must not be roused.
There were the Galileans, too, a large and powerful
number, many of them friendly to the healer who
had saved their sick, to the preacher whose eloquence
had thrilled the shores of their lake.　These fellow-
citizens of Jesus should be kept in ignorance of
what was happening.　It was thought best to dispense with the services of the Roman soldiery as
soon as possible, and the captive was hurried into
the hands of the Jewish authorities.

In the palace of the High-priest, the party were
ominously received.　They were evidently expected.
In the dead of night, the whole ecclesiastical family
were awake and up.　Annas, the ablest and coldest
officer of the national church, who had retired from
active service on his honors and his wealth, himself
met the prisoner.　The old man stroked his long,
white beard; he thought of his personal income, and
the revenues from the booths that the young fanatic

[1] Tradition.

had broken up ; for three years the Priest had cherished his grudge, but he said nothing about so low a subject. Jesus had quite forgotten it, at the moment ; he mildly returned the sarcastic gaze which frostily received him.

But the ex-Priest had no mind to commit himself too far, in a matter whose importance was evidently considerable : he turned the prisoner over to Caiaphas. One silent, significant, Oriental gesture carried the powerful weight of the pontiff's advice to his son-in-law.

The palace was well lighted and astir. Many church officers were to be seen ; in fact, a secret session of the Sanhedrin, irregular, incomplete, and unlawful, was convened. The High-priest of the Jewish nation appeared in full canonicals to judge the case. His sacred robes rustled, stiff with embroidery. The light from the hanging lamps caught the mitre on his brow ; across it blazed the jeweled words, " Holiness unto the Lord."

The eye of Jesus lifted and rested on the mitre, but he did not speak ; he had not spoken. With the instinct of the orator, his hand stirred as if it would have indicated, by an eloquent gesture, something of the emotion of the moment. But Annas had ordered that the prisoner be not unbound ; his wrists were crossed behind him. His flesh, more sensitive than that of a ruder man, had already begun to chafe beneath the ropes.

It suddenly occurred to him to ask himself why he was enduring this petty indignity. There surged within him the rush of his own peculiar conscious-

ness of power.   It needed but a thought's force to
burst these bonds as if they had been cobwebs caught
upon his fingers.   All his passionate love of liberty
leaped, — his foresight of worse humiliation to come,
his sense of wronged majesty, his insulted innocence.
His voluntary helplessness resented his conditions.
He thought how easy to be free, quietly to effect the
loosening of the rope, to point the finger silently at
the mitre, to blast the unholy brow that bore the
holy words, in a moment to turn his judges into his
prisoners, to convert the palace into the background
of such a scene as history had never witnessed.

He thought of that to which he gave himself over
if he accepted the natural course of events.   He
remembered how costly it all was. . . . " *Must I be
the sacrifice ?* " he asked.   His breath came fast ;
his color changed ; the pupil of his eye enlarged.
The Priest, who had begun irritably to cross-ques-
tion him, suddenly drew back before the expression
of his prisoner. . . .

There was a moment in which every man in the
hall was aware of an oppressive exigency whose nature he did not understand.   The swinging lamps
in the palace trembled on their slender chains.

.   .   .   .

Down the slopes of Olivet two timid figures stole
away from the groves where the eleven had hidden,
and like men who had been struck on the head and
stunned, suddenly gathering their lost senses, ran
through the valley and over the brook, hurried
through the Golden Gate, and across the Temple area.
Peter was ahead, and yet he kept falling behind as

impulsive people do, from misdirected energy. He stumbled and regained himself, and pushed on ; but, being now well within the walls, he ceased running, that he might not attract attention, and made his way westward as naturally as he could, towards the High-priest's palace. He was moaning openly, and his rugged young face looked old.

But the dearest disciple walked with his eyes upon the ground. He seemed to notice nothing. In the moonlight it could be seen that his lips moved dryly. "We all, — we *all* forsook him," muttered John ; "and we fled."

. . . .

Jesus stood before his judges with closed lips. They had not opened to blight his accusers, nor to defend himself. His momentary agitation had subsided into intense calm. The palace stood untroubled ; the council chamber was not disturbed ; the grim Hebrew faces, crowded in it, wore their natural expressions, touched only by unusual animosity. Nothing had occurred to startle.

It seemed to one who, having some acquaintance among the guards, had effected an entrance to the inner court of the palace that escaped catastrophe vibrated in the air. It seemed as if anything might have happened. But nothing had.

The Nazarene was suddenly aware that John was as near him as he could get, and a smile of recognition flitted over the white face of Jesus ; it was a warm smile, natural and sweet ; as if the prisoner had forgotten that he had been deserted, and remembered only that he was beloved.

John's face quivered; he felt as if he could have
died of shame. Trying to hide his emotion, he went
away and busied himself exerting some influence for
the admission of Peter, who stood in terror without,
among the servants and soldiers.

The night was growing very chilly, and fires were
burning in the courts. Peter crept up, shivering,
and began to warm his hands childishly. He was in
a panic. The servants began to badger him with
servile curiosity. Mortal fear mounted to his brain.

Jesus missed John, and experienced a deepening
loneliness that threatened every moment to unnerve
him. But his whole attention was now required to
the events of the night. These were moving with
malicious swiftness. The condemnation of the Nazarene was a whirlwind, not a process. Between
midnight of Thursday, and nine o'clock of Friday,
Jesus Christ was subjected to six distinct hearings
or trials; and the procedure was illegal from beginning to end.

Caiaphas had begun hotly enough, and without
much tact. Briefly, who and where were the disciples of the accused? In detail, what was his doctrine? Reply specifically to these questions. But
there was no reply. It seemed, for a time, that no
one could induce Jesus to break the remarkable
silence that he had elected to observe. Such scorn
of the High-priest, and of the Council, curled on
his sealed lips as might have withered Augustus,
the Emperor of the world. But unexpectedly came
these calm and unanswerable words: " I spoke
openly to the world. I always taught in the syna-

gogues and the Temple. . . . In secret have I said nothing. Why do you question me? . . . Ask those who heard me."

A stinging blow on the cheek from the palm of a hand — one of the utmost insults that an Oriental could receive — was the retort. A few impudent words accompanied it. Jesus, when he could recover himself, observed the servant who was responsible for this low thing. His reply came with the gentle dignity of a master:

"Have I spoken evil? Then testify of it. If well, why do you smite me?"

Irritated by the dignity or by the logic of the prisoner, Caiaphas formally turned him over to the council. The night was passing rapidly. The ecclesiastical dignitaries began to fret at the loss of their usual rest, and there was a general disposition to hurry the proceedings, so that these comfortable men could get to their beds.

He who had not slept for now many nights, and whose countenance was carved with the deep chisel of endurance approaching its limit, was the most self-possessed man in the palace.

Dawn was coming. Opaque purple grew to translucent gray beyond the windows, and showed past the edges of the curtains drawn to conceal the deeds of that night from the knowledge of the capital. The eye of Jesus turned to meet the rising of this last sun.

Witness after witness was forced to the front; but they were all preposterously perjured, and the case made little headway till one was found who

testified that the accused had been heard to utter
certain atrocities concerning the holy Temple. Then
Jesus remembered that in a moment of devout ecstasy, he had once cried: "Destroy it! I will build
it in three days," and his face changed subtly, so
that the Priest, believing him about to defend himself, angrily cross-questioned him afresh. But the
prisoner preserved his majestic silence still.

Then Caiaphas fell back upon a show of his full
pontifical authority; but his voice had more of the
shrillness of rage than the depth of dignity, when he
said:

"I adjure thee, by the Living God!" ·

At this appeal, the countenance of Jesus took on
a profound solemnity. He perceived that the crisis
of his fate was upon him. Should he reply? He
stood on trial for his life, unaided. Not a witness
for his defense had been allowed him. His stately
reserve had been his only friend, had proved his
best protection. Should he break that frail barrier
between himself and his doom? Now, when he was
expected to keep still should he speak, and take the
consequences? Silence was his one, last chance;
should he fling it away? *Then who would be the
sacrifice?* . . .

"Tell us," insisted the High-priest; "are you the
Christ, the Son of God?"

"You have said it," replied the Nazarene, in a
natural tone.

The council took up the challenge feverishly; several voices reiterated: "*Are* you the Christ?"

"If I tell you that I am, you will not believe me,"

returned the accused, "and if I ask *you*, ye will not let me go."

Now Caiaphas, pushing the point that he had made, followed up his brief advantage, repeating exultantly: "Are you the Christ, the Son of the Blessed?"

And Jesus, in a ringing voice, replied, "*I am.*"

A storm of execration half smothered his next words, which were of a mysterious and commanding character. Jesus grew mute again. He fastened his eye upon the mitre of the High-priest, where the jeweled inscription blazed which was understood to hold the pledge of atonement for the sin of blasphemy. Nor did he remove his gaze, while Caiaphas, in the presence of his council, tearing his priestly robe from throat to hem, in witness of the deadliest offense known to the Hebrew code, cried out passionately: "He hath blasphemed!"

A scene too piteous to portray succeeded. All capital cases must go to the Roman law, but the prisoner was practically considered as a condemned man. Dragged from the council hall to the inner court, he was given over to the malice of his accusers and of the spectators.

This took shocking forms. . . .

. . . .

Day was deepening. The air was so still and so clear that the crowing of a cock, far down the valley, outside the city gates, echoed to the palace and through it, with shrill distinctness.

The tortured man turned and looked into the court. There the bravest of his disciples, harried by servants, and livid with terror, stood gesticulating violently.   His hoarse voice penetrated quite plainly to his Rabbi's ears: "I tell you again, I do not know the man!"

When Peter raised his wretched eyes, they met those of Jesus, gently and mournfully regarding him.

He lived to be an old man, but it has been said of Simon Peter that never, from that dawn to his last, could he sleep past the hour that had known his shame; but rising from his bed, while the cocks called through the valleys, he prayed forgiveness for his sin, and found it.

It was morning, and the light was full, when the unresisting man, heavily chained, was led to the Roman court for his civil trial.   Pilate, the procurator, was on duty.   The politician had no special mind to condemn the prisoner; and a natural disinclination to severity in this case was deepened by the influence of a woman, his wife.   It was owing partly to her presence that Pilate was occupying the marble palace of Herod the Great, — a magnificent building, thought by good architectural judges to vie in splendor with the Temple itself.

The Roman matron, secretly merciful to the Nazarene, and much interested in his affairs since she and her husband had come from gay Rome to this dull Hebrew town, had slept but lightly on the night whose tragic events she more than half suspected.   A broken dream, in which the figure of the Galilean passed and repassed sorrowfully, had vexed the lady.   "He is a just person," she said to her lord; "have nothing to do with the case."

Pilate entered the judgment hall in an uncomfortable humor, being more than ready to dismiss the complaint against the Nazarene. But he perceived, at a glance, that he had to encounter the solid front of the inexorable Hebrew will. The nation had its mind made up. Great was Rome, but she should not save the heretic. The walls of the Prætorium told ready tales, and it soon began to be whispered in the streets that Jesus was actually, though still not formally, doomed.

It was then, when wavering hope first fainted in the hearts of his friends, that a cringing figure crawled into the presence of Caiaphas, and a shaking hand flung on the marble pavement at the High-priest's feet, the silver paid by the church for the betrayal of the great Rabbi, and hurled back into her treasury by a belated remorse. Who in the council of the nation had a moment to spare for the scruples of a cast-off tool? "Push him aside, like the blood-money rolling at his feet! Send a servant to gather up the silver, for it is accursed, being the price of blood. The holy treasury of the Temple may not receive it back. When we have attended to more important matters, we will devote the sum to some estimable charity, — such, for instance, as a burial-place for paupers, a worthy cause needing furtherance in Jerusalem."

Nobody noticed the most wretched man in Palestine, as he fled out of the city, and blindly pushed his way to the further edge of the Kedron valley.

But one thing was left for Iscariot to do; and he did it with a promptness which calls for a certain respect. The branch of the tree broke, and when he was found, he was deep in the gorge upon the jagged rock. But the fall had not marred his face, and identification was immediate and complete.

The morning opened pleasantly. It promised to be a fair day, warm and still. The city was soon alive, and it was still a very early hour when the rumors of the night's black story began to run through the capital. To these were added the presage of worse to come. It was said that Pilate had come off uncomfortably from the forced trial. The accusations of the Jewish church had not made much impression on the Roman procurator. These were chiefly three: the Nazarene had disordered the nation, he had forbidden his followers to pay their taxes to the Emperor, and he had put forth royal claims for himself. Pilate could make little or nothing of these points. He found the case against the accused so weak that he was at a loss how to handle it. When he personally put the question, "Are you the King of the Jews?" the Nazarene ingeniously replied: "You say so." The prisoner had added a few strange words: "My kingdom is not of this world, . . . else my servants would fight; I came into the world for this reason . . . that I might testify to the truth."

The cultivated pagan, not without some knowledge of the philosophy of his day, was interested in this reply. "What *is* truth?" he mused aloud. He regarded the remarkable Hebrew with fresh attention. Something about the man touched him.

It seemed a pity to execute such a person as this, a plain religious enthusiast, of a blameless life, and of unusual intellect. Really, what had he done, beyond rousing the jealousy of a sour lot of Jewish priests? The Roman was puzzled, and uneasy. He remembered the demi-gods of his own religion. "I find no fault in the man," he said. At that moment, some one in his hearing remarked that Jesus was a Galilean.

"Then," cried the procurator, with a smile of relief, "turn him over to Herod Antipas! The case belongs to his jurisdiction."

. . . .

Throughout the city, in little secret groups, were huddled the friends of Jesus. Matters had gone so far that they dared not now announce themselves for dear life's sake, and most of them found their lives dearer than his comfort.

One, a woman, separated herself from the others, and tried to get a footing near him, since access to his presence was totally denied her. But the crowd, that had begun to surge excitedly, forced her back. Loud voices round her said:

"They take him to Herod!"

She pushed on with the feeble step of a middle-aged woman, made old by suffering before her time. Now the current of the stream of people turned, and she found herself borne in the direction of the palace of the Maccabees, where Herod, having come to town to celebrate the Passover, had taken up his quarters.

The palace glittered in the sun with a forbidding

cheerfulness. Its broad approach was decorated by imported shrubs, and trees descended from the days of Solomon. Under their cool shadow a file of guardsmen tramped. The representatives of the Hebrew church followed remotely, with civic disorder of step. These did not enter the palace, nor did they set foot in the prætorium. They were excellent churchmen. They would not defile themselves on Passover week, by crossing a heathen threshold.

The watcher had one distant glimpse of a tall figure, chained, and closely guarded, and walking with difficulty.

"He will never know that I am here," she thought.

The woman followed blindly; she felt as if his chains dragged on her body, making one prisoner of the two. It was his mother.

A gentle hand touched her robe, and turning, she saw the protecting face of her son's dearest disciple. John stood silently beside her.

Painful rumors came from the palace. One could scarcely force the mind to believe them, they were so harsh. It was said that Herod, curious and talkative at first, had lapsed into petty mockeries and torments, unworthy of the meanest mind in Palestine. It was said —

Suddenly, down the marble steps, the people saw the military movement stirring once again. Tossed from the tetrarch to the governor, bandied between Rome and Israel, the worry of the law, the case went back.

The Nazarene was walking weakly down the long, shaded avenue. The toy of whim and spite, he bore himself majestically. But his face took on a mortal white, above the brilliant robe that taunted its piteous color.

CHAPTER XVII

THE tumult in the city mounted rapidly. Rumor, for once, was milder than the facts. These began to take incredible shapes.

It was quickly known that Pilate, clinging to his reluctance to condemn the Nazarene, had fallen back upon the politic Roman custom which pardoned one Hebrew criminal on Passover week. There lay in the dungeon of Herod a troublesome fellow, a noted revolutionist, under sentence for murder; and passing, strangely enough, by an ingenious alias, as Bar-Abbas, the son of the father. The procurator was bewildered when, having, in accordance with the traditions of the great anniversary, recommended the release of Jesus, there came back to him the demand that he should pardon the murderer instead.

Pilate was plainly at his wits' end; these had drawn him into a difficulty from which they proved unable to free him. It was said that he made earnest, even eager efforts to save the Nazarene from the fate that was upon him. It was noted that the governor vacillated over the case, and indeed, pleaded for the prisoner. It was known that but for the officers of the national church the Roman might have saved the life of the great Hebrew, —

to what a consequence, who can say? The story of
the world's future depended on the decision of this
one man. But Rome was passing her day of decided wills. Firmness was going out of fashion in
the enervated national character. Pilate was a politician, harried between a turbulent, coerced people and an unreasonable and exacting government.
Annoyed and unhappy, he threw up the game at
last, and yielded to the clamor of the Jewish nation.

He yielded to the people; but the people yielded
to the priests. These pious incendiaries fired the
popular feeling, steadily and stolidly. They would
take no alternative; they would listen to no compromise. They wrought the mob to a religious frenzy,
and the Nazarene went down before it.

The nearest friends of Jesus closed together.
They made a little band and kept as near him as
they dared, watching the prætorium for sight or
news of him. The streets were now full to bursting,
and movement became more and more difficult. It
was still early, with such monstrous rapidity had
the sham trial of the Nazarene proceeded. As the
morning advanced, the clamor in front of the palace
grew to alarming proportions. Suddenly the yells
and shouts of the mob became articulate. Two terrible words formed themselves out of the general
roar. Which among those who loved the Rabbi
best was the first to understand what those words
meant? They turned, each man and woman of them,
instinctively, to spare his mother. It was too late
for that. Were her ears a little dulled by time and
trouble? Who can tell? Mary of Nazareth said no

word, while the air of Jerusalem quivered to the laceration of the outcry : —

" *Crucify !* CRUCIFY him ! "

. . . .

Pilate came to the balcony of the great palace of Herod. The superb building blazed in the strengthening sunlight. The court room lay mistily within. Guardsmen covered every exposed spot, — porticoes, steps, avenues ; even the roof was armed. No one knew how the day's riot would result.

The Roman governor had a worried look. The people saw that he was agitated. A liveried slave brought him a basin and ewer, and began to pour water on his unsteady hands. Pilate held them up, dripping in the morning light. They were white, delicate hands ; the jewels on his fingers answered gayly to the sun.

" I wash my hands ! I have washed them of this innocent blood ! " said Pilate. He spoke theatrically. But he was in earnest, as the theatrical may be.

Then there rose from the throat of the Hebrew people, on their holy week, one long, sinister cry. Baser was never uttered by any nation.

" His blood be upon us, and upon our children ! "

. . . .

A centurion came up at this moment and roughly ordered back a little group of Hebrews who had attracted his attention by their agitated appearance, and their restraint of manner. A chance word of a bystander caused the officer to follow them with dark curiosity, but the person whom he sought was not among them. For their Lord's own sake, his friends at Bethany had not shown themselves. The presence of Lazarus in the capital would have infuriated the Sanhedrin, and would have hastened the end, or deepened the sufferings, of the gentle life with which his own was so marvelously inwound. Lazarus accepted the look of being neglectful and ungrateful, that he might offer the fact of loyalty.

But where was Mary? Bearing her part in this cruel dilemma, with strength, with sweetness, in silence, — hidden somewhere, invisible to Jesus, watching, listening, with eyes to which the mercy of tears was denied. No woman in Palestine — having set apart the mother of Jesus in her solitary sacredness — endured what the sister of Lazarus did that day, and lived to know that she had endured it, and yet that she could not die.

.   .   .   .

Again on the portico of the palace appeared the irresolute figure of the procurator. But this time he was pitiably accompanied. When the mob began to divine how, and by whom, the terrible cry arose once more: —

"*Crucify!* CRUCIFY!"

Pilate drew back with a gesture half dramatic, half sincere. At a sign from him, one in the background was thrust forward by military hands.

"Ecce Homo!" cried the Roman loudly.

There fell upon all the people a sudden and solemn hush. For the sight that they saw moved the basest soul in the multitude, and the witnesses of it who were the least unworthy painfully carried its reproduction to their last dream.

Jesus stood patiently, plainly to be seen, — a tall man, symmetrically formed, in the vigor of his youth. A robe of crimson purple dashed royal color upon him. There was blood upon his brow, and drops which his chained hands, hanging heavily, could not wipe away, thickened upon his cheeks. A mutter rustled through the crowd when it was seen that a chaplet of thorns, woven in semblance of a crown, had been violently pressed, by rude hands, into his temples. It was soon perceived, from his evident physical suffering, that worse had been done to the man. He had passed through what was called the "intermediate death." The penal scourge of the times was often a severe weapon, — a leathern strap, studded with spikes of iron or of bone; nor was it wielded with a merciful hand.

The sensitive flesh of the Nazarene quivered yet. . . . His body was slightly bowed as if it still bent forward in the instinctive attitude of one who would, but cannot, avert blows. This detracted somewhat from his height, but nothing from his kingly demeanor. His head rose nobly from his delicate, bared throat. His dark, brown hair and beard, curling and soft, finely framed a face that Palestine had loved before she hated, and which Rome respected while she feared. His features were strong, but as soon as one had said this, one perceived that they were fine. There was not a weak line in them, but there was not a rude one. There shone upon the man the light of such a stainless imagination, as seemed almost incompatible with the force and experience which he plainly possessed. This look

CHRIST AND PILATE—ECCE HOMO

was something before which the clearest heart felt clouded. It caused a strange, personal discomfort in one who was not too dull to be aware of it.

His lips, exquisitely cut, trembled to every stir of feeling; but his chin had the moulding of a great will. His eyes, large and luminous, burned from sockets sunken by suffering. In their expression was something ineffable. Not a spark of resentment sprang from their inner stars. Unfathomable pity, deep below deep, rayed from them. He looked as if he could have taken his torturers to his heart, and forgiven them before they asked it.

Signs of what he had endured he could not suppress, and his face was very haggard. The most pathetic thing about it was the indication that he had not slept; that he had endured much, and must endure worse, with nerves shaken to their utmost, and brain reeling. His whole physical system went to his therefore tenfold torment, unfortified by natural, human rest. Out of that mass of many thousands, this occurred, possibly, to two or three minds.

Now, full in his wasted face, from uncounted throats the roar went up again :

" We have a law ! . . . He made himself the Son of God. He ought to die ! "

.   .   .   .

It was between eight and nine o'clock in the morning when the word went forth that even the allowable respite of two days between sentence and execution was refused ; and that the man and the cross — his last, his dumb companion — had come together.

Crucifixion was not a Jewish death-penalty, nor was it, at that time, the favorite that it later became with Rome, when Hebrew souls went up by thousands from Roman crosses; and when one of those ghastly, historic retributions, which nations, like individuals, sometimes undergo, avenged the Nazarene.

For this blameless man had been reserved the exceptional death; that of the lowest shame, that of the sorest torment.

The day was as fair as it had promised, and there was a show of happy sunlight upon his face and figure when he was led out of the palace of Herod towards the narrow, arched street, known for his sake, from that time, as the Via Dolorosa.

The mob had a glimpse of his peaceful, melancholy face as the cross was adjusted by leathern straps to his arms and shoulders. A few, more thoughtful than the mass, observed how exhausted he looked.

He had but a very short distance to walk to the hill then in use as the place of common execution. It lay in a northwesterly direction from the Temple. It was scarcely a quarter of a mile away. Great surprise was felt, when the cry came up from the following crowd:

" He cannot do it! He has dropped. The man is too weak to carry his own cross ! "

It was soon known that a stranger from Cyrene, coming into the city, and meeting the brutal procession, had been arrested, and forced by the Roman

guards to bear the burden, under which the condemned had sunken. No one had understood before how far the strength of the Nazarene was gone.

In every mob there is hidden the warmth of some
human mercy ; and as the gentle prisoner went to
his death, the voices of the Hebrew women arose,
wailing. He had cared for them, and blessed their
wretched lives in so many ways that it was hard to
say which of all his kindnesses was the kindest, or
which of his wonders had been the most wonderful.
He had cured their sick, he had saved their dissipated, he had loved their children, he had poured
out his exquisite sympathy upon their unknown
griefs. For the heart-break that only women know,
for the woe that women of their times endured, as
a matter of course, without complaint, he had been
divinely sorry. He had been the only man who ever
understood.

The women sobbed and moaned bitterly, and covered their faces with their robes, and their cry went
up to heaven against the men who had done this
murder.

Then Jesus, when he heard the women weeping,
forgot himself, and turned to comfort them. And
he guarded them and warned them against troubles
and perils of the future, known, it seemed, only to
himself ; but which afterward, as he had said, fell
heavily upon them and their hapless children.

And the women wept the more, — not for their
own sakes, but for his, — because he forgot himself
and remembered them, in an hour when all men
would have called it only natural if he had forgotten

everything in heaven and earth, except his own emergency. This was now past all human hope. For the great heretic there could be no reprieve.

.   .   .   .

There was in Jerusalem something like an association of Hebrew ladies, organized for the purpose of relieving the sufferings of those condemned to lingering deaths. The use of anodynes was their chief or only practical method of doing this ; and a mixture of myrrh and strong wine was found most helpful to the tortured. The executive department of this feminine charity was delegated to men.

The women who had followed Jesus, loving and mourning him, were distressed when they learned that the Nazarene declined their anodyne. After he had been told of its nature, no one could persuade him to touch it. At whatever cost, he chose consciousness as the road to death. It was said that his convictions refused him the right to curtail any form of suffering which God allotted him. This was a strange thing. Who could understand it ?

It was now nine o'clock in the morning. The little, sarcastic revenge of Pilate, on the prominent Jews who had forced him into an unpleasant position, had been affixed to the top of the cross. It was ingeniously written, for the benefit of a mixed population, in three languages, — Latin, Greek, and Aramæan. This inscription set forth, as was usual, the charge under which the condemned was to die.

A committee of Hebrew priests had hurried angrily to the procurator.

"Take down the titulus!" they demanded; "it

is offensive to us to say that he is King of the Jews. Say that he *claimed* to be. Re-write the titulus!"

But Pilate laughed.

Baffled and stung, a number of very religious Jews ran up towards the place of execution, to see for themselves what was happening. The priests could not follow, for it was unlawful to defile themselves with the associations of death, and at Passover time. These pious persons climbed to the walls of the Temple area; and there, as the April morning broadened cheerfully, they sat in the pleasant light and feasted upon what they saw. Golgotha was quite within their range of vision. They watched the scene, in all its details, as long as they could see.

A messenger, running, came breathless back to them. They hurled ravenous questions at him.

"When the cross was lifted, — what did you hear?"

"Strange words."

"Tell us them! Give us the words! What did he say?"

And the messenger, dropping his voice for uncontrollable awe, gave them the words. "As the Lord liveth, the man did say: 'Father, forgive them, for they know not what they do.'"

The priests glanced over their shoulders, and each man saw that the others had turned white to the lips. The oldest averted his face. The rest gazed on.

.   .   .   .

Jesus, on Golgotha, looked down and off. He

saw the city and the Temple shining in the light of life and spring. . . . On the walls and pinnacles he saw moving figures, and perceived that his agonies were studied by the clergy of his church.

Below, he saw his worn, blue robe in the hands of the soldiers, who were casting lots for his tunic.

Beyond, up the wooded slopes of Olivet, lay unseen Bethany. His dimming eye wandered over the crest of the horizon towards beautiful Galilee; there came upon his confused senses a breath from his dear lake, seventy miles away.

He seemed, for a moment, to be preaching in his own boat. Some sick persons were brought to him, on the shore, and a merciful instinct caused him to move his hands, as if he would heal the sufferers.

The anguish of the form of death which forbids the victim even to writhe recalled his drifting mind. It could not float far, for his brain was strong and clear. He retained throughout his torment his own self-possession. He looked upon the people, thinking of them in his favorite word. What a "multitude" they were! Had they all come out to see him suffer? It would have been something if they had not taunted him so!

He recognized faces among them, — this one he had comforted in a great sorrow; that one he had cured of a cruel disease; he identified persons whom he had seen often in his audiences, and who had believed in him and trusted him. He saw that they were classifying him, now, with the common felons who occupied the crosses at his right hand and at his left.

Suddenly he saw women pressing as near the cross as they were allowed; faces familiar to his childhood were in the group; and there was one — she came from Magdala; he had saved her from great misfortunes. She had remembered it, and had cared enough to be near him at the end. He was touchingly grateful for this sign that he was not quite forgotten. And there — God pity her! — there was his mother. Who was beside her? The dear disciple stood looking at his Lord. The face of John was like a cast moulded out of love that cannot act.

Across the countenance of Jesus passed the semblance of one of his most radiant smiles, such as those remembered who knew him in the affectionate relations of life. Many persons distinctly heard the faint words by which he commended his mother to the protection of his friend, —

"He is your son." . . . "Take her; she is your mother."

It was not unusual for the crucified to linger for days, and surprise penetrated the onlookers when they perceived that the sensitive Nazarene was already sinking. He had not been under torture for yet six hours, but the signs of coming dissolution were apparent even now.

Since noon the brilliant sun had deadened. At first there were no clouds, and observant persons cast anxious glances at the sky which had taken on a coppery color. Darkness had indeed begun. It was not yet mid-afternoon, but all the world was blackening fiercely. Lurid redness gashed the heavens ; it was as if they had been splashed with blood.

Between the crucified, high above the heads of the living, an awful conversation was taking place. From one of the condemned felons, taunts were overheard :

" Then, why do you not save yourself, and us ? "

Reproaches for this brutality issued from the dry lips of the other, a compeer in some dark past. It was observed that this man addressed the sinking Nazarene. He replied faintly, offering some devout comfort to his low companion in agony.

This exquisite self-forgetfulness did not stop the ghastly hilarity, which still amused the mob at intervals, as it had all day.

" Why do you not come down from the cross, you Son of God ? "

.   .   .   .

Why did he not ? How simple a deed that were !

Where were the forces of which he had spoken in Gethsemane, in which he believed, but with whose mystical reinforcement he chose to dispense ? Silent, in unseen spaces, obeying unknown laws, marshaled but unsummoned, thrilling for his command, they awaited it.

The taunts came up :

" You saved other people ! Now let us see you save yourself ! "

His lips, parching with the thirst of crucifixion, moved painfully. There drove across his tortured brain the thought of the consequences if he said the word that burned for utterance, if he gave the sign that battled through his being for expression.

What did he hear? Was it the dying throb of his own great heart? Was it the voice of God? or the wail of man?

"*Thou shalt carry the sins of the world. . . . Thou Lamb of God!*"

. . . .

Jesus opened his closing eyes. They were fading fast, and the figures in the moving mass before him were scarcely visible. He could see his mother's upturned face. He could yet feel upon him the eyes of John, whose expression bore to him the yearning of the frail, human love that might fail him, and grieve him, but which loved him still, and only asked to be trusted in its weakness and forgiven for its faultiness, because it was human, and because it was love.

But the faces of his dearest passed on into the universal darkness, and went out. They were replaced by ineffable visions. The stored strength of a lifetime of prayer lifted all his nature, and shut it in with God. Who forgot? Who deserted? His Father loved . . .

Now all the woe of souls unborn thrust itself upon his consciousness. His own age, his own people, had slain him. But he was not dying for his own age. All times, all peoples, counted in the cost of his anguish. He felt the human exigencies in which belief would be hard, and scorn of the invisible natural; he thought of the weakened, and the pursued by trouble, and of those who would find their suffering greater than their endurance. He remembered that it was his to show them how to trust in God. . . .

A deadly darkness had swept down upon the crosses; a roar that was neither tempest, nor thunder, occupied the air. In the swift and startling gloom his face could be seen, struck out distinctly by inexplicable light. Before its expression, all the people fell upon the ground, those who had hated him praying Jehovah to spare their brutal souls; but those who loved him thought only of his, and prayed for him.

Ah God, what a cry!

. . . Uttered with the last energy which assists dissolution, spoken in the tongue of his youth, and of the lowly people for whom he had cared, the piteous words which one who loves him sensitively would not, even yet, urge the refusing lips to repeat, carried the last surprise of his broken heart.

As his unanswered question went up from the cross to the heavens, the darkness deepened to fright. The wind arose, but fell at once to ominous calm. Then the lips of the earth opened and spoke.

In the unnatural dark, all the people ran hither and thither, and could not see one another's faces. But his upon the cross remained still visible, hanging a little higher than their own, and smitten out in light.

The earthquake tore the rocks of Golgotha, and the walls of the city reeled, and stones which sealed the tombs in ancient burial gardens were loosened. In some instances they were thrust off, and sepulchres left open to the recoiling gaze.

The panic on Golgotha shook from centre to circumference of the half-blinded crowd. The people

GOLGOTHA

fled in horror, anyhow, anywhere, as they could; as they ran, they beat their breasts, and uttered short, terrified sounds.

The Roman officer, who had been posted at the foot of the cross, fell flat with shame and terror.

" It *was* the Son of God ! " he cried.

When the priests, groping through the prolonged darkness, huddled together in the Temple, they found a fearful thing. The great and sacred veil, hanging before the Holy of Holies, was rent across its blue and purple, white and crimson folds, straight through its embroidered, golden cherubim — torn from end to end.

CHAPTER XVIII

THE RESURRECTION AND THE LIFE

WHEN the darkness lifted from the land, the crucified Nazarene did not stir.

Was he dead so soon? There were those who were inclined to complain of him, because his sensitive and exhausted frame did not support torture longer. Even in death, he offended his tormentors. They took the quickest possible steps to make sure of the fact that he was gone, beyond a question.

"Not a bone of him shall be broken" had sung an ancient poet of his people, in the days when prophecy and literature clasped strong hands.

A Roman soldier stood on Golgotha with upraised arm to apply the test of the *crurifragium* to the motionless body of Jesus. But he laid his mallet down with uneasy surprise, and took his spear instead. Did there linger in the vigorous Galilean the innermost ember of life? The trained military hand made no mistake in giving the vital wound. Then the spear dropped as the mallet had, and the Roman wished he had not marred the man. For there was something that he could not understand about the manner of this death.

It has since been said that there were certain physiological evidences that the crucified Rabbi had, indeed, died most piteously, yielding to a mental agony which, in rare cases, has been known to cause a lesion of the central organ of life. It has long been believed by many who would have wished to believe otherwise, that Jesus, in the literal sense of the words, died of a broken heart.

The broken-hearted keep their own counsel; and the secret is his yet. By whatever road he trod the last wilderness that lay between his lonely life and its appalling end, the end had come. Follower and foe, Jew and Gentile, accepted the fact: Jesus the Christ was dead.

Now, upon the murdered man was poured a swift tenderness which was offered to him — as it is to many a sensitive and deserted soul — too late.

A prominent Hebrew who had long loved the Rabbi in silence pushed his influence to the full, demanded the body of the Nazarene, and obtained from the Roman government its immediate possession. He offered his own family burial place, a new tomb, that death had never occupied. The eminent citizen achieved what lowlier friends could not have accomplished, and the last dignities were offered without disturbance to the body of Jesus before the Sabbath sun had set. This was as the law compelled.

The trembling fingers of his chosen friends drew out the spikes from the feet that had trodden Palestine over only to do it kindnesses, and bathed the hurts in the hands that had healed and blessed, but never harmed. As these were composed for their rest, one who had cared for him very much thought how often they had been seen lifted over the heads

of the people, while he prayed that happiness, and
health, and holiness might come to them. The tears
of loving women dashed upon his face, when it was
drawn down within their reach. They who had
never ventured or thought to touch him while he
was alive, begged permission to lift his cold hand to
their lips. But his brow was so majestic that no
kiss could intrude upon it. In death, as in life, he
passed alone.

They bore him to his garden tomb as the light
was striking low upon the leaves of trees and plants,
and upon the petals of the closing flowers. They
carried him in haste and fear. Only his bearers and
two or three friends accompanied him. With tired
feet and tender thoughts he had followed many a
burial procession. But Jerusalem was ashamed to
follow his.

Rudely embalmed, or wrapped in such spices as
could be hastily procured, and folded into fair linen,
his noble body was left in the outer chamber of the
pure, new sepulchre. He was not interred.

As the round stone rolled into its place the sun
sank. And the Hebrew nation piously set itself to
the observance of High Sabbath; for it was Holy
Week.

.   .   .   .

But there were ingenious minds among their
priests and leading men, and the Roman governor
promptly received one of the anxious committees
that had tried his patience all the week.

" Give us a watch at the tomb," urged the spokesman shrewdly, " for the man has said strange things;

he did claim that he would not stay in it three days. He has his friends. They would steal his body to save his reputation as a prophet. Give us guards!"

So Pilate yawned, and gave them guards, for he was weary of the subject. And the tomb was barred with a small stone, which, adjusted to the disk, held it in its place. A tablet of moist clay, so placed that the least movement would break it, was stamped with the imperial seal. The officers of Rome sat without and guarded the tomb.

They sat there all night on duty. The next day they were relieved by other guards, and the next night the watch went on again. So the Sabbath came to its end, and midnight of Saturday to Sunday followed.

The watch were brave men, and accustomed to grim duties, but they had uncomfortable thoughts. The night was long, and there was no wind. It was so still that their own hearty breathing startled them. The garden was in bloom all about the beautiful new sepulchre. The stalks of shrubs seemed to stir as if they had been hit by passers; but no one moved. Now and then a flower stooped, as if it had been brushed; but it had not been touched. The air was faint with perfume; the place was heavenly bright. The white disk that locked the sepulchre gave back the light, as if it were a gate of pearl.

Within the vault, Jesus of Nazareth lay in state.

It came on to be the hour when the night dies and the day is not yet, but is seen to be approaching. The moon was set. The cheek of the East had begun to pale.

The watchmen in the garden moved uneasily. Who stepped? There was no one. What stirred? Surely, nothing.

They passed to and fro, and came together at the mouth of the sepulchre, where they stood on guard.

In any two comrades picked for united duty, there is liable to be one finer and one braver than the other. Of these two men, he who was the quicker of eye suddenly went the color of terror, pointed with his spear, and fell.

The stone that closed the tomb was moving.

The other guardsman sprang, with a Roman oath, and struck at the stone with his sword, but he did not hit it. The great disk began to stir in its groove and slowly rolled out to one side.

The moon was down, but the sun was not yet up; yet the garden glowed; a light that was neither of the dawn nor of the sunset rayed upon the tomb. The leaves of the vines that clung about it had the look that foliage has when it is aflame, and every flower in the garden was a bell or cup of fire. ∴ . . Glory became translucent; translucence softly outlined —

But the bolder of the guards turned as faint as his mate, and dropped beside him.

.   .   .   .

Mary called Magdalene came to the garden, and it was Sunday's dawn. She had not slept. The night had been so brilliant, that it seemed as if she had sat at the walls of Heaven. Her soul was floating; — had it wings? She wondered why she had not wept. She thought of her miserable past without a pang. With a flight of joy she remembered what the Rabbi had done for her. Other women had ministered to him, and loved him: let them mourn him! They had not suffered as she had; she felt as if it were hers only to bless him. She felt as if she outloved them all — as, indeed, she had out-walked them all, and so came first into the garden.

Silver gray was sweetening to rose along the east, which was still dim; but the prelude of the morning had begun with pomp. It would be a stately sun-rise. The city lay melted in an unusual and beautiful mist. This had a gentle color, and gave a grateful indistinctness to the outlines of the palaces and the Temple.

In the garden the dew was heavy. The scent of the opening flowers was delicate. There was such purity in the air that it was a delight to breathe. The trees were full of song birds. Music, perfume, light, color, flooded the garden, and rose against the solemn shape of the sepulchre.

The woman crept up on tiptoe, as one does who fears lest she might disturb a dear sleeper. She held her breath — ah, what had happened? What had happened?

The guards were nowhere to be seen. The great disk was rolled from its position. The woman looked in at the mouth of the vault; the tomb was open and empty.

With her hands upon her heart, Mary glanced, and sped out of the garden. This was a matter for men. She ran to the lodgings of Peter and the dear disciple.

" They have stolen him ! " she gasped.

Her breath was gone, and her courage with it. All her high mood of the night and of the first dawn had broken down. She came back, walking weakly. She could not keep up with John, or with Peter, who ran on without noticing her. She entered the garden drearily.

The other women were not organized like Mary. They came up more deliberately, with their myrrh and spices in their arms, thinking to finish the burial preparations that the Sabbath law had interrupted, and to do for their Lord what should be done, before it was too late. They were less sensitive, or more brave than she whose early misfortunes had shaken body and soul; and when they saw the great disk rolled away, they did not run. They put the myrrh carefully down upon the turf, and stooped and crept into the tomb. And so it befell them to see that which some of them were afraid to speak of, and it happened to them to hear that which others were more afraid not to tell. To these last, the world owes the record of some of the wonderful words in whose radiant hope the Christian dead of centuries have been laid to rest.

So the women came out of the tomb, for he was not there, and they, too, went away.

John came running to the sepulchre, and stopped. Peter, panting heavily, pushed straight in. The other followed him more slowly, and the two men examined the tomb. It was to them but an empty

vault. They saw no blinding sights; they heard no
mysterious words. They saw the linen cloth lying,
as fair and fresh as when it had been wound about
his dear body — but nothing more. With shaking
hands they reverently examined the grave-clothes.

"He is not here," they said. And they, too,
had gone away.

. . . .

Mary was alone at last. She knelt down, gathering
her strength, and looked into the tomb for herself.

The marble slab was bare. There he had lain
in state, awaiting his burial. Beyond was the crypt
where they had meant to inter him to-day. The
air breathed in and out of the new tomb, as pure
and strong as dew and youth. The morning sun
streamed in. The sepulchre was empty.

Was it ? Look again! At the head and foot
of the long, white slab, brilliance began to form.
The woman held her breath, and called her courage.
She was ready to believe in the inexplicable, but
she was sore afraid of it. Yet, as she gazed, she
ceased to be afraid. What she saw seemed to her
more natural than any common, usual thing, that
could be explained.

Call them spirits, call them angels, or name them
as one would, these strange, beautiful visions, with
eyes like the arrows of the storm, were messengers
of God. And God had never been explained.
Mary looked at the spirits confidingly. Her tears
ran down into a sudden, childlike smile.

"They have taken away my dear Lord," she
said, "can you tell me where to find him ?"

A shadow fell over her shoulder, and entered the tomb. There it lay solemnly. It was the shadow of the figure of a man.

She had thought it was the keeper of the burial garden, and began to explain to him how and why she was there. Her sobs tore from her now so that her words were hard to understand, and her own ears were deafened by them. Her eyes were blinded, too, by the tears which she had kept back so long that they would have their way at last.

She did not recognize the stranger, while she tried to talk with him, until he called her by her own name.

Then a cry went up to the morning skies, that arched like a dome of joy above the tomb.

" *My Master !* "

She sprang towards him, crying and laughing, and her words began to fall fast, like drops pouring from a flagon of delight.

" It is my dear Lord ! *He is alive !* "

She fell at his feet, and stretched up her arms. But he motioned her back.

.   .   .   .

Now, about the city, and throughout Judea, and in all Palestine, great things were said ; and as great were never said, but took place in silence and in secrecy ; while others were whispered under oath of honorable persons, and so came into record.

Past many an ancient tomb whose stones the earthquake had loosened at the hour when the Nazarene gave up his ghost, stole silent figures ; into many a home where the bereaved sat desolate, trod soundless footsteps. The latch lifted, the curtain stirred, the casement opened; and one who had been mourned for years came in and took his old, familiar place, and smiling, looked about the room, to see if he were remembered.

"The Resurrection" had been a theological phrase in Palestine, accepted by some, refused by others, and a puzzle to all. Now it came to be called a fact of history. For the dead had been seen abroad, and recognized.

It also came, but not at once, to be understood that this mystery had some connection with the other, mightier one, which, in time, absorbed the interest of all thoughtful men.

There were those who bowed their heads, and smote their breasts and said : " We have crucified a man. But we could not slay a God ! "

There were others who mused, and knew not what to say. These were less afraid of not recognizing a God than of deifying a man ; for this was their nature. And to all natures, the life and death of the great Nazarene remained a mystery.

To none did the wonders which directly succeeded his death seem more mysterious at the time than to his chosen friends. The women came with their joyous testimony ; but they were women. The men listened to them in masculine incredulity ; *they* had found only an empty tomb. No disciple had seen angels ; and the Roman watchmen, for fear of their lives, and being heavily bribed, withheld their star-tling witness, and thrust out the report that the body had been stolen by the followers of the Nazarene while the guards slept at their posts. This childish tale was instigated by the priests, and the pardon of Pilate to the offending watchmen was a part of the price.

Thus matters stood immediately after the death of Jesus. Then that happened which changed everything.

It was the late afternoon of the first Easter, when two of the eleven,[1] restless with sorrow, went out by the western gate for a country walk. They took the direction of a little place called Emmaus — a lovely village set over the hills in bloom and green. Life and light throbbed in the soft wind, in the gentle scenery. Thousands of birds were in the air. The soul of spring swayed by dreamily. But the hearts of the twain were as heavy as the clods of the grave. Their Lord was dead.

In the bewilderment of fresh bereavement, they talked drearily, — of him, of his great life, of his piteous death, of all that was precious and of all that was confusing to them in his history ; of the failure of his purposes, of the ruin of their hopes and of his.

A stranger joined them as they were walking, — it seemed that he was one of the festive bands with which the suburbs of Jerusalem had been peopled the past week — and entered into their conversation. They thought him a very ignorant man, though he had not that appearance, for he questioned them

---

[1] Cleopas, and (by tradition) Luke.

minutely about the life and death of their Rabbi.
Was there a foreigner in Jerusalem who had not
heard what had happened? They answered him
with a sort of surprised condescension, but they
readily began to talk about their Lord; indeed, they
could not speak of anything else. And as they
strolled and talked, their feeling about the stranger
underwent one of the swift transformations which
simple minds experience in the presence of a superior. This was no ordinary tourist. This was a
master of knowledge. He spoke of the Hebrew
Messiah; of the meaning of ancient prophetic poetry; of the possibilities hidden in the scriptures
of the race. He spoke of the recent events that had
shaken Palestine — of the national hopes and of the
national shame.

The two disciples felt deeply drawn to the stranger;
their thoughts took a high turn; courage and faith
swept back upon their despairing hearts, like fire from
heaven upon an abandoned altar. They clung so to
the stranger that, when he would have left them and
passed on up the country road, they could not, would
not, have it so. They begged him, nay, they compelled him, to accept their hospitality. So he indulged them, smiling, and went to supper with them
in their simple house of entertainment. There, it
seemed the only right thing for him to do to take
the head of the table; his hosts did not even wonder
why. And it seemed to be wholly expected that
he should ask the blessing of God upon the bread.
Then it seemed not strange, in any way, when the two
began slowly and quietly to understand who he was.

How did this recognition come about? Was it of the mind, or of the heart? Was it of the senses, or of the spirit? Had they been blinded or deafened? Had he changed, or was it they? The secrets of approach between the living and the dead were God's, — were God's and *his*.

Like so much else that had been inexplicable, this, the utmost mystery, now yielded to his control. And they who loved and mourned a dead Christ, lifted their eyes and perceived that he was alive.

.   .   .   .

Ah, the radiance! the rapture! The countenance that had been overstrained with suffering was blinding bright. His wan and wakeful eyes had taken on a look of rest which nothing could disturb again. His tormented body shone with such vigor that it seemed as if every nerve had forgotten that it had ever known a pang. His fine lips quivered — not with pain. When he smiled, it was as if the heart would break with joy to see him. . . .

For forty days he whom Palestine had tortured and slain, trod her dust, elate and wonderful.

It pleased him to reveal himself on many occasions, and by the witness of many eyes and ears. It has been recorded that five hundred persons, at certain places and times, met with personal knowledge that the dead Nazarene lived again.

But it was to his own friends that his heart hurried, and his own received him rapturously. Once, in a manner not known, he is thought to have found his way to comfort heart-broken Peter. Once, and

THE SUPPER AT EMMAUS

once again, in a fashion that the whole world knows, he came into the upper chamber of the stone house [1] at Jerusalem, where the disciples sat behind doors closed and bolted, fearful of priests, of Rome, and of the people, hiding from they knew not what perils, and consumed by misery. Here he saluted them audibly: " Peace be unto you ! " he said. Here he shared their evening meal, and they saw him eat, before their eyes, the poor man's fare of fish and honey which was all they had to offer. Here a mysterious solemnity took place, dimly understood by those who witnessed it, but reverenced by them and by all who have loved him since, because it proceeded from him.

After this, he took the pains to come back the second time, to the same place and company, because on his first appearance the skeptic of the group was absent. He called on the distrustful disciple who demanded for assurance of his Lord's identity such exacting proofs as history has been careful to specify, to employ his own methods of satisfying his doubts. Jesus yielded his incomprehensible personality, while Thomas, — being of the type of mind that would to-day put the case of the resurrection of Jesus Christ into the hands of experts in psychological research, — investigated the marvel as he would. The doubter thrust out his trembling fingers. . . .

There was the spear-wound made by Rome. There were the torn hands and feet, mutilated by Israel. The apparition could be touched. It had form, sub-

[1] Tradition.

stance. It was a body. It bore the likeness of the torments with which life had seared it. . . .

As the skeptic fell upon his knees, the upper room echoed with the low cry with which the groping belief of all men and all times will go reaching up to mystery: "*My Lord and my God!*"

.   .   .   .

The beautiful part of the wonder was that Jesus seemed to care for the same things that he used to care for before he had died; not only for the truths and the friends, but for the places that he had loved.

He went joyfully into Galilee, which had been dear to him; and there he expressed wishes that his disciples should meet him; as they did. He came to the lake and loved it and remained by it for a while.

And when the puzzled fishermen, coming back to their old duties, went out on an unsuccessful trip, and put about, tired and discouraged, he who had so often met and helped them met them once again upon the shore. And he cared for them and for their disappointment, and did them one of his own strange kindnesses, and ate a meal with them, as he had done once or twice before since his reappearance.

But Peter dashed into the water, as he was apt to do if he were afloat on any startling occasion, and hurried, longing, to his Lord. A solemn and memorable conversation took place between them.

Upon these radiant scenes there fell not the soft footfall of a shadow. All was as natural, as peaceful, as pleasant, as a safe and happy life. Indeed, happiness was a paltry word by which to speak of

the demeanor and expression of him who seemed to
know celestial delight upon terrestrial ground.

Beautiful Galilee, that had been kinder to him or
less unkind than any other province in the land, received and kept the secret of his movements, when
those who loved him best and saw him most often
knew not where he had gone or whence he came
again.   He appeared and disappeared as he would,
peaceful and majestic.

He wore something of the look of mysterious joyousness which a spirit might, if it had the opportunity, after death, to come back to the scenes that were
best beloved in life.   But they who saw him, and
conversed with him, and touched him said :

" It is not a spirit."

What sacred romance, what solemn delights and
surprises came into the lives of those fishermen for
a six weeks' span !   There passed upon the shores
of Gennesaret a celestial drama, grand and still.
With every dawn these rugged men, grown gentle
and dreamy, hushed to awe, trembling with expec-
tancy, awoke to say : " Will he come to-day ? "   At
nightfall they asked one of another, "Have you seen
him ?   Have *you ?*

.   .   .   .

But the time came when it was no longer possible
to say of his appearance that it was like anything
known to men, or imagined by them.   Nor was it
possible to think that the earth could continue to
hold a presence such as his had now become.

There fell a day when he had bidden his friends
with him into the hills, and had talked with them

tenderly, and directed their future, and glorified their souls with love and faith, till they felt that they could die for him and be happy; as some of them did, and were.

Then it was made known to them that he would lead them away, and out of Galilee, towards Jerusalem. Mutely they followed the mysterious call.

Near Bethany, where he had been so beloved, he paused. It was as if he would come to the home of his heart before he went.

There the little group understood suddenly that they were to lose him. It needed no parting words, although he spoke them. His eye, his smile, his outstretched hands, became remote. Ecstasy enwrapped him. Mistiness began to blend upon him. The air between himself and them trembled.

They dared not entreat him. . . . Now something graver than joy, but which was not sadness, touched his expression. His eyes followed them wistfully; pity was the last look, as it had been the first, that they saw upon his face. Then love unutterable blinded all other consciousness, whether in himself or in those whom he left. His voice ceased. His features dimmed. His form faded. A delicate cloud received him. He melted into it, and was not.

Thus vanished from the earth Jesus of Nazareth, the Son of God.

Evil never touched his spirit. Corruption did not approach his body. Even his ashes were not permitted to remain in the soil of the land that had slain him.

THE ASCENSION

He was born in denial of the laws of life.   He died in defiance of the laws of death.   He was Lord of law.   Ideal of sacrifice, Master of suffering, the grandest intellect, the purest heart that this low world has known — its Supreme Soul — he passed.

He has left us the faith which bears his name. He has left us the august opportunity of everlasting life.

" Many other signs . . . did Jesus . . . which are not written in this book ; but these are written that ye may believe that Jesus is the Christ, the Son of God." — THE DEAR DISCIPLE.

The Riverside Press

CAMBRIDGE, MASSACHUSETTS, U. S. A.
ELECTROTYPED AND PRINTED BY
H. O. HOUGHTON AND CO.